(Dec. 2005)
Samuel Turner
Property

To
Charles

THE WESTERN PURSUIT
of the American Dream

I think I've know you as long
as I've been collecting this stuff

Best wishes

Ken Rudell

WASHINGTON IRVING, July 13, 1831. "One of the most striking characteristics of an American is his self dependence. Born to no fortune he knows, from his earliest years, that he has nothing but his own mental and bodily exertions to rely on in the great struggle of existence. This self dependence produces a remarkable quickness and versatility of talent. He turns his mother wit, as the Indian does his knife, to all purposes, and is seldom at a loss. At his first outset in life the world lies before him, like the wilderness of his own country, a trackless waste, through which he must cut his own path; but what would be a region of doubt and despondency to another mind appears to him a land of promise, a region of glorious enterprize tinted with golden hope."

THE WESTERN PURSUIT
of the American Dream

EXHIBITION

National Heritage Museum

2004–2005

Selections from the Collection of

Kenneth W. Rendell

Historical Publications, 2004

Library of Congress Cataloging-in-Publication Data

The western pursuit of the American dream / selections from the collection of Kenneth W. Rendell.
    p. cm.
  Includes index.
  ISBN 0-8061-9954-7 (alk. paper)
    1. Frontier and pioneer life—West (U.S.)—Sources. 2. Overland journeys to the
Pacific—Sources. 3. Pioneers—West (U.S.)—History—Sources. 4. West (U.S.)—Social life
and customs—Sources. 5. Material culture—West (U.S.) 6. West (U.S.)—History—Sources.
I. Rendell, Kenneth W.

F596.W51255 2004
978—dc22   2004047867

Design: Janice Moore Design & EXP Typographics
Editing: Ellen Persio
Photography: Eric L. Johnson

Copyright © 2004 by Kenneth W. Rendell
Published by Historical Publications
46 Eliot Street, Natick, MA 01760
Distributed by the University of Oklahoma Press, Norman,
Publishing Division of the University.
All rights reserved. Manufactured in the U.S.A.

Thanks

Bill Reese has been of extraordinary assistance in selecting rare books for my collection. His descriptions and placements of the books in the context of the development of the West have been used extensively.

Dave Bowers, the premier rare coin dealer and my lifelong friend, has provided expert guidance over the years as I assembled my collection of Indian Peace Medals and Colonial coins.

I enjoyed many discussions about Western Americana with Mike Kokin, owner of Sherwood Americana and my neighbor many years ago when I operated a gallery in Beverly Hills, and I've acquired a number of guns and artifacts in my collection from him.

Don Ellis has been the source of not only the most important Indian artifacts in my collection, but also indispensable advice and comprehensive scholarly background on these pieces.

Shirley McNerney, my wife and business partner, has always encouraged my collecting. At a financial low point many years ago, she argued strenuously against selling any of the collection. Somehow we struggled through that time — I've forgotten how, but I've not forgotten her support of my collecting.

The historical letters, documents, manuscripts, and diaries in the collection are all part of the field I regularly deal in through my New York gallery. These pieces come from hundreds of different sources, frequently from descendants of the original recipients.

ALSO BY KENNETH W. RENDELL

History Comes to Life: Collecting Historical Letters and Documents, 1995
Forging History: The Detection of Fake Letters and Documents, 1994
With Weapons and Wits: Propaganda and Psychological Warfare in World War II, 1992
Autographs and Manuscripts: A Collector's Manual [co-author], 1978

Contents

Preface viii

1. Early Exploration 1

2. First Eastern Settlements 11

3. Crossing the Appalachians 21

4. Louisiana 43

5. Lewis and Clark 59

6. The Fur Trade 67

7. The Indians 85

8. Santa Fe 123

9. Exploration and Scientific Expeditions 133

10. Texas 147

11. California 163

12. Overland Trail 171

13. Northwestern Settlements 193

14. The Mormons 205

15. California Gold Rush 217

16. Crossing the Continent 241

17. Prospecting, Settling, and Wonderment 267

18. Outlaws and Lawmen 293

19. Cowboys 309

20. Indian Wars 317

21. Klondike and Alaska: Last Frontiers 335

22. The West of the 20th Century 343

Index 353

Unlike my interest in World War II,* my fascination with the American West has a very simple origin. The Boston neighborhood where I grew up was a cramped and confining place of two- and three-family houses, tiny yards, and a suffocating Irish-Catholic atmosphere. My family spent summers north of the city in a lakeside cabin without plumbing or electricity — and I loved every minute of my life there.

This was during the late 1940s when movies and radio, and, eventually, television, abounded with stories about the American West. My vision of the West during those early years must have been highly romanticized, but that image didn't last long. I'd soon read enough history to realize that the West of Roy Rogers, Gene Autry, and Hopalong Cassidy was a fantasy world with no relation to reality except for the scenery. In fact, it wasn't this fantasy world that captured and held my attention, but rather the beauty and openness of the landscape and, most important, the dream of freedom and opportunity that inspired me with a sense of adventure not unlike the spirit of the first pioneers. While I never longed to be a cowboy or a gunfighter, I did yearn to escape from my neighborhood to the wide-open spaces of the West, where a man could be whatever he could do. I always liked Thoreau's words — "Eastward I go only by force, but westward I go free."

In 1961 I drove through the West, camping out along the way, but my first direct encounter with "real" West — the untamed frontier that so intrigued me — was in 1967 when I drove to Alaska and the Yukon. During a month-long stay on a homestead in Northern British Columbia, I met a pair of true modern-day pioneers and observed the challenges they faced. Morley and Grace Clark lived a self-sufficient and very tough life. He hunted, fished, farmed, raised horses, and in the winter set trap lines and traveled by dogsled. His wife cooked, scrubbed, and laid up provisions without any of the conveniences we take for granted. My acquaintance with them was as close as I could come to a first-hand experience of the nineteenth-century American West.

I continued my pursuit of the West on subsequent summer vacations, exploring the Oregon Trail and then the Santa Fe. My western travels reached a pinnacle when Steve Ambrose and I, my wife, and twelve other friends hiked, canoed, rode on horseback, and drove across Montana. Our journey followed the route forged by Lewis and Clark, and included readings of the explorers' journal notations on the topography, the weather, the flora and fauna, and other details of the spots where we stopped along the way. It was the ultimate Lewis and Clark experience.

The steps in my Western journey seemed to evolve naturally, as my reflections on past trips inspired new adventures. I once spent a week exploring the original railroad tunnels in Donner Pass. When I shared my recollections of this trip with Steve Ambrose during a conversation about a book he was planning on the transcontinental railroad, we decided to find a way to travel over the Sierra Nevadas from Sacramento to Reno in a diesel locomotive. Much of our route was identical to the original one carved from the mountains with pickaxes and explosives by Chinese immigrants in the 1860s. As we drove the locomotive up to the Donner Pass, each of us took a turn as the engineer — but coming down the mountain was another matter. For that, we had to turn the controls over to a Union Pacific engineer.

The Sierra Nevada trip, in turn, gave rise to the railroad trip of a lifetime. Steve, his wife Moira, and I traveled from Council Bluffs, Iowa, to Cheyenne, Wyoming, in the private railway car of nineteenth-century railway magnate Edward Harriman. From Cheyenne, where two Union Pacific steam locomotives were brought out, we continued along the original route to Sacramento. To ride along in the cab of a steam locomotive with one foot on the platform and the other on the tender (full of oil rather than wood as it once would've been) and watch the unfolding of a landscape almost unchanged since the building of the railroad was incredible. As I imagined the first transcontinental railway passengers looking out their window at these same prairies and mountains on their way to new lives and opportunities on the American frontier, I felt intimately connected to their pursuit of the West. It was out of this experience that the idea of an exhibition that would tell the story of the Old West through the words and artifacts of the explorers, travelers, and settlers who followed their dreams there was born.

All the illustrations and quotations in the exhibition and catalog are taken from the collection of letters, diaries, books, and artifacts I've collected over the course of fifty years. In addition to books that inspired these pioneers to go west and letters about their dreams, plans, and experiences, I've included examples of the things they used, both in their everyday lives and for special purposes, to provide a close-up glimpse of their world through their own eyes. These remnants of the past express — as no historian can — the realities, anxieties, and, above all, the hope of a new life that the West represented not only to the people who actually went there, but also to those who merely fantasized about escaping to the frontier.

In contrast to this historical evidence of what life was like in the West, items from my collection such as Currier & Ives lithographs of pioneer homes, Davy Crockett almanacs, and Dime Novels illustrate the fantasy version of this time and place that most people are familiar with today. The need to embellish reality is certainly nothing new. Long before John Wayne movies, romantic fantasies of the West dominated the public's imagination. In the days when the immigrant guides, expedition reports, and similar books in this exhibition were first published, however, the unrealistic notions they popularized were often mistaken for truth.

The first pieces in my Western collection were a group of very fine Indian artifacts I acquired from the widow of a collector in New York in the late 1950s. I was stunned by the quality of his collection and spent every dollar I could afford and then some, and even now remember all the pieces I couldn't even think of purchasing at the time.

Equally unforgettable was the first Western book I acquired. After seeing a copy of Alexander MacKenzie's *Voyages* in Michael Ginsburg's catalog, I mentioned to him how excited I was by the book, even though its $300 price tag put it far beyond my reach. Despite the fact that $300 was then as significant a sum to Mike as it was to me, he sent me the book and said I could pay him in a year. This extraordinarily kind gesture marked the beginning of my Western book collection and a friendship with Mike that has continued for over forty years.

Acquiring this collection has provided me with nearly a half-century of adventure, as well as a continual source of pleasure and inspiration. I hope this exhibition and catalog enable you to share my adventure.

*The World War II collection is now on exhibit in The Museum of World War II, a 10,000-square-foot museum just outside Boston (www.museumofworldwarii.com).

Chapter 1

EARLY EXPLORATION

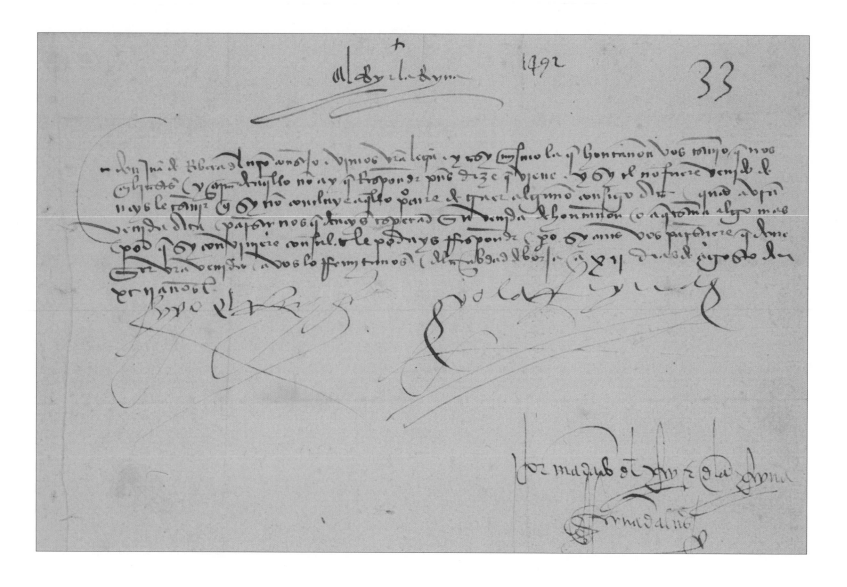

FERDINAND AND ISABELLA, patrons of Columbus. Document Signed by both, August 12, 1492, nine days after Columbus set sail for the New World. The document is addressed to the commander in chief of the frontiers of Navarre, ordering him to prepare for a mutiny.

Columbus's discovery of the New World was followed by the arrival of conquistadors — generally former soldiers in the wars that ended in Spain in 1492 — whose main interests were gold and, to a much lesser degree, silver. The islands of the Caribbean were soon passed over, and their exploration of Florida, and later the Southwest, were in vain. Central and South America provided vast mineral wealth, and Mexico City by the mid-16th century, had become the principal city of New Spain.

The French were the first to challenge Spain, but their attempts at colonization in Florida met with defeat by the Spanish forces. By the late 16th century, Spain was setting up missions and sending Franciscan friars to the Southeast to convert natives. At the same time, the French were exploring the Gulf of St. Lawrence and establishing various fishing settlements there.

Early exploration is a very difficult area to collect; it has always been considered a very important historical subject and consequently has been collected for centuries. There was never very much material to be collected. Today, manuscript material from this era is extremely rare. The important books that are occasionally available fetch significant sums, and artifacts, except for silver bars, are almost nonexistent.

Not everyone was seeking only gold or souls. Louis Hennepin wrote of his reasons for traveling to America in *A New Discovery of a Vast Country in America…*, 1698:

"Men are never weary of pursuing the objects they have in view; such as present them with millions of ravaging qualities capable to afford 'em both satisfaction and instruction. The wonders they there meet with are so surprising and enchanting that they are necessarily engaged to survey the same with all possible exactness in order to satisfy their natural curiosity and inform their minds.…They're never weary of making new discoveries. They are indefatigable in rambling through unknown countries…not mentioned in history; feasting their minds with the satisfaction of gratifying and enriching the world with something unheard of that no thought could ever reach before. 'Tis true, such enterprises expose 'em to infinite fatigue and danger; but the hopes they've conceived of contributing thus to the public good and advancing the glory of god and at the same time gratifying their natural inclinations are their chief solace and comfort encouraging them to suffer all with the constancy and pleasure."

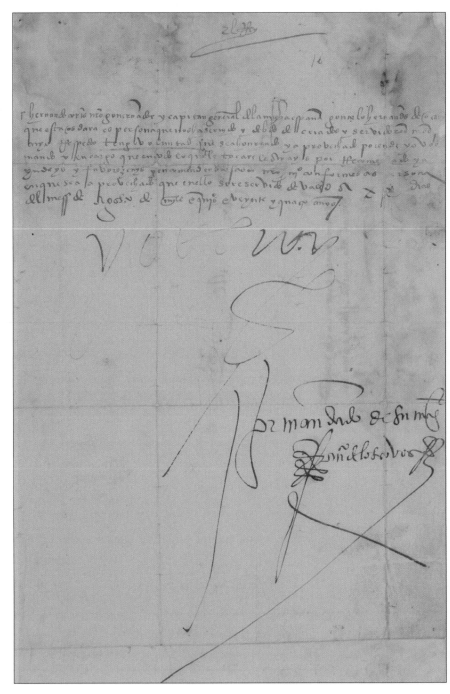

KING CHARLES I OF SPAIN wrote to Hernando Cortéz, who was then governor and captain general of New Spain, August 19, 1524, recommending Gonzalo Hernandez de Ocanpo. This is one of the earliest surviving letters from Europe to the New World.

Silver bar cast from silver artifacts taken from the natives during the conquest of Mexico. This bar was recovered from a Spanish shipwreck off Grand Bahama Island. The name of the ship taking the treasure to Spain is unknown, but the stamps on the ingot show it to have been cast between 1521 and 1558; we can assume it is most likely from the earlier period because of the crudeness of the bar, which has signs of other metals, and indeed the objects themselves, still visible.

This ingot weighs 6.9 pounds, measures 9 by 27 by 2 centimeters, and contains two partial tax stamps of King Charles I of Spain (Charles V the Holy Roman Emperor). During the early 1500s, native silver and gold artifacts were hastily melted into bars, and then shipped to Spain in this crude form of impure ingots, which were then remelted and divided into silver, gold, and copper ingots.

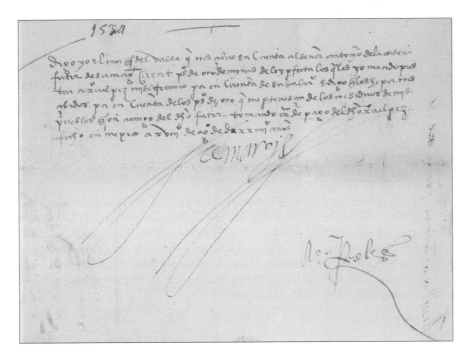

HERNANDO CORTÉZ. Document Signed, Mexico, August 18, 1534. A receipt and payment order for 100 gold pesos.

William Prescott, in his *History of the Conquest of Mexico,* remarked that *"the history of the Conquest…is necessarily that of Cortez, who is…not merely the soul, but the body, of the enterprise, present everywhere in person, in the thick of the fight, or in the building of the works, with his sword or with his musket, sometimes leading his soldiers, and sometimes directing his little navy. The negotiations, intrigues, correspondence, are all conducted by him; and like Caesar, he wrote his own Commentaries in the heat of the stirring scenes which form the subject of them…. Cortez was not a vulgar conqueror. He did not conquer from the mere ambition of conquest. If he destroyed the ancient capital of the Aztecs, it was to build up a more magnificent capital on its ruins…. If he was greedy of gold, like most of the Spanish cavaliers in the New World, it was not to hoard it, nor merely to lavish it in the support of a princely establishment, but to secure funds for prosecuting his glorious discoveries."*

Outina Gallorum auxilio Potanou ſuum
hoſtem ſuperat. XIII.

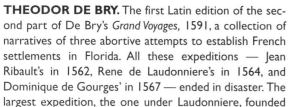

Columnam à Præfecto prima navigatione locatam VIII.
venerantur Floridenſes.

Ceremoniæ à Saturioua in expeditionem adverſus XI.
hoſtes profecturo, obſervatæ.

THEODOR DE BRY. The first Latin edition of the second part of De Bry's *Grand Voyages,* 1591, a collection of narratives of three abortive attempts to establish French settlements in Florida. All these expeditions — Jean Ribault's in 1562, Rene de Laudonniere's in 1564, and Dominique de Gourges' in 1567 — ended in disaster. The largest expedition, the one under Laudonniere, founded the present-day St. Augustine and was later massacred by the Spanish. The narrative of this expedition was written by artist Jacques Le Moyne, who escaped the massacre and managed to return to England. His extraordinary illustrations of the Florida Indians, which appear on forty-two leaves of this work in their first published form, rank with the best visual record of American Indians before the 19th century. They show all aspects of Indian life, including settlements, ceremonies, wars, agriculture, hunting, and preparation of food. They also show scenes of the French settlers and their involvement with the Indians. These images, along with those of White, which appear in the first part of De Bry, were widely copied for illustrations.

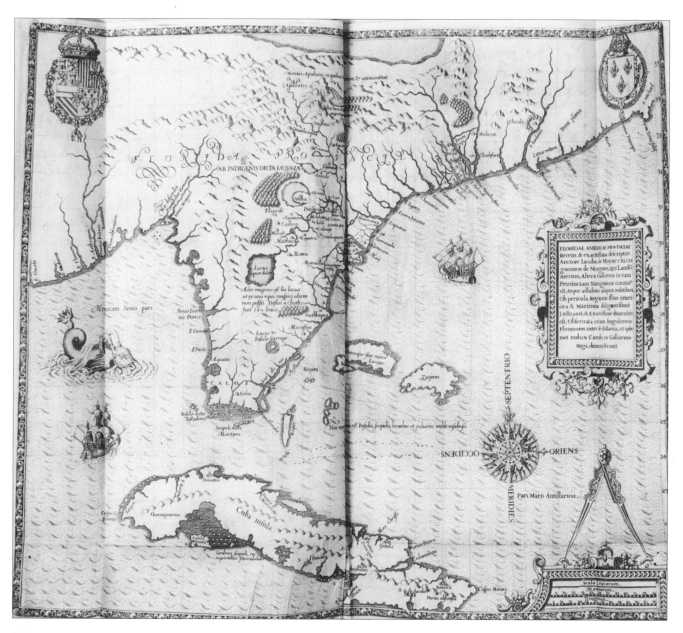

This map is one of the most elaborate of the Florida peninsula to appear in the 16th century using the names assigned by the French and Spanish.

Christopher Columbus's heir, the Duke of Veragua, presents to the Queen of Spain his case for compensation in the loss of the Island of Jamaica to the English. Jamaica had been given to Columbus by Ferdinand and Isabella as part of his compensation for his discoveries.

Columbus had negotiated a settlement with Ferdinand and Isabella as payment for his discoveries, but it did not provide the extraordinary wealth and colonies that were to develop in coming decades. By 1508, colonists could not be controlled, and Columbus's son, Diego, began a series of lawsuits with Spain to clarify the terms and make them workable. These lawsuits were inherited by Christopher Columbus's grandson, Luis, who in 1556 settled them. He received the title of Duc of Veragua, the island of Jamaica, and an annuity of 17,000 ducats.

During the 17th century, Jamaica was gradually colonized under the control of Columbus's heirs, the dukes of Veragua. Eight Spanish families created large plantations on the island, and immigration there was discouraged unless controlled by the Columbus family. By 1650 only 3,000 people, including slaves, inhabited Jamaica.

This peaceful and profitable situation changed abruptly in June 1655, when England invaded Jamaica. The Spanish were ejected by 1658, and the Columbus family lost its most valuable asset.

This autograph manuscript, 1671, is the petition to the queen to compensate the family for this loss.

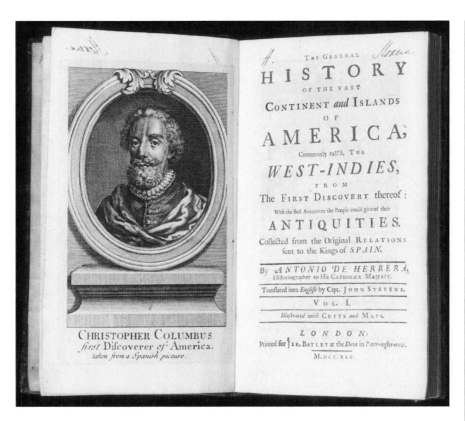

Antonio de Herrera, *The General History of the Vast Continent and Islands of America, Commonly Call'd the West Indies, from the First Discovery,* London, 1725–1726.

The first edition in English of one of the primary accounts of the early Spanish conquest of the New World, originally published in Madrid in 1601–1615. Herrera was the official historian to Philip II, and was able to examine many documents that were later destroyed, making his work a primary research source.

He wrote, *"The generality of mankind were so far from imaging that there could be any such regions as the West Indies, that it was look'd upon as an extravagant notion* to think of any such thing; for it was believed that the land terminated at the Canary Islands and that all beyond them to the westward was sea; and yet some of the ancients gave hints that there were such countries…. The admiral…Christopher Columbus had many reasons to believe that there were other countries because being a great cosmographer and having much experience in navigation he considered that the heavens being round and moving circularly above the earth that the water compacted together formed a globe or ball of the two elements and at the part discovered was not all the earth but that there was still much undiscovered…and ought to be inhabited because God had not created it to lie waste."*

Four manuscript accounts describing a voyage in 1699 down the Mississippi River, two written in Kansas and two in Chicago. They provide a remarkably detailed description of a voyage made by Montigny, St. Cosme, La Source (all missionaries), and Albert Davion along the northern shore of Lake Michigan, across the present-day state of Illinois, and down the Mississippi as far south as the encampment of the Taensas Indians in what is now Louisiana. The group had been sent by the church in Quebec to establish missions along the river.

Chapter 2

FIRST EASTERN SETTLEMENTS

SIR WALTER RALEIGH sponsored three expeditions from 1584–1587 to the southern coastal area he named Virginia. Document Signed, August 5 [1587], transferring the title of Leigh Manor in Derbyshire to Richard Wharton and John Hopkinson. This estate, which Queen Elizabeth granted to Raleigh, was part of the forfeited holdings of Anthony Babington, who had been executed for masterminding a plot to assassinate Elizabeth and replace her on the throne with the imprisoned Mary Queen of Scots.

By 1610 Spain was at the peak of its power in the New World. France, its main potential rival, had been establishing trading posts in the interior to develop the fur trade and had shown little interest in land. When England began sending expeditions to America in the early 17th century, their interest focused not the gold and silver sought by the Spanish or the development of trade, but on acquiring land for settlement.

Jamestown in Virginia was established in 1607, and by the time of Sir Walter Raleigh's death on the scaffold in 1618, it had a population of 600. Like Massachusetts, the Virginia colony had taken root under the leadership of Captain John Smith. Virginia flourished under both under a system of religious freedom (for its inhabitants) and free enterprise. Both colonies traded American products for English goods. By the end of the 17th century, English colonists from various settlements along the Eastern Seaboard had begun a steady migration westward. While the movement from New England was very orderly, resulting in systematically organized new towns, the movement from the south had a more informal flavor of a "real west," with many kinds of groups, small and large, founding new settlements.

Collecting the artifacts, manuscripts and books from this period is less difficult than acquiring material from the early exploration but the availability of such items is still very limited. Some early colonizers, such as William Penn, signed many land grants, but the material of others, for example, Roger Williams, the religious freedom leader who founded Rhode Island, is virtually unique in private ownership. John Smith's books on Virginia and New England are very rare and expensive. Perhaps the least expensive artifacts are the coins of these early colonies, and they offer a window into these early times for relatively modest sums.

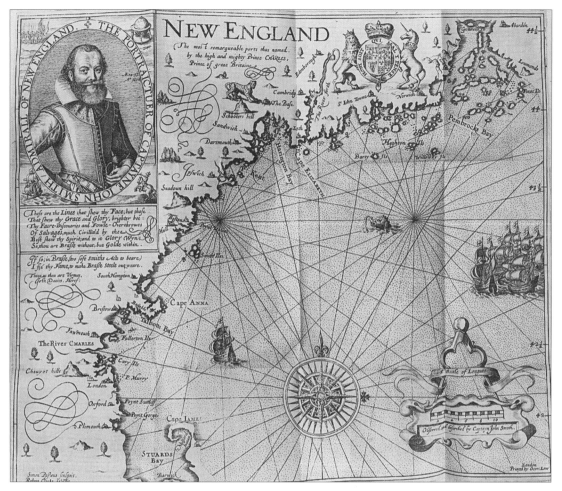

JOHN SMITH. *A Description of New England: Or the Observations, and Discoueries, of Captain John Smith, 1616.*

Smith's *New England* was the English pilgrims' principal guide to their American haven. Based on Smith's two visits to the New England coast in 1614 and 1615, this book did much to encourage later settlement in New England, preceding by four years the sailing of the *Mayflower*. Smith named Plymouth, and described the place as *"an excellent good harbour, good lands, and no want of anything but industrious people."* The primary objective of Smith's first voyage, which was financed by a group of London merchants, was to search for whales and gold mines. The first visit was relatively brief but afforded ample opportunities for trading with the Indians and for collecting much geographical and natural history information. On his second voyage in 1615, Smith met with less success. Thwarted by storms and pirates, he was eventually taken prisoner by sailors on a French warship. During his captivity, Smith wrote his *Description of New England,* which was destined to inspire future adventurers with descriptions of the opportunities awaiting them in the region.

This map from 1616 was based on surveys made by Captain Smith for the Council for New England. Considered the foundation of New England cartography, it stands as the first map to bear the name New England (the region was known as North Virginia before the publication of Smith's book). The names of the settlements were changed by Prince Charles from their original Indian names to those used today. The map depicts the area from the present-day Penobscot Bay in Maine to Cape Cod.

Smith wrote, *"And of all the foure parts of the world that I have yet seene not inhabited, could I have but meanes to transport a colonie, I would rather live here than any where: and if it did not maintaine it selfe, were wee but once indifferently well fitted, let us starve… here every man may be master and owner of his owne labor and land; or the greatest part in small time. If hee have nothing but his hands, he may set up this trade; and by industrie quickly grow rich; spending but halfe that time wel, weh in England we abuse idlenesse."*

This New England Shilling, minted in 1652, was the first coin produced in the English New World. Originally, the Massachusetts Bay Colony operated on a barter system. The most frequently traded items included dried fish, furs, grains, musketballs, and, after 1627, wampum. Wampum, which were strings of beads made from certain types of shells, circulated as a form of currency among Indians. During this period, civil unrest in England leading to the execution of King Charles I and the defeat of royalist forces gradually emboldened the New England colonies to become more independent, and in 1652, colonists passed an act establishing their own mint. Ten to fifteen coins from this mint are believed to have survived.

The earliest coinage minted for any English-speaking region in the New World was the shilling coin made for the Sommer Islands (Bermuda), 1615/16. The hog shown on the obverse commemorates the day in 1532 when the island was overrun by hogs from a wrecked cargo ship; the reverse shows a sailing ship. Crudely made on thin planchets, the surviving examples are heavily eroded by salt spray.

Massachusetts Pine Street Shilling, dated 1652, minted 1667/74.

Lord Baltimore Sixpence, 1658/59. For decades after Catholics seeking religious freedom first colonized Maryland, tobacco remained its main crop and medium of exchange, with musketballs and gunpowder serving as small change. By requiring every one of Maryland's 5,500 householders and freeman to exchange 60 pounds of tobacco for ten shillings of the new silver coins, the colony put 2,750 pounds into circulation. Eventually the coins vanished, the colony reverted to barter, and in 1706 hemp, a staple crop, became legal tender.

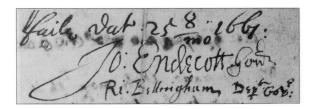

JOHN ENDICOTT led a group of colonists who landed at Salem, Massachusetts, in 1628. He served as governor at various times, including the year 1661, when he signed this document.

RICHARD BELLINGHAM, who co-signed the document as deputy governor, also served three terms as governor of the Massachusetts Bay Colony.

JOHN WINTHROP arrived in Salem in 1630 and, like John Endicott, served as governor of the Massachusetts Bay Colony for many years. He signed this document as governor in 1647.

SIR EDMUND ANDROS, governor of New York, New Jersey, Virginia, and New England. Autograph Manuscript in his name, June 17, 1687, giving instructions for the exploration of the inner regions of New England.

Deed of land from Paupsunnuck, wife of Panneasum, to John Pynchon of Springfield, Massachusetts, May 4, 1663. *"The sd Paupsunnuck wife of Pannesun [sic]... in consideration of 150 fadam of wampum & some Coates & other thing...& sell...aforesd tract of land...for ever free from any Incumbrance & molestation of any Indian."*

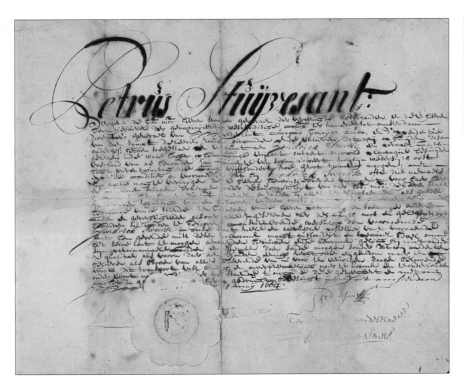

PETER STUYVESANT, administrator of Dutch settlements in America who had forced the Colony of New Sweden (present-day Delaware) to surrender, and was later forced by the British to surrender New York. Document Signed, New Amsterdam (New York), May 15, 1664. Four months before surrendering New Amsterdam to the English, Stuyvesant confirmed a grant of land to Hendrick Sweerse on Long Island. 16½ by 13 inches.

William Bullock, in his 1649 guide for prospective immigrants to Virginia, wrote, *"The principal motive, that drew the author to this work was…finding many gentlemen have unsettled themselves with a desire to better their fortunes in remote places…. Men are dispersed abroad in several small numbers at great distances from each other which is very uncomfortable…whereas if they had been all directed to any one good place they might have been in this time a great and flourishing people: in finding also…that this country of Virginia is abundantly stored with what is by all men aimed at…health and wealth so there wants nothing to their happiness…but good instructions… I thought that man should take the stranger by the hand and lead him to it showing him not only the richest mines but also how to dig them."*

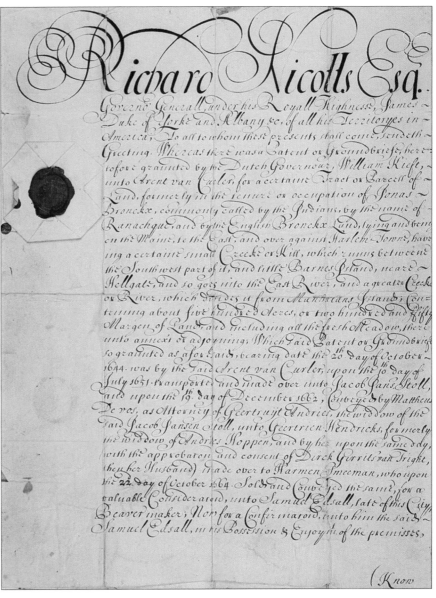

RICHARD NICOLLS, the first English governor of New York. Document Signed, 1668, reaffirming the rights of proprietorship for 500 acres of land purchased under the Dutch from Jonas Bronck, who had purchased present-day Bronx from the Indians in 1639.

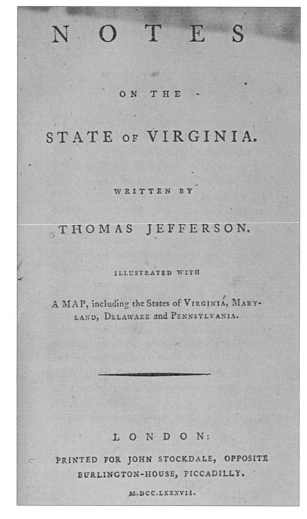

Regarded as Jefferson's great literary and intellectual work, *Notes on the State of Virginia,* 1787, was written as a series of answers to questions about the natural history of the state and many aspects of life there.

George II Indian Peace Medal, 1757, depicts an Indian and a Quaker sharing a peace pipe. This medal was struck and distributed by a Pennsylvania Quaker group known as the *Friendly Association for Regaining and Preserving Peace with the Indians by Pacific Means.*

The London Elephant Halfpence, 1666/94, is believed to have been brought to Pennsylvania in 1682 by the Quakers. The origins of this coin are unknown; variations circulated in different colonies.

Dr. Samuel Higley discovered copper in Simsbury, Connecticut, and in 1737/39 began striking copper coins of such purity that jewelers melted them down for alloying gold and silver.

Map and illustration of the Swedish settlement on the Delaware River, from Campanius Holm's *Account,* published in Stockholm, 1702.

The Swedish colony of Fort Christina was established in what is now Wilmington, Delaware, in 1638. After years of rivalry with both the English and the Dutch, the Swedes were driven from their colony by the Dutch in 1655.

BENJAMIN WORSLEY, English Secretary for Trade and Plantations. Autograph Letter Signed, December 14, 1668.

A long and important letter in which Worsley gives his reasons for fearing the king's resolution *"not only to disowne but to Restraine ye Trade of ye Privaties"* of Jamaica, *"especially if ye said order should be…directed to be executed with Rigour or hastinesse"* and estimating the connivance of the Jamaican government *"in ye profitt so in ye Guylt of ye said Roving trade."* He insists the pirates should not be driven into the French camp and that a deal should be made to keep them loyal.

WILLIAM PENN, founder of Pennsylvania. Document Signed, October 28, 1681, conveying 5,000 acres of land 12 miles north of Newcastle Town in Pennsylvania for 100 pounds. 27 by 21¼ inches. Penn's colony was founded on Quaker ideals.

Chapter 3

CROSSING THE APPALACHIANS

Henry Popple, "A Map of the British Empire in America with the French and Spanish Supplements Adjacent Thereto…," London [1732].

The best and most famous map of colonial North America issued up to the date of its publication. The map, which is divided into twenty sections, is on a grand scale and, if assembled results in a rectangle, over eight feet square. Its coverage extends from the Grand Banks off Newfoundland to about ten degrees west of Lake Superior, and from the Great Lakes to the north coast of South America. Several of the sections are illustrated with handsome pictorial insets, including views of New York City, Niagara Falls, Mexico City, and Quebec, and inset maps of Boston, Charlestown, Providence, Bermuda, and several other areas.

Popple produced the map under the auspices of the Lord Commissioners of Trade and Plantations to help settle disputes arising from the rival expansion of British, French, and Spanish colonies. Despite its importance and large scale, the map does contain a number of inaccuracies, reflective of the state of cartography at the time, and all the more noticeable because of its large size.

By the mid-18th century, America was dividing into two groups: those who lived in the coastal settlements and were oriented toward European—specifically English—thinking along class lines, and those living inland bordering the mountains. The back-country settlers thought in terms of north-south, not west-east, because the barriers of the mountains united these settlers with a common interest in fur trading, hunting, fighting Indians, and farming and a shared dislike for land titles and boundaries.

They also shared a contempt for those on the East Coast, who controlled legislation, especially regarding trade, for their pacifying attitude towards Indians and their legislative action giving vast tracts of land to favored friends.

In 1763, in response to an Indian uprising, British negotiators offered the Proclamation of 1763, which prohibited settlement west of the crest of the Appalachian Mountains. This was ignored by the back-country settlers, who had no regard for agreements made by England. The land speculators from the East, including George Washington and Benjamin Franklin, ignored it as well.

The settlement of the land over the mountains began midway in the mountain chain, as Daniel Boone led settlers over old hunting trails into Kentucky. The movement through the Cumberland Gap was the greatest westward movement of the time (between 1775 and 1800, it is estimated that 300,000 people "went west" through the gap). During the American Revolution, the Indians sided with the British, who could produce manufactured trade goods that the Americans could not. The Westerners fought their own battles, led in the Northwest by George Rogers Clark, and in the Southwest by local leaders, and their victories saved the West for the United States in the 1783 peace negotiations.

The most imperative task of the new American government was organizing the western lands. The older colonies, such as Virginia, had huge claims on the wilderness, while Maryland claimed nothing. The nonclaimant colonies threatened the Union and prevailed. The wilderness would be divided and sold by the federal government under the Terms of the Ordinances of 1785 and 1787.

Collector interest in this area is focused on documents of the leading participants, most of which are rare but occasionally obtainable. Letters of settlers are very rare, but less sought after. Contemporary books are generally available, as are artifacts such as Kentucky rifles, at reasonable prices. It is an interesting area to collect with almost as many peaks and valleys of rarity and cost as the terrain this material is concerned with.

One of the best descriptions of America at this time appeared in 1797 in Gilbert Imlay's *Description of the Western Territory*, the most informative work on the West at the end of the 18th century. It was entitled *Remarks for the Information of Those Who Wish to Become Settlers* and was written by Benjamin Franklin:

"The governments in America give every assistance to strangers that can be desired from protection, good laws and perfect liberty. Strangers are welcome because there is room enough for them all and therefore the old inhabitants are not jealous of them, the laws protect them sufficiently so that they have no need of the patronage of great men; and everyone will enjoy, in security, the prophets of his own industry: but if he does not bring a fortune with him he must work and be industrious to live…. The government does not hire people to become settlers. Land being cheap…so that the property of a hundred acres of very fertile soil may be obtained at an easy rate; hearty young men…may easily establish themselves…. Multitudes of poor people from England Ireland Scotland and Germany have…in a few years become wealthy farmers; who in their own countries where all the lands are fully occupied and the wages of labor low could never have emerged from their low position wherein they were born…. The increase of inhabitants by natural generation is very rapid in America…. Hence there is a continual demand for more artisans of all the necessary and useful kinds to supply those cultivators of the earth with houses and with furniture and with utensils…which can not so well be brought from Europe. Tolerable good workmen in any of these mechanic arts are sure to find employ and to be well-paid for their work; there being no restraints preventing strangers from exercising any art

they understand nor any permission necessary. If they are poor they begin first as servants or journeymen; and if they are sober industrious and frugal they soon become masters, establish themselves in business, raise families and become respectable citizens. Persons of moderate fortunes…who having a number of children to provide for are desirous of bringing them up to industry and to secure estates for their posterity have opportunities of doing it in America which Europe does not afford.

"The establishment of manufacturers has rarely succeeded in America, the country not being yet so ripe as to encourage private persons to set them up; labor being generally being too dear and hands difficult to be kept together, everyone desiring to become a master and the cheapness of land inclining many to leave trades for agriculture. Things that are bulky and so small value as not well to bear to expense of freight may often be made cheaper in the country than they can be imported and the manufacturer of such things will be profitable whenever there is a sufficient demand…. The government of America does nothing to encourage such projects; the people are by this means not imposed on either by the merchant or mechanic: if the merchant demands too much profit on imported shoes they buy of the shoemaker; and if he has too high of a price they take them of the merchant; thus the two professions are checks to each other. Shoemaker however has on the whole a considerable profit upon his labor in America beyond what he had in Europe as he can add to his price a sum nearly equal to all the expenses of freight and commission…and the case is the same with the workmen in every other mechanic art. Hence it is that artisans live better and more easily in America than in Europe.

"In the old long settled countries of Europe all arts, trades, professions, farms, etc. are so full that it is difficult for a poor man who has children to place them where they may gain or learn to gain a decent livelihood. The artisans who fear creating future rivals in business refuse to take apprentices but upon conditions of money…which the parents are unable to comply with…. In America the rapid increase of inhabitants takes away that fear of rivalship and artisans willingly receive apprentices from the hope of profit by their labor during the remainder of the time stipulated after they shall be instructed, hence it is easy for poor families to get their children instructed.

"The almost general mediocrity of fortune that prevails in America obliging its people to follow some business for subsistence, those vices that arise generally from idleness are in a great measure prevented. Industry and constant employment are great preservations of the morals and virtue of a nation."

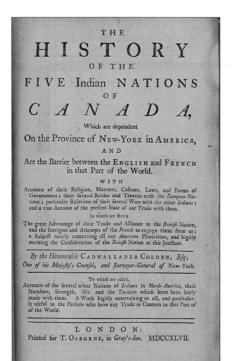

A MAP of, the Country of the FIVE NATIONS, belonging to the Province of NEW-YORK; and of the LAKES near which the Nations of FAR INDIANS live, with part of CANADA.

N.B. The Tuscaroras are now reckon'd a sixth Nation, & live between the Onondagues & Oneidos; & the Nicariages of Misilimakinac were received to be the seventh Nation at Onny May 30th 1723: at their own desire, as Men of that Nation being present besides Women & children. The chief Trade with the far Indians is at the Onondagues rivers mouth when...

Cadwallader Colden, *The History of the Five Indian Nations of Canada, Which Are Dependent on the Province of New-York in America, and Are the Barrier Between the English and French in That Part of the World…,* 1747. For decades, the only reliable colonial history of the Iroquois. The book influenced British and American policy throughout the 18th century.

SIR WILLIAM JOHNSON, superintendent of Indian Affairs in the American colonies, concerning Indian relations with the French; Letter Signed, undated.

"To Brethren & Freinds [sic] of Oshquago,

"…I have no news now worth sending you, only what the Senecas & Oneidaes brought me a few days ago, about the French's threat[e]ning to cutt of[f] all the Six Nations, which as I am sure you have heard from the Oneidaes…. I have often told the Six Nations that the French would some time try to do such a thing, as I know they have it in their Heart altho they speak fair with their Lips. The Oneidaes have asked me & the 2 Mohawk Castles to be ready when called to go to the meeting at Onondaga, where the Belts now are from the Chenundadies, Twightys & other Nations from the Westward. I hope [the] On[on]dagaes or Oneidaes will call y[ou]r People to [the] Meeting and some of every Nation living on Susquahana; if not, I will invite them there myself If I go. There was a great Alarm at Scohare lately, but I did not beli[e]ve a word of it, for I expected if there was any Enemy to come that Way against us, you would let me know it. So I did not mind it; I was angry with the Germans for makeing such an Alarm."

JASPER YEATES. Autograph Letter Signed, Pittsburgh, September 19, 1776. To Edward Shippen in Lancaster, Pennsylvania. A very detailed report on the frontier and the defense of western Pennsylvania against the Indians.

"We had received advice that 1500 Chippewa and Ottawa were to meet in a few days at a place…about 90 miles from hence, in order to attack us… We had before heard of a number of…warriors making incursions of the settlements about Kentucky, and we had undoubted accounts of their killing and wounding some of the inhabitants and taking others prisoners…. [T]he British partisans stuck at nothing to increase their fears of inflame their passions. The testimony from all quarters…satisfied our judgements that Pittsburgh was in an uneasy situation…and of too much importance to be neglected.

"[In regard to] volunteers…it is surprising what a noble spirit these woodsmen have. They are generally armed with rifles and are accustomed to all kinds of hardships. The Indians know and confess them their superiors in their own mode of fighting, and if well supported this c[orps] may defy the savages…. We have now in this town and garrison about 350 men properly equipped for action, and have no great apprehensions from the savages. If they do commence hostilities…I will not fall an easy prey."

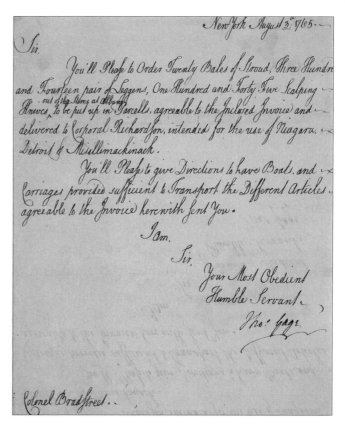

THOMAS GAGE, British commander in chief of North America. Letter Signed, New York, August 3, 1765.

"Order Twenty bales of Stroud, Three Hundred and Fourteen pair of Leggens, One Hundred and Forty Five Scalping Knives…delivered to Corporal Richardson intended for the use of Niagara, Detroit & Misillimackinack.

"You'll please to give directions to have Boats, and Carriages provided sufficient to Transport the Different Articles."

GEORGE WASHINGTON. Letter Signed, Headquarters, Middle Brook, March 2, 1779. To Brigadier Gen. Potter.

"I have recd… your Ideas of the kind of War necessary to be carried on against the Savages for the more effectual Security of our Frontier; with your opinion of the most practicable Route of penetrating the Indian Country. Your ideas correspond in a good measure with my own…. I have t[urn]ed my thoughts and taken some measures towards carrying on an expedition against the Indians of the Six Nations…the m[o]re suddenly a Blow of this kind can be struck especially against the Indians, the more will the weight of it be felt."

Washington's expedition broke the power of the Six Nations and freed the frontier from the horrors of Indian warfare.

THOMAS JEFFERSON. Autograph Letter Signed, Philadelphia, December 24, 1791. As secretary of state, to General Daniel Smith.

"The opposition made by Governor Blount [of North Carolina] & yourself to all attempts by citizens of the U.S. to settle within the Indian lines without authority from the General government is approved, and should be continued.

"There being a prospect that Congress, who have now the post office bill before them, will establish a post from Richmond to Stanton, & continue it thence towards the S.W. government a good distance, if not nearly to it, our future correspondence will be more easy, quick & certain."

On July 12, 1792, Jefferson wrote, "I think we shall have no campaign against the Indians this year. There is some ground of expectations that they will accept of peace, as we ask nothing in return for it."

DANIEL BROADHEAD, early Pennsylvania settler. His survey book, drafting tools, letter to him from George Washington, and miniatures of Broadhead's wife and himself, the latter purported to be by Charles Wilson Peale.

29

The earliest Indian Peace Medals of the United States were individually engraved by silversmiths and bear the date of George Washington's inauguration, 1789. See page 114 for the history of Indian Peace Medals.

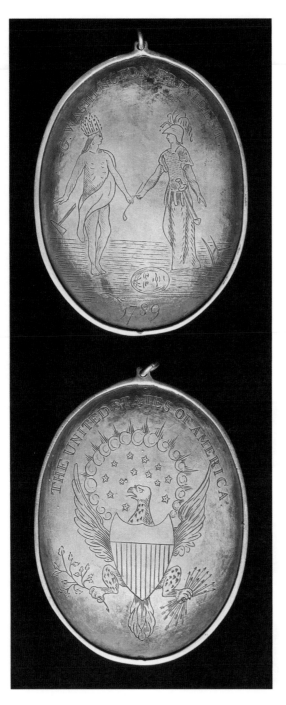

The second American Indian Peace Medal, 1792; George Washington replaces the female figure.

The Treaty of Grenville Medal, 1795, was given to chiefs who signed the treaty, August 3, 1795. The treaty was negotiated by General Anthony Wayne and the chiefs of twelve tribes.

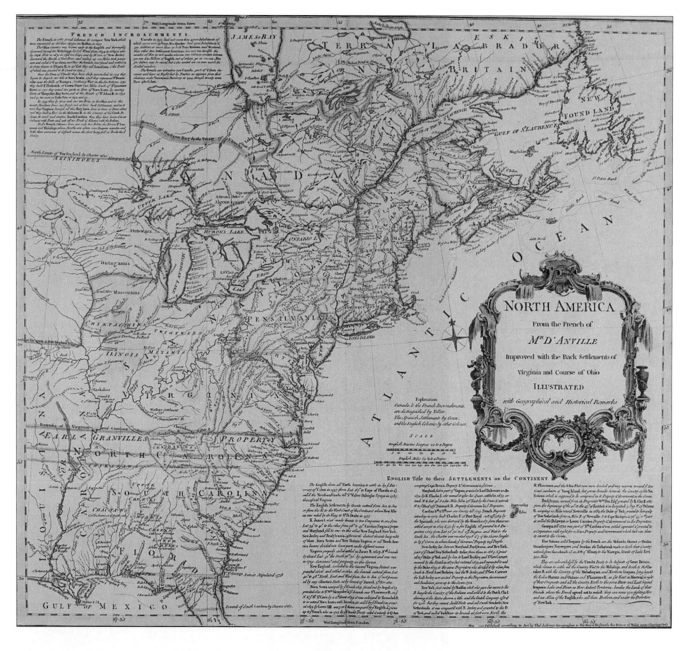

Jeffrey's map of "North America from the French of Mr. D'Anville Improved with the Back Settlements of Virginia and Course of Ohio," 1755. 19½ by 23 inches.

Kentucky rifle by Jonathan Dunmyer, *ca.* 1850s, .30 caliber bore.

Flintlock pistol attributed to Peter and Daniel Moll, Allentown, Pennsylvania, early 19th century.

A powder horn engraved with a map of Boston, Brookline, and Roxbury, April, 1775.

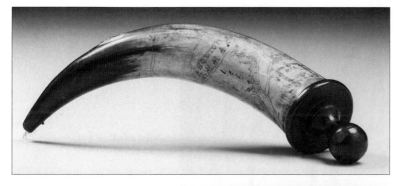

Original barrel of Kentucky Rifle Gun Powder, *ca.* 1840, 13 inches long.

A powder horn inscribed *"MY LIBERTY ILE HAVE OR DEATH, 1773."* The horn is also carved with a rough sketch of some hills, three houses nestled in a valley, and a small compass with an arrow pointing north. 8½ inches long.

Beginning during the French and Indian War and continuing throughout the Revolutionary War, regular soldiers, militiamen, farmers, and others used horns to hold the black powder used to fire their muskets and rifles. Because the horns were a highly visible part of their accouterments, they would often have them decorated by professionals or would carve them themselves. There were all kinds of designs: there were horns showing a map of a particular region, others referring to a particular campaign or battle, horns depicting specific locations, some showing when and where the owner served in the war, examples commemorating a particular regiment or company, and others referring to a particular ship or naval battle.

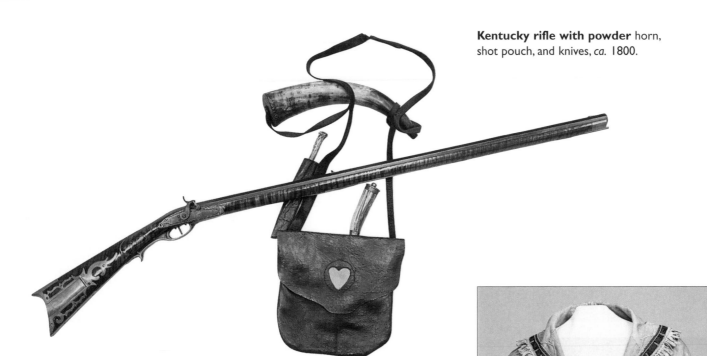

Kentucky rifle with powder horn, shot pouch, and knives, *ca.* 1800.

Athapascan poncho-style shirt, most likely owned by a trapper, mid-19th century.

An Eastern Woodlands frontier jacket, linen, lined with silk and decorated with bead work, *ca.* 1825–1850.

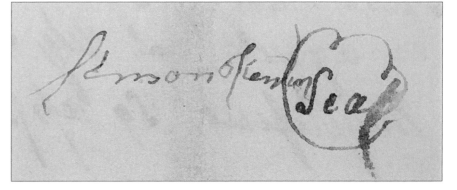

DANIEL BOONE. Signed transfer of 125 acres in Kentucky, 1788. Boone had heard about Kentucky from hunters, about 1766; in 1769, he and a group of hunters went through the Cumberland Gap and were captured by the Shawnee. After escaping, he spent several years exploring Kentucky. By 1773, land speculators became interested in Kentucky for settlement, and the conflict with the Indians, who saw Kentucky as their hunting area, was constant. In 1775, Boone cut the Wilderness Road through Cumberland Gap and founded Boonesboro. Settlers followed Boone in such huge numbers that they soon overwhelmed the Indians.

SIMON KENTON. Signed agreement to arbitration over a disputed land deed by the scout for Daniel Boone and George Rogers Clark, 1812. Virtually illiterate, Kenton was captured and escaped from Indian captivity eight times, running the gauntlet each time; he was three times tied to the stake for burning but survived to become embroiled in many controversial land dealings.

F. A. Michaux wrote in *Travels to the West of the Allegheny Mountains*, 1802:

"More than half of those who inhabit the borders of the Ohio, are again the first inhabitants, or as they are called in the United States, the first settlers, a kind of men who cannot settle upon the soil that they have cleared, and who under pretence of finding a better land, a more wholesome country, a greater abundance of game, push forward, incline perpetually towards the most distant points of the American population, and go and settle in the neighbourhood of the savage nations, whom they brave even in their own country….

"Such were the first inhabitants of Kentucky and Tennessee, of whom there are now remaining but very few…. They have emigrated to more remote parts of the country, and formed new settlements. It will be the same with most of those who inhabit the borders of the Ohio."

His Tribe;

Given under my hand at Louisville State of Kentucky this 15th Day of October 1792.

G R Clark

A. R. Dn.

L Am. Legion

Head Quarters. Cincinati

We the Subscribers Commanding the Kentucky Volunteers now in Service No West of the Ohio do certify that we have every reason to believe from information as well as from our personal knowlege that Baptiste de Guoin Chief of the Kaskaskies has ever been a friend to the Whites together with his Tribe. John Adair Capt

Given Under our hand Geo: Madison Lieut

Oct 27th 1792. Job Hale.

GEORGE ROGERS CLARK organized and led frontiersmen in defense against Indian raids (1776–1777); gained the approval of Governor Patrick Henry for the expedition to conquer the Illinois country; and saved the Kentucky region for the colonies. Document Signed, Louisville, Kentucky, October 15, 1792.

"Baptists de Guoin Chief of the Kaskaskias Tribe of Indians has ever been a friend to the Whites together with his Tribe."

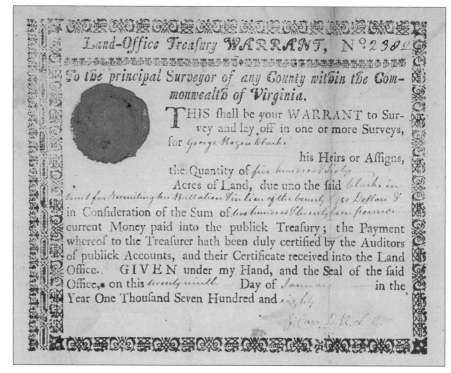

Land-Office Warrant made out to George Rogers Clarke, January 29, 1780, for *"five hundred & Sixty Acres of Land…for recruiting his Battalion & in lieu of the bounty of 750 Dollars & in Consideration of the Sum of two hundred & twenty four pounds."*

[Facsimile of handwritten letter, page 1]

[Facsimile of handwritten letter, page 2]

Davy Crockett. An entertaining almanac containing the story of Mike Fink, the Ohio boatman, and a number of yarns concerning fights with bears, snakes, and wildcats. 1838.

DAVY CROCKETT. Autograph Letter Signed, House of Representatives, January 3, 1829. To the Hon. James Clark of Kentucky.

Shortly after the opening of Congress on December 3, 1827, the freshman congressman from Tennessee, Davy Crockett, was invited to dinner at the White House. Crockett had already attracted attention in the capital for his backwoods appearance and rough-and-tumble manners, and rumors that he had behaved boorishly in front of President Adams were soon circulating among his Whig detractors. When the story found its way into print, Crockett was moved to refute it publicly in this letter.

"Forbearance Ceases to be a virtue, when it is Construed into an acquiescence in falsehoods or a tame submission to unprovoked insult. I have seen published…a Slander…purporting to be an account of my first visit to the President of the Nation.… I presume Sir that you have a distinct recollection of what passed at the dinner…and you will do me the favor to say distinctly, whether the inclosed publication is not false. I would not make this appeal, if it ware not, that, like other men, I have enemies who would take much pleasure in magnifying the plain Rusticity of my manners in to the most unparalleled grossness and indelicacy. I have never enjoyed the advantages which many have abused; but I am proud to hope that your answer will show, that I have never so far prostituted the humble advantages I do enjoy, as to act the part attributed to me."

37

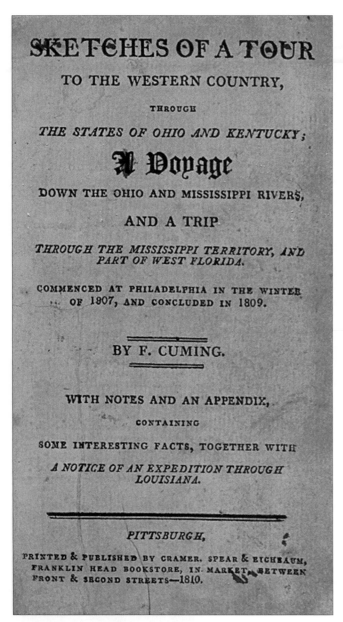

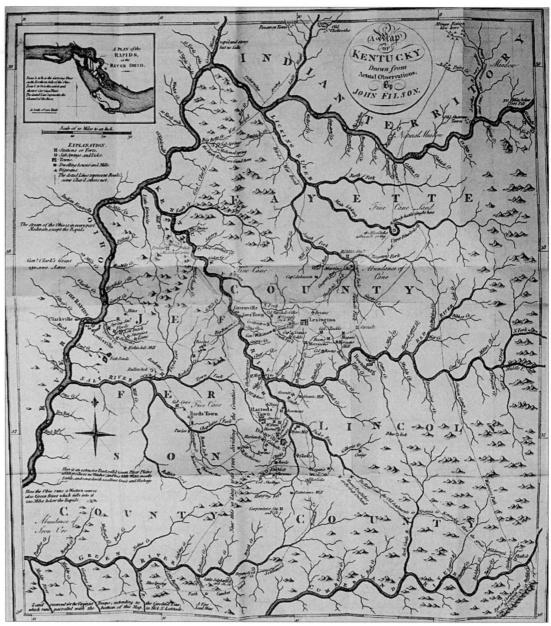

Fortescue Cuming, *Sketches of a Tour to the Western Country, Through the States of Ohio and Kentucky; A Voyage Down the Ohio and Mississippi Rivers, and a Trip Through the Mississippi Territory, and Part of West Florida…*, Pittsburgh, 1810.

The first map of Kentucky, from John Filson's *The Discovery, Settlement, and Present State of Kentucky. And an Introduction to the Topography and Natural History of That Rich and Important Country; Also Colonel Daniel Boon's [sic] Narrative of the Wars of Kentucky*, 1793.

...nold acres No 20 lies in Section No 6 Town No 1 Range No 8 about 6 mile above Marietta, the second lot from the Ohio and corners with Section No 1 Town No 2 Range 8 and is first rate bottom Land —

3 acres No 94½ in Section No 25 Township No 3 Range No 8 about 2 mile North of Marietta, poor broken hill.

Horse lot No 1115 — 26 mile below Marietta on the bank of the Ohio & ¼ of a mile above the mouth of the Hockhocking River, contains half an acre, the Situation is good, but a few families in the Town at present but it is probable in time to become a place of some Business.

160 acres 835 — viz 88 acres in Section No 9 Town No 2 Range No 10 on Slim's run bounds North on the line of donation Land about 10 mil North west of Marietta, flat & hill Land — also 72 acres in Section No 31 Town No 3 Range No 8 about one mile above Marietta & ½ of a mile west of the Muskingum river, chiefly hills, some flat land —

400 acres No 666 in Sections No 35 & 36 Town No 12 Range No 15 on the Hockhocking river, lies 2 mile long & 8159 wide about 20 acres of bottom, balance first & 2d rate hill land, about 42 mile west of Marietta & about 15 mile above Athens on the road to Lancaster —

640 acres. Is Section No 6 in Town No 7 Range No 15 about 75 mile below Marietta & 6 mile from the Ohio, & 14 mile North of Gallipolis, and about 16 miles Southerly from Athens, on the head waters of Kigens Creek, about 3½ mile Westerly of Judge Higleys, on Leading Creek, on which are several mills & a large Settlement, the Section is believed to be of the middle quality of upland, capable of cultivation & excellent for wheat —

262 acres No 6 Lies in Section No 15 of the Same Township with the above Section & about 2 mile Southerly on the waters of Campaign Creek & the quality is supposed to be nearly the Same —

Certified agreably to the minutes of Survey &c

Rufus Putnam Sup—

Marietta october 13d 1810

RUFUS PUTNAM, one of the organizers of the Ohio Company effort to colonize a tract on north bank of the Ohio River; he also laid out the town of Marietta. Autograph Document Signed, Marietta, 1810. Description of a Right of Land in the Ohio Company. Putnam lists six sections of acreage and a house lot, giving the location of the property and the types of land.

"The Hunter's Shanty in the Adirondaks," a lithograph by Currier & Ives, 1861, romanticizing life in the mountains; 14½ by 21 inches.

When a canal across New York State was first proposed, Dewitt Clinton (then mayor of New York City) supported the idea. President Thomas Jefferson thought it was a "little short of madness" and Clinton's opponents called the proposal "Clinton's Folly." But when Clinton became governor of New York State in 1817, $7 million in funds for a canal from the Hudson River to the Great Lakes were quickly approved. On July 4, 1817, unskilled workers broke ground in Rome and started west. The Erie Canal (between Albany and Buffalo) opened on October 26, 1825, and was hailed as the greatest engineering marvel in the world. Three hundred sixty-three miles long, forty feet wide, four feet deep, with eighteen aqueducts and eighty three locks, the canal shortened travel time from the East Coast to the gateway to the West (the Great Lakes) by half and reduced shipping costs by 90 percent.

More than an engineering feat, the Erie Canal proved to be the key that unlocked an enormous series of social and economic changes. Its effect was immediate and dramatic — it opened the only trade route west of the Appalachians, prompted the first great westward migration of American settlers, turned Rochester into the nation's first boom town and made New York City the busiest port in the United States. The explosion of trade was spurred by freight rates from Buffalo to New York of $10 per ton by canal, compared with $100 per ton by road. In 1829, 3,640 bushels of wheat were transported down the canal from Buffalo. By 1837 this figure had increased to 500,000 bushels; four years later it reached one million. In nine years, canal tolls more than recouped the entire cost of construction. Prior to construction of the canal, New York City was the nation's fifth largest seaport. Within fifteen years of its opening, New York was the busiest port in America, moving tonnages greater than those shipped by Boston, Baltimore, and New Orleans combined.

ANDREW JACKSON. Letter Signed, June 17, 1827. The President writes about the Erie Canal, *"I have witnessed with delight the progress of the New York canals."*

ANDREW JACKSON. Autograph Letter Signed, Nashville, April 3, 1821. The future President takes Florida from the Spanish: *"Duty will compel me...to set out for...Pensacola, to be ready to receive the Floridas, and to organise the Government thereof."*

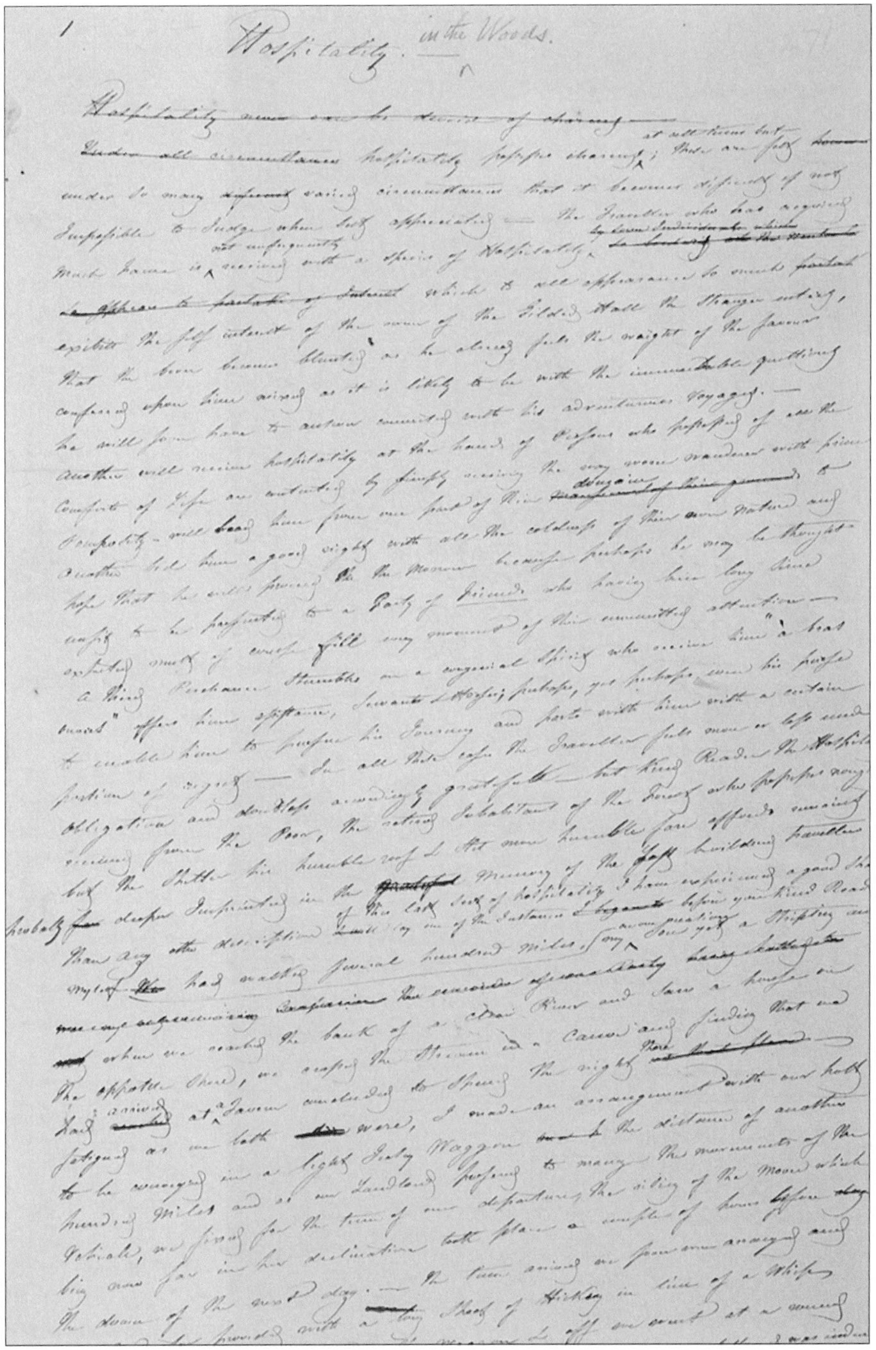
Hospitality. in the Woods.

JOHN JAMES AUDUBON. Autograph Manuscript, *ca.* 1830, entitled "Hospitality [in the Woods]."

Probably written while Audubon was in Edinburgh in late 1829 or early 1830, the manuscript was originally published in that city in 1831 as Episode XV of the first volume of *Ornithological Biography*, as the text accompaniment to *Birds of America*. In this episode, he vividly describes an incident of frontier travel in the Kentucky woods, where he and a fellow traveler were royally entertained by settlers after having lost their way in a storm. It provides Audubon with the perfect anecdote to illustrate the pure and frank hospitality of the American frontier.

"Snowy Heron or White Egret," plate 49 (page CCXLII), from *Birds of America, Drawn from Nature,* by J. J. Audubon. Engraved surface 22 by 18¾; overall 36¼ by 24¾.

This illustration, which shows Audubon in the lower right, is the only one in *Birds of America* in which the artist has portrayed himself.

Chapter 4

LOUISIANA

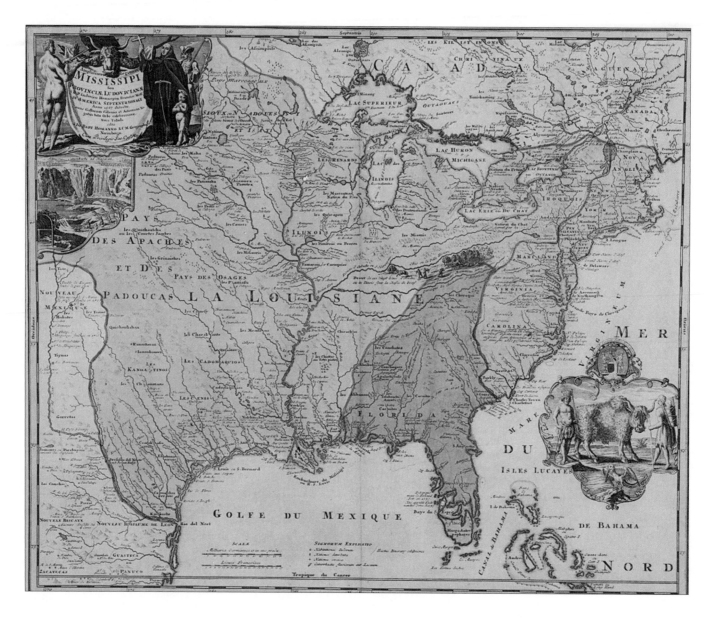

Map of the Mississippi Valley [Homann, Nuremburg, 1759–1784] with insets showing
Niagra Falls and an Indian family with a buffalo and an opossum. 19½ by 23 inches.

The settlement of the Mississippi River Valley by Americans was a lengthy process. The new United States had to solve a number of major problems before it could deal with how to distribute the land and settle the area.

In the early 18th century, Spain owned the west bank of the Mississippi River, and French trading posts occupied much of the land to the east. The French and Indian War, 1755–1763, resulted in a treaty that forced out the French. The Treaty of Paris, 1783, which ended the American Revolution, had recognized the right of the new United States to these lands but left Britain with seven frontier posts. These outposts enabled the British to both continue the fur trade in what would be American territory, and maintain their relationships with the Indians there. Those relationships acted as a buffer between the U. S. territory and the waterway systems vital to England's fur trade in the West and around the Great Lakes.

The Ordinances of 1785–1787 established the methods for developing the area and provided that only the government could negotiate treaties with the Indians to obtain land. While states such as Virginia were claiming huge tracts (Virginia claimed most of the Northwest), settlers were moving into the Mississippi River Valley without regard to land titles or whether the land still belonged to the Indians.

By 1790, settlers were moving north across the Ohio River, and Congress was being pressured by settlers and speculators to acquire lands from the Indians. The extensive forests that covered the present-day states of Ohio, Indiana, and Illinois were rich in furs, and the Indians had no desire to give up the lands that supported their livelihood.

American frontiersmen firmly believed that the British posts providing arms, ammunition, and other supplies to the Indians incited the attacks on American settlements.

The Indians could be formidable enemies. In the fall of 1791, when General Arthur St. Clair, governor of the Northwest Territory, tried to build forts on the Maumee River to counter British influence, a surprise Indian attack near today's Fort Wayne inflicted over 900 casualties on his 2,000 men. St. Clair, laid up in his wagon with gout, was hauled to safety, but few other officers survived. News of the defeat struck fear along the frontier, intensifying the clamor for removal of the British.

The Treaty of Grenville, after General Wayne's victories over several tribes, opened most of the territory to settlement by forcing the Indians to give up much of their land. Other treaties forced other tribes to give up their lands in the Mississippi River Valley, which was about to be overwhelmed with speculators and unscrupulous promoters. The biggest problem confronting the United States — navigation of the Mississippi River — still remained. Negotiations with Spain resulted in the Pinckney Treaty, which gave Americans free navigation of the Mississippi and the right to ship goods through New Orleans for three years free of customs duties.

Suddenly, with three treaties — Jay's, Grenville, and Pinckney's — the Mississippi River Valley was open — until the War of 1812 closed the frontier once more.

During the intervening seventeen years, Americans who were crowded into the area east of the mountains exploded into the West. It was the first opportunity they had to go west and fertile farming land was selling for $2 to $3 an acre compared to $14 to $50 an acre in New England. Other emigrants wanted to escape the religious establishment, taxes, or the rigid social order. In the southern states, farm soil was exhausted and yields had declined. This, in addition to the same incentives motivating Northerners, propelled Southerners westward.

The corrupt practice of distributing land grants to politicians makes one wonder if our present-day corruption isn't just part of the way it's always been. The land companies controlled virtually all of the land, reselling it to squatters and new settlers at an enormous profit. Only pockets of Indian land remained, and in 1830, Andrew Jackson solved this problem for the settlers by signing the Indian Removal Act pushing the frontier to the Mississippi River.

This is not an area popularly collected. In my experience, most artifacts, books, and manuscripts are modestly priced.

Henri Joutel, *Journal Historique du Dernier Voyage Que Feu M. De Lasale Fit Dans le Golfe de Mexique, Pour Trouver L'Embouchure, & Le Cours de la Riviere de Missicipi, Nommee a Present la Riviere de Saint Louis, Qui Traverse le Louisiane....,* 1713.

The premier account of La Salle's tragic last voyage, compiled from the diary of La Salle's close subordinate. It chronicles the unsuccessful attempt to found a French colony on the Gulf of Mexico in 1684, when La Salle's expedition established itself on the Texas coast. The next two years were spent awaiting reinforcements that never came while internal tensions in the party grew. In the end, La Salle and his men determined to return to Canada via the Mississippi, but one of the company assassinated La Salle near the Trinity River, and the company split up. Some of the survivors, including Joutel, pressed on, reaching Canada by way of the Mississippi and Arkansas Rivers.

KING LOUIS XIV OF FRANCE. Letter Signed, ordering Count de Estucca to report on the building of fortifications in the Mississippi Valley, 1676.

Philip Pittman, *The Present State of the European Settlements on the Mississippi; with a Geographical Description of that River....* London, 1770.

The author of the most authoritative work in English on the Mississippi Valley on the eve of the Revolution explored and surveyed the length of the Mississippi. Pittman spent 1763 and 1764 in West Florida and from 1765 to 1768 in Illinois. The book describes the French villages he found there, the country along the Mississippi River, and the commerce of the region. The excellent maps, including the plan of New Orleans, one of the earliest published, are some of the most accurate and detailed produced up to that time.

Nine deniers minted in France, 1721, and shipped to French colonies in North America, especially the newly founded city of New Orleans.

JOHN JAY's notes for the treaty that opened the west. Autograph Manuscript [London, September 1794]. Jay's list of objections to Grenville's proposals for the Treaty of Amity, Commerce and Navigation [1794], better known as Jay's Treaty.

In response to Jay's first draft, which was filled with proposals most advantageous to the United States, British Foreign Secretary Lord Grenville countered with proposals that were given to Jay on August 30, 1794.

The manuscript written by Jay is marked by him "Notes of Objections to Settlement Project." It details the points the United States and Great Britain had not resolved in September 1794. The treaty was signed on November 19, 1794.

The first seven (of eighteen) objections Jay noted are

"1. In what Capacity are they so to remain? As british Subjects or American Citizens? If the first, a Time to make their Elections shd. be assigned.

2. If his Majesty's Subjects are to pass into the American Territories for the Purpose of Indian Trade, ought not american Citizens to be permitted to pass into his Majestys Territories for the like Purpose.

3. If the Am[erica]n Indians are to have the Priviledge of trading with Canada, ought not the Canada Indians to be priviledged to trade with the U.S.?

4. If Goods for Indian Trade shall be introduced Duty Free by british Traders, how is the Introduction of other Goods with them to be prevented? And for this Priviledge, operating a Loss to the Am[erica]n Revenue, what reciprocal Benefit is to be allowed?

6. Why confine the mutual Navigation of the Mississippi to where the same bounds the Territory of the U.S.?

7. Why shd. perpetual commercial Priviledges be granted to G.B. on the Mississippi etc., when she declines granting perpetual Commercial Priviledges to the U.S. anywhere?"

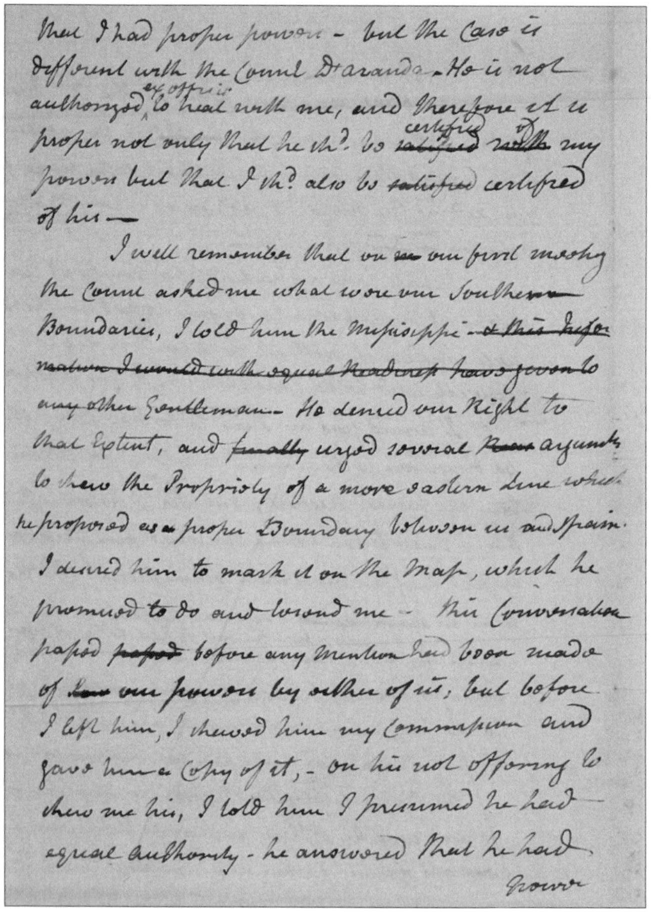

that I had proper powers - but the Case is
different with the Count D'Aranda. He is not
authorized ex officio to treat with me, and therefore it is
proper not only that he sh.d be ~~satisfied~~ certified ~~with~~ of my
powers but that I sh.d also be ~~satisfied~~ certified
of his —

I well remember that on ~~on~~ our first meeting
the Count asked me what were our Southern
Boundaries, I told him the Mississippi ~~& this infor~~
~~mation I would with equal Readiness have given to~~
any other Gentleman. He denied our Right to
that Extent, and ~~finally~~ urged several ~~Reas~~ arguments
to shew the Propriety of a more eastern Line which
he proposed as a proper Boundary between us and Spain.
I desired him to mark it on the Map, which he
promised to do and leave me - this Conversation
passed ~~passed~~ before any mention had been made
of ~~his~~ our powers by either of us; but before
I left him, I shewed him my Commission and
gave him a Copy of it, - on his not offering to
shew me his, I told him I presumed he had
equal authority - he answered that he had
power

An extraordinarily important letter by John Jay, who was at that time negotiating the Treaty that ended the American Revolution, demanding that Spain recognize the Mississippi River as America's western boundary [Paris, September 1782].

"The count asked me what were our southern boundaries and I told him the Mississippi.... He denied our right to that extent, and urged several arguments to show the propriety of a more eastern line which he proposed as a proper boundary between us and Spain."

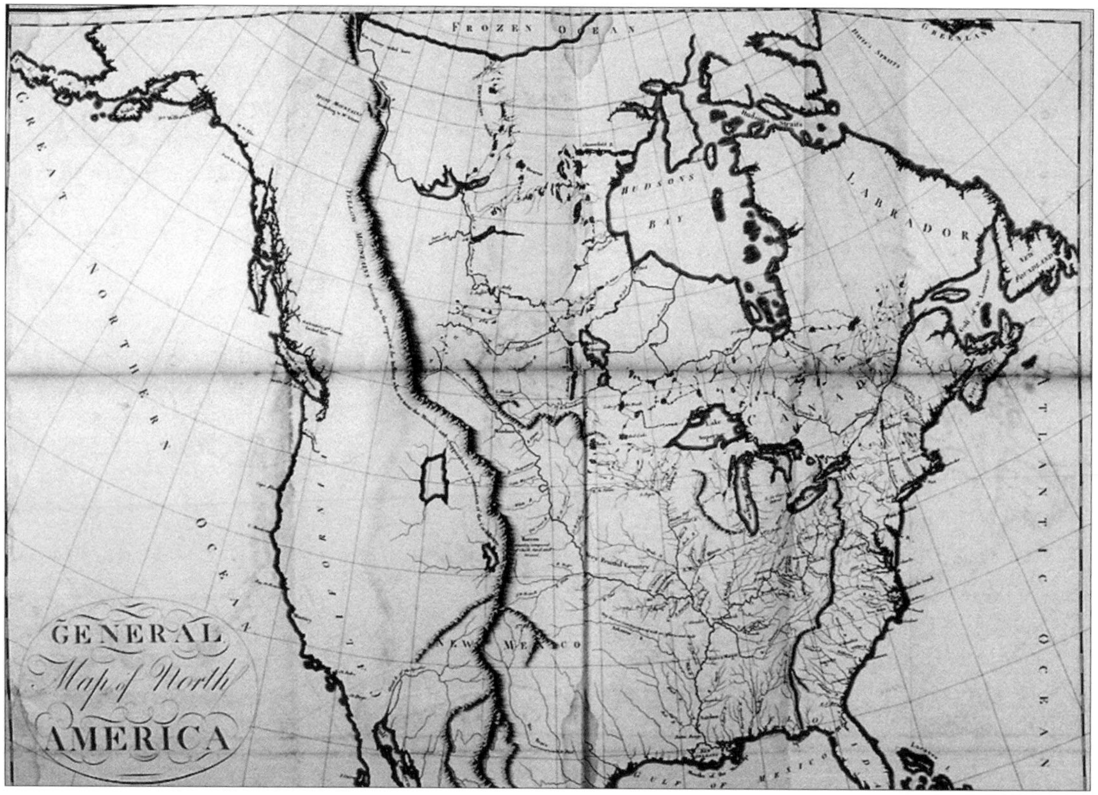

Collot's map from his *Voyage in America,* 1804. In 1796, Collot was sent by the French government to make a general reconnaissance of the Ohio and Mississippi valleys, both to gauge the military situation on the frontier and to gather a view of the strength of secessionist sentiment among the American frontiersmen. His mission was undertaken during a period of great tension between the weak Spanish government in Louisiana and the rapidly expanding power of the United States in the West. Collot performed his mission admirably, creating a wealth of maps and views, as well as soundings of the frontier population.

The emigrations to the Waters thereof, are astonishingly great; and chiefly of that description of People who are not very subordinate to Law & good Government.—Whether the Prohibition from the Court of Spain is just or unjust—politic or otherwise; it will be dificult to restrain a people of this class from the enjoyment of natural advantages.—It is devoutly to be wished that Mr. Gardoqui would enter into such stipulations with Congress as may avert the impending evil, & be mutually advantageous to both Nations.

After the explicit declarations of the Emperor, respecting the navigation of the Scheldt, and his other demands upon Holland he will stand I think, upon unfavorable ground; for if he recedes, his foresight & judgment may be arraigned—and if he proceeds, his suit may be involved.—But probably I am hazarding

GEORGE WASHINGTON. Autograph Letter Signed, June 21, 1785, to the French chargé d'affaires, expressing his opinion on one of the most important issues of the time: the right of free navigation of the Mississippi.

"I wish disagreeable consequences may not result from the contentions respecting the navigation of the River Mississippi. The emigrations to the waters thereof, are astonishingly great; and chiefly of that description of People who are not very subordinate to Law & good Government. Whether the prohibition from the Court of Spain is just or unjust, politic or otherwise; it will be difficult to restrain a people of this class from the enjoyment of natural advantages. It is devoutly to be wished that Mr. Gardoqui would enter into such stipulations with Congress as may avert the impending evil, & be mutually advantageous to both Nations.

"After the explicit declarations of the Emperor, respecting the Navigation of the Scheldt, and his other demands upon Holland, he will stand I think, upon unfavorable ground; for if he recedes, his foresight & judgment may be arraigned, and if he proceeds, his suit may be involved. But probably I am hazarding sentiments upon a superficial view of things, when it will appear, ultimately, that he has had important objects in view, and has accomplished them."

Washington's letter, expressing his views in favor of the free navigation of the Mississippi River, reflects explicitly on the negotiations that were currently taking place between the Spanish minister, Don Diego de Gardoqui, and John Jay. His support was based on his belief that if "trade would go down the Mississippi as soon as Spain had the wisdom to welcome it, this was an indirect argument for the development of the Potomac…. [Goods]…could be delivered to the Ohio far more cheaply and more quickly via the Potomac than by the long, long voyage back up the Mississippi against the current." (Douglas S. Freeman, George Washington).

The issue of free navigation was, of course, "important to the inhabitants of the interior Mississippi Valley at a time when the river was their main highway of commerce and its mouth was owned by a foreign power. The establishment of the right was an important step in the world wide liberation of commerce. It was first granted by France, which then owned Louisiana, in favor of Great Britain and was a by-product of the territorial settlement at the end of the French and Indian War…. At the same time France ceded Louisiana to Spain…. During the American Revolution both British subjects and American citizens claimed the right of free navigation and Spain permitted both of them to navigate it for a time — the British until 1779, when Spain went to war with Britain, and the American until 1784, when Spain closed the river to all foreigners, mainly in the hope of checking the growth of American settlements in the West." (Dictionary of American History)

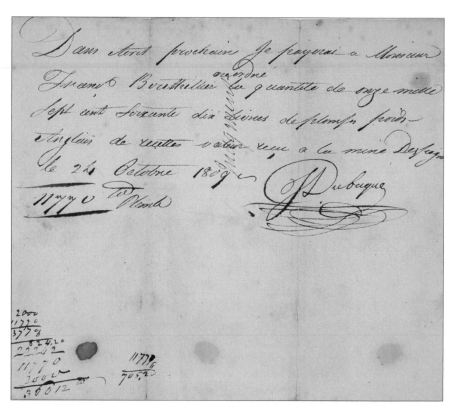

JULIEN DUBUQUE, the first white settler in Iowa, promissory note signed, 1809.

THOMAS JEFFERSON wrote July 11, 1806, *"All…you see…about danger of Indian Hostilities is entirely false. The French part of the N. Orleans legislature have proved clearly that that people is not yet capable of self government."*

The governor of Upper Louisiana, Benjamin Howard, reflected the Western perspective when he wrote to Robert Wickliff from St. Louis on May 26, 1812, discussing at great length his actions *"for the defences of the frontier…. When they hear of the late [miseries] in Indiana, and the deplorable state of the Country, the people running off…the Govr. sending his wife away and fortifying his own house. What would have been our situation if no preparations had been made. We have not the strong and intrepid populations of Kentucky to call upon in the moment of difficulty and confusion. Our strength is not great but our plan of defence is settled and now understood by the people. Each man on the frontier is fixed and has made up his mind to make a stand, and altho we may be attacked and injured yet the enemy will feel too, but perhaps I feel more alive on this subject than you."*

In another letter to Robert Wickliff, September 5, 1813, he wrote, *"organizing about 1000 men for an Expedition against the Indians in the neighborhood of Peoria, they have come down and settled at their former village…. If I had those men I could*

have taken high ground with our numerous enemies in this quarter; with my present force, to annoy them partially is all I can expect."

Not everyone found the Indians the only problem. Andrew Chute, a physician, wrote to his sister and brother-in-law from Independence and Westport, Missouri, 1835: *"I am living snugly in a log hut in the West…. Business of all kinds is very profitable and none more so than the practice of medicine, but physicians are exposed more than all others to the various causes of disease, and the sickness and mortality among them are very great."*

Concerning the state of religion among the Indians and other Westerners, he wrote, *"The great mass are sunk in the grossest ignorance and indifference to religion. There is certainly a field for Christian effort…. It is lamentable to see a population sufficiently large to constitute an entire state…almost entirely destitute of moral instruction…. Though Sabbath breaking, intemperance, profanity, falsehood, and impurity prevail… I never heard one syllable uttered by a preacher against them."*

The constant problem of white settlers moving onto Indian lands was a concern of fair-minded Easterners.

Thomas Jefferson in a letter to General Smith on December 24, 1791, wrote, *"The opposition made by Governor Blount & yourself to all attempts by citizens of the U.S. to settle within the Indian lines without authority from the General government is approved, and should be continued."*

General Arthur St. Clair, the governor of the Northwest Territory, was frequently faced with the issue. He wrote from Cincinnati on July 16, 1796, to General James Wilkinson concerning Zachariah Coxe, who had started an illegal settlement on the Ohio River.

"It is important to the public interests the settlement made by Coxe, below the mouth of the Cumberland, should be broken up, and that he himself should be made prisoner…. Upon the presumption that the Lands, upon which the Settlement is formed, are a part of those allotted to the Chickasaws by the Treaty of Hopewel in 1786…[i]t is declared to be lawful for the military force of the United States to apprehend every person who shall be found in the Indian Country over and beyond the boundary-line between the United States and the Indian Tribes."

HENRY R. SCHOOLCRAFT, explorer and ethnologist; Indian agent in the Lake Superior region from 1822 to 1836. Autograph Letter Signed, Sault Sainte Marie [Michigan], June 24, 1826. To Robert Stuart of the American Fur Co. on Mackinac Island, discussing delivery of various goods and other business.

"My express canoe returned…having performed the voyage in 24 days…. The Governor's canoe left on the 16th, & from the state of the wind, probably reaches Detroit on the 20th. You may therefore look for His Excellency about the 4th of July."

Percussion rifle, .50 caliber, sold to settlers in the Mississippi Valley by Louis Hoffman, Vicksburg, 1850s.

Remington "over and under" pistol commonly used by riverboat gamblers.

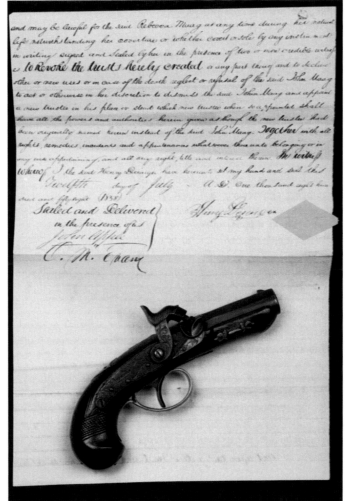

A flintlock pistol made by Henry Deringer, with a document signed by him, 1838.

The Immigrants Guide to the Western States of America, by John Regan, published in Edinborough in 1852 begins, "America is the land of freedom, not withstanding her Negro slavery! Freed from the antiquated and absurd traditions of European states which weigh like an incubus upon the energies of their people and in the enjoyment of an unencumbered energy she stands forth the most favored land under the broad heavens…. The great immigration field in the Mississippi Valley consisting of the states of Illinois, Iowa, Minnesota, Wisconsin, Michigan and Indiana, embraces a territory 360,000 square miles or three times the extent of Great Britain and Ireland of surpassing fertility watered by a system of rivers unequaled in the world. To this fine country would I direct the attention of immigrants…. There is all the difference in the world between the American seaboard and the interior in the manners of the people. On the coast the manners of older countries in some measure prevail and a just estimate of the true character of the people can not be formed from that source…. In the United States an industrious man has a tenfold better opportunity of improving his condition than here. How few working men in this country are laying up anything for old age and infirmity? Do they not find that all their weekly earnings are barely sufficient to meet their weekly wants? What must they expect when sickness and old age come upon them?…. There was once upon a time when one might have said 'the hand of the diligent maketh rich' and relied upon it under all circumstances. We have come to a poor pass indeed when in our native land such an axiomatic proverb as that must be taken with many exceptions…. He who will not arise…and make the proverb good deserves the fate that awaits him."

The author then outlines the basic rules for immigrants to America:

"To purchase land there is as easy as to rent it here…. The country is everywhere well-watered…. The country is fertile to a remarkable extent…. The people are essentially democratic, like their institutions: they are an educated people without which a democracy could not subsist…. That Work! Work!! Work!!! Must be the order of the day with all who immigrate to better their fortunes. To honest and prudent industry everything will be conceded. To indolence and imprudent movements nothing but disappointment. The roughness of first appearances must not be minded. The vigorous and resolute hand put forth in all discouraging appearances will melt as the mists of the morning before the rising sun…. The New World supplies territory while the Old World supplies people…. To all who feel themselves pinched and straitened in this Old World from no fault of their own I would say WESTWARD, HO!"

Another book written for Europeans is Laurence Oliphant's *Minnesota and the Far West in 1855.*

"The impressions of a traveler visiting the United States…for the first time are so totally unlike those which he has experienced in the course of his rambles in the Old World that he at once perceives that in order to the due appreciation of the country he is about to explore an entire revolution must be effected and those habits of thought and observation…. Instead of moralizing over magnificence in a process of decay he must here watch resources in a process of development. He must substitute the pleasures of anticipation for those of retrospection, must be more familiar with pecuniary speculations than with historical associations — delight himself rather in statistics than in poetry-visit docks instead of ruins."

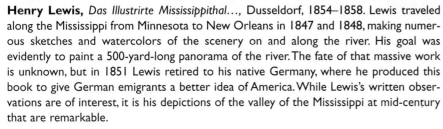

Henry Lewis, *Das Illustrirte Mississippithal…,* Dusseldorf, 1854–1858. Lewis traveled along the Mississippi from Minnesota to New Orleans in 1847 and 1848, making numerous sketches and watercolors of the scenery on and along the river. His goal was evidently to paint a 500-yard-long panorama of the river. The fate of that massive work is unknown, but in 1851 Lewis retired to his native Germany, where he produced this book to give German emigrants a better idea of America. While Lewis's written observations are of interest, it is his depictions of the valley of the Mississippi at mid-century that are remarkable.

"This book is famous for its colored plates of places and scenes along the Mississippi in the second quarter of the nineteenth century. These include views of such well known cities as St. Louis, St. Paul, Dubuque, Burlington, Keokus, Memphis, Vicksburg, Natchez, and Baton Rouge. At the end is a magnificent folding plate of New Orleans." (Thomas Streeter). The Graff catalogue calls this *"one of the half-dozen great and rare illustrated books relating to North America."*

"The Jolly Flat Boat Men." From the original painting distributed by the American Art Union in 1847. Published exclusively for the members of that year, 1847. Painted by G. C. Bingham. Engraved by T. Doney. 26½ by 23 inches.

Chapter 5

LEWIS AND CLARK

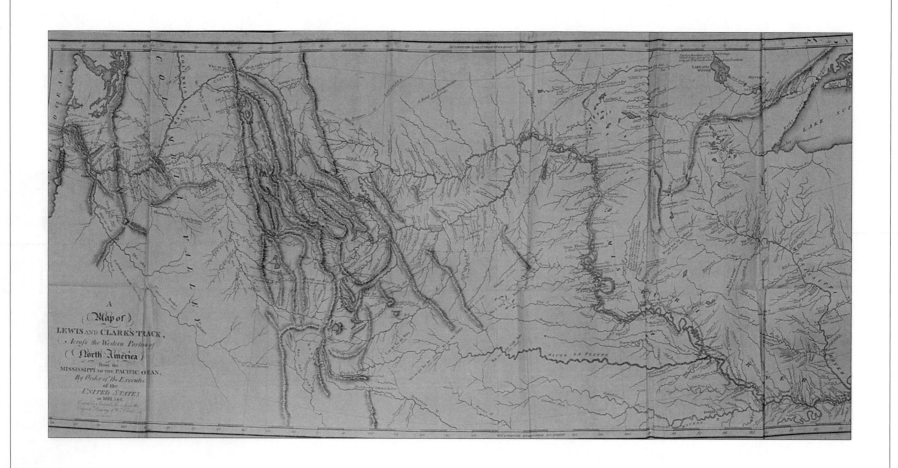

The most important part of the Lewis and Clark report was their map, which was sold separately from the two volume account of the expedition. It is extraordinarily rare and is not usually found in the first edition. 12½ by 27 inches.

After Louisiana had been ceded by France to Spain during the French and Indian War, the Spanish had allowed Americans free navigation of the Mississippi River. This right was vital to the settlers of the Mississippi Valley, Kentucky, Ohio, and Tennessee for whom the river provided a waterway to the rest of the world.

When Napoleon demanded that Spain, which he had virtually annexed, give Louisiana back to France, the Spanish readily agreed — there was no choice, and Louisiana was not a profitable colony. Before the transfer was made public — just before Jefferson became President — Spain closed the Mississippi River to Americans. The American West realized the threat to their commerce, and Jefferson realized Napoleon's potential threat to America.

If France owned the land west of the Mississippi, and France and England went to war (as seemed inevitable), England would likely move into Louisiana and close the Mississippi River — much more serious than Spain's doing so.

Jefferson was surprised by Napoleon's offer to sell Louisiana, and a deal was struck for $15 million that doubled the size of the United States.

The Lewis and Clark expedition had many important scientific objectives and Jefferson arranged for Lewis to be tutored in the sciences. The a primary objective was to find a water route across the continent. Lewis and Clark could succeed in the former, but no one could find a water route that didn't exist.

This Season Medal, representing the family, depicts a family scene in a typical American room, *ca.* 1796. In the background, a woman is weaving on a large vertical loom. In the foreground another woman, dressed in a flowing skirt uses a foot-treadle–powered spinning wheel. At the left, a young child beside the spinner's chair watches an infant in a cradle. At the right is an open fireplace with andirons and, above it, a kettle suspended on a chain and several utensils.

John Trumbull, who designed the medal, said, *"It is meant to convey an idea of domestic tranquility and employment."*

Although the specific pedigree of this medal is not known, it is quite likely that it was taken on the Lewis and Clark expedition and was presented to an Indian. Their journal records that fifty-five specimens were taken along on the trip. Pieces made for collector purposes were not fitted with suspension loops.

Meriwether Lewis and William Clark, *History of the Expedition Under the Command of Captains Lewis and Clark, to the Sources of the Missouri, Thence Across the Rocky Mountains and Down the River Columbia to the Pacific Ocean. Performed During the Years 1804–5–6...,* Philadelphia, 1814.

First edition of the definitive account of the most important exploration of the North American continent. It is the official account of the first major exploration of the Transmississippi by the United States.

HISTORY

OF

THE EXPEDITION

UNDER THE COMMAND OF

CAPTAINS LEWIS AND CLARK,

TO

THE SOURCES OF THE MISSOURI,

THENCE

ACROSS THE ROCKY MOUNTAINS

AND DOWN THE

RIVER COLUMBIA TO THE PACIFIC OCEAN.

PERFORMED DURING THE YEARS 1804—5—6.

By order of the

GOVERNMENT OF THE UNITED STATES.

PREPARED FOR THE PRESS

BY PAUL ALLEN, ESQUIRE.

IN TWO VOLUMES.

VOL. I.

PHILADELPHIA:

PUBLISHED BY BRADFORD AND INSKEEP; AND

ABM: H. INSKEEP, NEWYORK.

J. Maxwell, Printer.

1814.

Book D. N° 16

Paris, June 7th 1803.

Sir,

We have the pleasure to forward you by Mr. Jay the ratification by the first Consul of the Treaty and Conventions which we concluded on the 30th of April with this Republic. We have heretofore forwarded to you the original Instruments & two Copies by different routes, the original by Havre, under the care of M. Hughes, who sailed about two weeks since, expressly charged with that object, and instructed to proceed with the greatest possible dispatch, after his arrival in the United States, to the City of Washington, to deliver the same in person: the second by the way of England, under the care of Mr. Reid, son of the late President of Pensylvania, who was instructed to forward it, immediately on his arrival in England, by the most prompt & safe opportunity that offered; the 3d by Mr. Derieux, who sailed from Bordeaux. We flatter ourselves that you will receive those several Communications in the course of the present month, and this by Mr. Jay early in July, as it is highly important that our governt. should receive and act on the subject of them as soon as possible. The

R. M. Osborne, a United States agent in the newly acquired Louisiana Territory wrote to the chief of the Osages on the River Arkansas, August 10, 1805, that he was forwarding to the governor of Louisiana, James Wilkinson, the chief's request for official recognition of his tribe:

"[A]s it seems to be your wish to have both a commission and flag from the American government as a testimony of their friendship towards the people of your nation, I shall by the first convenient opportunity transmit to the governor of Louisiana & commander in chief of the army a copy of your commission with the substance of your message to me. Until his pleasure is known I would recommend to you to live in perfect friendship with the white people who may occasionally come among you, and endeavor to cultivate the friendship and esteem of your neighbours. It is a duty encumbent on you to keep the young men and women of your tribe in habits of industry & sobriety and prevent as much as possible the introduction of ardent spirits and such other kinds of merchandise as tend to corrupt their morals, their minds, and dispositions. Should the white people of America learn that your conduct is such as merit it, they will no doubt feel every disposition to treat you as friends wherever they meet with you."

ROBERT R. LIVINGSTON as American minister to France, and James Monroe as special envoy. Letter, unsigned [retained copy], Paris, June 7, 1803. To Secretary of State James Madison. In late April 1803, France agreed to sell the Louisiana Territory to the United States. Five and one-half weeks after the Treaty of Cession and its two accompanying conventions had been signed, Livingston and Monroe, in this twelve-page letter, discuss the final stages of the Louisiana Purchase and express their anxieties that France might back out of the deal as it appeared that she was experiencing seller's remorse.

63

MERIWETHER LEWIS. Autograph Letter Signed, Louisville, Kentucky, November 9, 1806. To Henry Dearborn, the Secretary of War.

"My bill of exchange No. 115 of this date in favor of Capt. William Clark for the sum of four hundred dollars is in part monies due him for his services while on the late expedition to the Pacific Ocean, and which when paid will be charged to me on the faith of my final settlement with the United States relative to the said Expedition…"

Six weeks earlier Lewis and Clark had returned to St. Louis after the expedition. Lewis arrived in Washington on December 28. There, he made recommendations to Congress to reward the participants.

Stephen E. Ambrose in *Undaunted Courage* wrote that Lewis had already, in an initial report to President Jefferson, paid tribute to Clark, stating that "'he is equally with myself entitled to your consideration and that of our common country.' …That put it directly before the president: Lewis wanted him as captain and co-commander. This was what he had promised, what Clark had earned. To Lewis, any other action was unthinkable." Lewis and Clark each received a total of $7,262 in compensation.

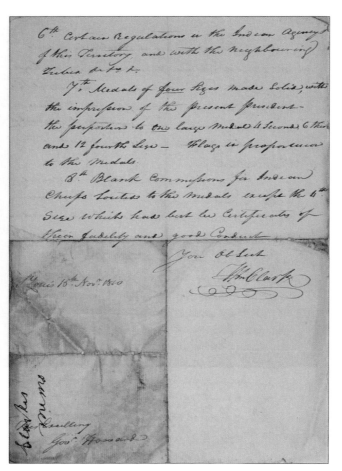

WILLIAM CLARK. Autograph Letter Signed, written as superintendent of Indian Affairs, St. Louis, November 15, 1810.

"When you are at Washington, your attention to certain points…would conduce much to the safety and quiet of this detached part of the Country…. A Military Establishment & Factory at pra[i]rie de Chien…. The Boundary line run in conformity with the Sae & Fox Treaty. The Osage annuities given them at the Factory on the Missouri, at the time of running the line agreeably to the Osage Treaty which is indispensable, arrangements made to build Blockhouses & a Horse mule, and a Black smith furnished at the Fort…. Medals of four Sizes made solid, with the impression of the present president, the proportion to one large medal 4 second 6 third and 12 fourth size. Flags in proportion to the medals. Blank commissions for Indian chiefs [suited] to the medals."

U.S. Model 1803 Harpers Ferry flintlock rifle, dated 1805. This model rifle was carried by the Lewis and Clark expedition.

The large-size Jefferson Indian Peace Medal in silver. Lewis and Clark carried three of this size (4-inch diameter) for the chiefs of the Mandans, Arikaras, and Omahas. Jefferson himself also presented prominent chiefs brought to Washington with the largest medal. Less than ten specimens are known. Lewis and Clark also carried thirteen medium-size silver medals and sixteen smaller ones.

Gaining the friendship and respect of the Indian tribes they would encounter was one of Lewis and Clark's major goals. Indian leaders in the Mississippi Valley and especially along the Missouri had long been accustomed to gifts of silver medals from the British, French, and Spanish, so Lewis and Clark had to be prepared.

Chapter 6

THE FUR TRADE

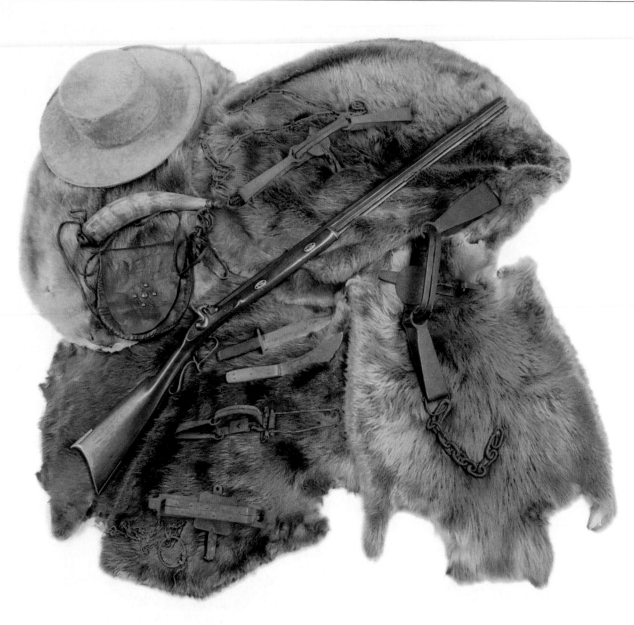

Tools of the fur trade: Plains rifle by H. E. Dimick, St. Louis, .44 caliber, *ca.* 1850s, various traps and knives, together with beaver skins and a beaver hat.

The fur trade, and to a lesser degree, fishing were France's principal interests in the New World. The Indians' knowledge that France didn't want their lands (Quebec was founded on unoccupied land) gave the French a distinct advantage over the English.

France's competition with the English and Dutch increased as the Indians' desire for European trade goods continued to grow, and European countries played on intertribal rivalries, at first in the East, and then further west as the pelts were depleted. The Iroquois, backed by the English, attacked French traders to keep them out of the fur-rich Mississippi Valley. In 1701, the French and Iroquois made peace, and the English took on open competition and warfare with the French, eventually driving them out of North America.

The Hudson's Bay Company became the dominant force, later rivaled by the North West Company, but after the Louisiana Purchase and the Lewis and Clark expedition, the Americans became an important factor. One of the first American expeditions was led by Manuel Lisa, and the other by William Henry Ashley. Both expeditions went up the Mississippi and Missouri Rivers establishing trading posts. They created regional monopolies but their competition, John Jacob Astor's American Fur Company, which had started dealing in furs on the New York frontier, was designing a global monopoly. Astor intended to take over the western fur trade by setting up trading posts across the West and establishing his major trading post at the mouth of the Columbia River. From there, his ships would take furs directly to the Orient and bring back trade goods. His plans might have worked if not for the War of 1812.

After establishing Astoria, a post at the mouth of the Columbia River, Astor's ship went north to trade, where all of the crew was killed and the ship blown up by natives. Astor and his partners thought it best to sell out to the Canadian North West Company, when they learned of the outbreak of war and were threatened by British ships. Astor was essentially out of the western fur trade.

Eventually the Hudson's Bay Company took over the North West Company. In the United States territory, the Rocky Mountain Fur Company came to dominate the fur trade. Their success was fueled by the innovative practice of the annual rendezvous. Instead of establishing posts throughout the west, the company brought trade goods to annual meetings in various mountain locations, allowing the trappers to stay in the mountains and trap without having to travel east with their furs. The company prospered (see the document on page 82) until the mid-19th century when the silk hat became the fashion rage in Europe and the beaver hat's popularity declined.

Some of the artifacts, specifically trade axes and guns, except for Hawkens, are available to collectors. Very few documents or letters are ever offered on the market. Generally, while almost everything related to the fur trade is rare, collector interest is not so overwhelming as to make offerings as rare or as expensive as the rarity and interest of the pieces might otherwise warrant.

The island of Michilimackinac (present-day Mackinac) between lakes Huron and Michigan was at the center of the fur trade from its beginning to its decline in the 19th century. It contained the vital waterways to the West, as well as to the Chicago area and to the Mississippi River. Trade goods were assembled in Montreal in the winter and then sent by boat to Michilimackinac, where the island trading post was the distribution and trading center for the entire fur trade in the northern part of the continent.

ROBERT GIGUIERE. An exceptionally early Document Signed, August 1, 1661.

"Messrs. Giguiere will load the surplus of pelts that they will be able to carry in the canoe that…Perrot must furnish them for their trip, without having to leave when the pelts belonging to…Perrot have been loaded. Drawn at Michilimackinac."

HENRI DE TONTY, pioneer fur trader and explorer. Contract signed with two voyageurs, August 18, 1686, together with the inventory of trading goods. The contract gives Tonty (the holder of one of only twenty-five Royal permits) half the proceeds of their fur trading and allows the two voyageurs to take general trade items of their own on the trip. The inventory of trade goods illustrates what they believed would be most appealing to the Indians at this early time. Tonty had just returned from a voyage down the Mississippi in search of Las Salle's lost expedition when he wrote this document.

Hudson's Bay Company. Letter Signed by Prince Rupert, Sir George Carteret, one of the proprietors of New Jersey, and other members of the Admiralty Board, March 9, 1673/74. To the Principal Officers and Com: of his Ma: Navy, concerning the early affairs of the Hudson's Bay Company, which was organized by Prince Rupert and other influential Englishmen and chartered in 1670 as *The Governor and Company of Adventurers of England Trading into Hudson's Bay,* for the purpose of seeking a northwest passage and engaging in fur trade in the untapped vast area northwest of Lake Superior.

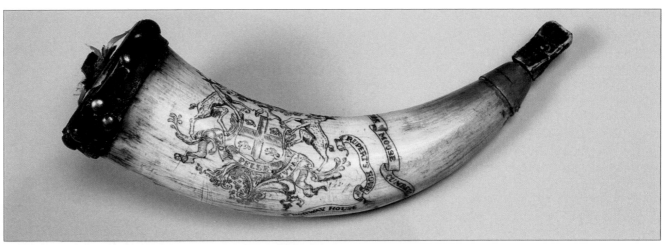

Powder horn engraved with the symbol of the Hudson's Bay Company, 19th century.

Hudson's Bay Company silver Friendship Medal with the likeness of King George III, late 18th century.

Hudson's Bay Company medal, after 1801, used as a gift to friendly Indians.

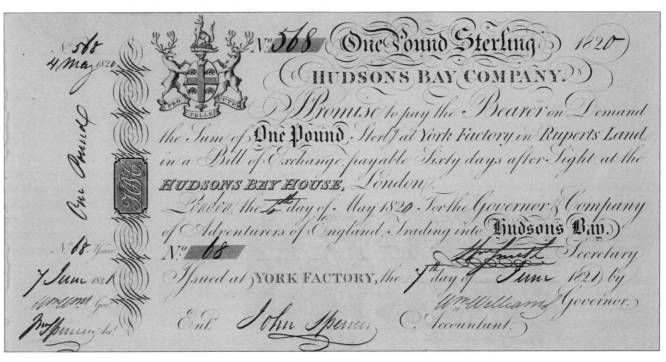

Hudson's Bay Company script for one pound, issued at York Factory on Hudson Bay, 1821.

The classic beaver tall hat, *ca.* 1800–1815. The label on the silk lining inside, depicting two beavers on a river-bank, reads, *"Stillman, Manufacture and Dealer in Hats, Caps and Furs…Hartford, Conn."*

In a very interesting *Memorial of Sundry Manufacturers of Hats in…Philadelphia,* 1806, forty-six hatmakers in Philadelphia petitioned Congress to make more furs available to American hatmakers, rather than sending them to Europe.

"That your memorialists are engaged in a branch of manufactures of considerable importance; that owing to the regulations with the Indian tribes on our frontiers, they are obliged to depend for a very large proportion of furs, the raw materials of their manufacturers, on the government of the United States; that the mode at present adopted by the agent for Indian affairs in vending these furs is, in the opinion of your memorialists, improper and disadvantageous to the manufacturer, and to the interests of the government.

"By the plan now in operation, the agent for Indian affairs exercises a complete control over the sale of these furs, and may dispose of them at what places, for what prices, and in what quantity he may deem most proper. Thus are your memorialists dependent on the will of an individual, for the raw materials of their manufacturers; and have been, and still may be, obliged to witness the exportation of these furs to Europe, to enrich and encourage foreign, to the injury and ruin of domestic manufactures. This your memorialists consider a hardship and a serious evil to their country, and to remedy it, humbly request the serious attention of Congress.

"[We] suggest to the wisdom of congress, the propriety of regulating by law, the mode of selling the furs belonging to the United States, so as to insure a better supply today to *the manufacturers and a fair price to the government. The mode which your memorialists beg leave to suggest is a sale by public auction, at such times and places as may enable the manufacturers and others generally to attend….The government will receive a full price, and the American manufacturer, whether of large or small capital, be enabled to obtain a sufficient supply."*

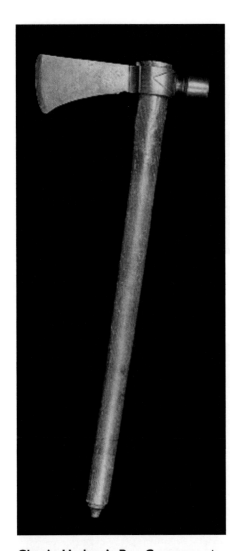

Classic Indian fur trade musket with the brass dragon sideplate, 1851.

Indian trade musket made by Barnett, 1828.

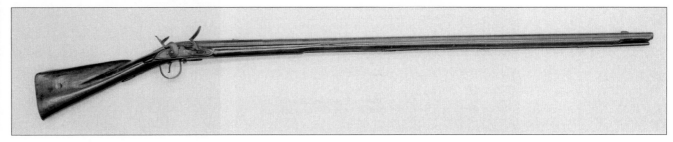

Classic Hudson's Bay Company pipe tomahawk, *ca.* 1770–1790, marked "Parkes" with British Broadarrow on reverse, used as a treaty gift.

Fur trade musket, with an exceptionally long barrel (47½ inches), made by Barnett, 1800, for the North West Company.

A Contract for Voyageurs. Document Signed, Montreal, January 17, 1820. A contract in which Allard and LaFleur agree to *"make the journey in winter for three years in the dependencies of the Northwest of Upper Canada."* Archibald McLeod, who played a leading role in the struggle between the North West Company and the Hudson's Bay Company for control of the western fur trade, signed on behalf of the company.

The North West Company's 1820 Beaver Token was the only circulating currency in the Pacific Northwest. It is believed to represent one Beaver skin; all known examples were unearthed in the Columbia and Umpqua River Valleys in Oregon.

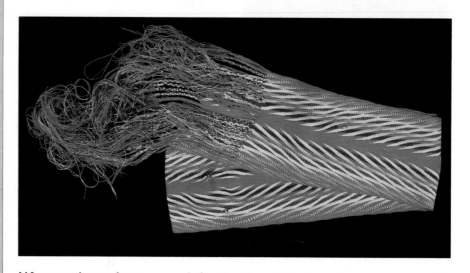

L'Assomption sashes are named after the village in Quebec where many were made. They were traded extensively throughout North America by fur traders, and many voyageurs wore them as part of their regular attire. The sashes were not only decorative but also functional — the key to an individual's trunk, in which his every possession was usually stored, was often attached to one end.

A draft of the Articles of Association of the North West Trading Company, Boston, 1808. The articles state the plans for a proposed enterprise, whose principal objective was to establish a permanent settlement at the mouth of the Columbia River as a site to deposit trade goods and a safe haven for ships.

North West Company. Invoice Signed, McTavish Frobisher & Co., Agents NW Co., Montreal, May 5, 1806. Sundries forwarded from Montreal by the North West Company to River St. Maurice, including blankets, cloth, Russian sheeting, cotton, Irish linen, colored thread, stitching needles, scalpers, awls, fire steels, gun flints, fishing lines, round beads, cod lines, files, scissors, blank books, paper, ink powder, quills, lead pencils, sealing wax, tea, oxhide shoes, portage collars, men's Montreal hats, wool hats, beaver ruffs, corn, peas, gunpowder, molasses, pork, butter, spirits, wine, brandy, sugar, carrot tobacco, salt, soap, mattresses, a tent with poles &c, biscuits, flour, pork, and kegs.

ALEXANDER HENRY. Autograph Letter Signed, Montreal, January 10, 1823. To John Haynes, Indian agent at Fort Wayne, Michigan Territory.

Henry entered the fur trade in 1761. When a venture for mining copper near Lake Superior proved unsuccessful, he returned to the fur trade and made many expeditions between Montreal and the Rocky Mountains. In 1809, he published his valuable *Travels and Adventures in Canada and the Indian Territories Between the Years 1760 and 1776.*

Robert Stuart, head of the American Fur Company in the Upper Great Lakes Region, handwritten report to Ramsay Crooks, the head of the New York division, Mackinac, November 10, 1822. A lengthy report on activities in Stuart's area:

"I have had a letter from Rolette of 19th Sept_ with 23 Packs, principally Deer skins, but the season is so far advanced, that the navigation of the North River must be closed…. I would therefore keep them here until spring…. McKinzie has arrived at the Prairie with $40,000 worth of Goods — Lockwood with $18,000 worth; the Grignons…have bent their course that way; and a young man belonging to Stone or Dousman, went up the St. Peters 'some time ago.'… He begs that Mr. Matthews be requested to bring him next spring from Montreal, 1 pr: fine linen made into shirts: and to get from Gibby 3 prs: Pantaloons of cloth_ 1 Body Coat & 1 suitout, all of fashionable colors…. You will have to watch McKinzie, this winter yet, for I have direct and positive information, from a person from one of the Bureauz [sic], that an attempt is to be made to trammel the trade…. Holidays…has a very strong opposition this season, and the consequence will of course be, no return, for you know his maxim in such cases is to prevent the Indians hunting altogether…. Do not neglect to let me know as soon as practicable all you may learn of the new opposition, as it may be of conse-

quence to know what their movements are likely to be, early…. We are to have a monthly express this winter, so you can write often….

"The letter which Dousman got last summer to join the great Boston Co. was written him by Stone, from Detroit, and I have not the least doubt but he is at the bottom of the whole affair; although perhaps not deeply interested, he may suppose it would be an effectual method of embarassing our operations at St. Louis etc: but if we understand our own interest it ought to have the contrary effect; and I give it as my candid opinion, that unless we crush their ambitious views in that quarter at once, (which you can easily effect at present, from the disgust the people of that place express toward them,) they will soon show themselves in every section of the country. Could you reconcile the interests at St. Louis, and make a general arrangement, it would give them death blow to all their hopes; and depend upon it, they would quarrel and all go to flinders. But this I suppose the old Gentleman cannot be made to understand, as it would require some enlargement of means etc: but should you lay the whole ground open to his view, he has too much sagacity not to further the 'project' for it would at once give us the controul of the whole country; and the additional sum requisite is not so alarming as at first sight might appears; of this enough you will of course do for the best."

RAMSEY CROOKS. Head of the American Fur Company in New York, to Robert Stuart, Great Lakes Partner, March 12, 1828. A detailed discussion of company affairs and plans:

"On the subject of Mr. Rolettes present Outfit[:]… His disposition to have always at command more than enough of goods…to his extravagant notions in regard to his supplies for the trade. Mr. H. L. Dousman informs us that there are many unsaleable articles at Prairie des Chiens which merely serve to swell the annual inventory of the upper Mississippi Outfit. I have…advised Mr. Rolette to carry back all such goods to Mackinac, and you will use your best endeavours to get them off our hands on the most favorable terms…. Dousman['s] orders amount to about $800, laid out in Iron, Wampum, Garnets, Common Broaches, Wine, Brandy, Tea, Medicines…. We have furnished these things so that he may not have the most remote cause to complain…. I have no doubt it will be much for our interest that he should in the future depend on Mackinac alone, for all his supplies of merchandize…. At the request of the parties 2 Kegs Port Wine will go up from Montreal for Judge Doty…. Mr. Franchere has all the Boatmen, and nearly all the mechanics engaged, and will have everything ready to move by the 1st. May, or earlier if the season permits…. If any part of your Buffalo Robes had come here, the whole of the article would have been taken to account_ but Mr. Matthews sold all at Buffalo (except the 36 sent up by him to Detroit Department) and you were credited for proceeds of the sale…. You will therefore have to debit Detroit Dept. for these 36 Buffalo Robes…. My letter of 23 January will tell you everything about the _Traps_ I am truly sorry that the German Steel…is so very bad…. I think it possible your Blacksmith does not understand work…. [A]ll the Tobacco you want was at Detroit last October in anticipation of your order…. Mr. Hubbard has drawn for $160 on account of skins he purchased, and he has sent a memo of goods which will amount to probably $1300. It will be cut down to the $1000, and I am truly sorry you ever authorized him to commence this demi-savage traffic, for I think we have sufficient evidence to conclude we would be the gainers by attending…exclusively to the trade with the Indians, or if with the Whites, for such articles only as we usually furnish the Natives: but I have no opinion of carrying among the civilized border population an assortment of goods adapted to a different state of society…. Mr Rolette advises that he will send 2 Boats to Green Bay early in the Spring, and requests that you will forward by the first vessel 40 to 50 barrel bulk of Salt, Sugar, Whisky & Pork to meet them at Green Bay and load them back to the Prairie. The season on the upper Mississippi has been favorable for hunting Muskrats…. Judge Doty has not paid his account yet…. It appears that nearly half the amount which stands at his debit in the Company's books, is a claim of your own against the judge — and I will just remark that this office can not recognize any such transfers_ With your own means you of course do as you please, and although we incur no risk of loss, because in the event of non-payment the amount can always be charged back to you, still it is a practice we cannot approve of…. If you will lend your money, you must make your own collections…. While on the subject of accounts I…understand you credit yourself 7 percent per annum on all money you individually furnish the Company…. If you prefer placing your money in our hands, you must conform to the terms on which we keep such deposits…5 percent."

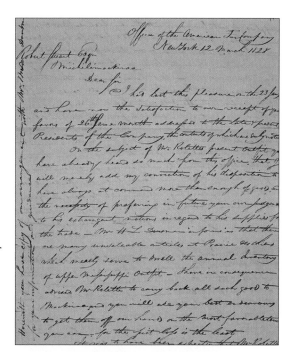

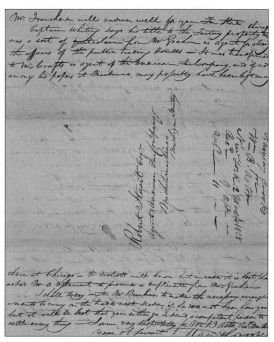

WILLIAM H. ASHLEY, pioneer fur trader and explorer.

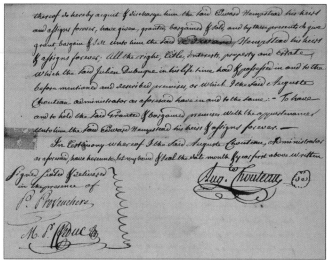

RENE AUGUSTE CHOUTEAU, cofounder of the city of St. Louis and important fur trader. Document Signed, July 2, 1811, as administrator of the estate of Iowa pioneer Julien Dubuque.

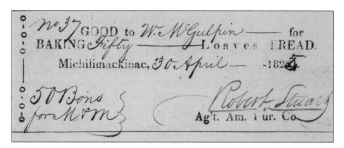

ROBERT STUART. Document Signed, Michilimackinac, April 30, 1825. As agent for the American Fur Company, Stuart issued a coupon *"Good to W. McGulpin for Baking Fifty Loaves Bread."*

In 1810, Stuart became a partner in John Jacob Astor's Pacific Fur Company. During an 1812 expedition to the Columbia River, he was chosen as a courier to carry dispatches overland to Astor. After a perilous journey, attended by extreme privation and suffering, over a route which in considerable part had never before been seen by white men (he discovered South Pass which became the gateway through the mountains), he arrived in St. Louis on April 30, 1813. From 1820 to 1834, he was the head of the American Fur Company for the Upper Lakes Region.

MANUEL LISA, early fur trader and explorer. Document Signed August 25, 1817, selling land north of the town of St. Louis.

John Jacob Astor's American Fur Company silver medal bearing his profile was given by the company's Upper Missouri Outfit ("U.M.O." on the reverse) to the tribes it traded with — the Mandan, Hidatsa, Assinoboin, and Yankton Sioux. Fort Union, the Upper Missouri Outfit's base, was a square-shaped stockade just north of the confluence of the Yellowstone and Missouri Rivers (late 1832–1843). There are six known examples.

The American Fur Company's post, Fort Union, was in competition with the Hudson's Bay Company. In 1831, the agent in charge of Fort Union proposed to Pierre Chouteau, Jr., who managed the company in the West, that they obtain Peace Medals from Washington. The secretary of war replied that the company could issue its own "ornaments," but they would not be considered official medals. Astor had these medals struck in late 1832. In 1843, the government prohibited the company from minting and distributing any more medals after the Hudson's Bay Company complained that Astor's company had usurped the authority of the federal government by minting and distributing the medals. The number minted is unknown.

Pierre Chouteau, Jr., & Company, Upper Missouri Outfit's Indian Presentation Medal, 1843. A copy of the Van Buren Indian Peace Medal, this medal was made in St. Louis at Chouteau's direction after the distribution of the Astor medal was prohibited by the government. Chouteau's blatant copy of the government's design was noticeably larger and cast in pewter rather than silver. Chouteau was ordered by the secretary of war to cease distribution of the medals almost as soon as he started presenting them to tribes. Four to six examples are known.

JOHN JACOB ASTOR. Fur trader and financier. Autograph Letter Signed [Germany], October 7, 1823. To Robert Stuart at Michilimackinac.

"Of our deer skins of 1822/1823 nearly all are sold but all the furrs & most of the Beare skins of that year as well as all the Deer of this year Remain unsold....The pepol are everywhere & every Day getting Poorer & as many articls of manufactor which are now very low can be used in place of Deer skins & fursrs th[e]y Rec[eive] the prefference.... [I]t is absolutely necessary that our Imports & our expences be lessend....

"Go on steadily & as sparingly as possible. Perhaps next season our hatters will use Raccoon and that some of them may com your way to buy them at 40 cents. I would rather sell than purchas. Otter are allways good & worth from 3¼ to 3¾ or even 4$ to us. Beare 3$. Costs have got to be very low & we should only pay 1½, for good fisher 1$, Lynx 1 to 1½$. Deer should [be] 33 cents Red 30 & gray 24. Beaver & musrat as the Price may be in New York."

The Rocky Mountain Fur Company. Thomas Fitzpatrick and Edmund T. Christy. Document Signed, July 20, 1833. Also signed by Robert Campbell, the veteran mountain trapper and supplier, as witness. Concerning the co-partnership between the Rocky Mountain Fur Company and Edmund T. Christy, Jim Bridger, and others.

This contract forming a new company was signed in the midst of Rendezvous 1833, which started at the mouth of Horse Creek in Green River Valley, Wyoming, on July 15 and lasted about ten days.

Classic Bowie knife by Rochus Heinisch, *ca.* 1850s. 18½ inches overall.

Jacob and Samuel Hawken percussion conversion pistol, .48 caliber, *ca.* 1825. The earliest known pistol produced by the Hawken's St. Louis workshop.

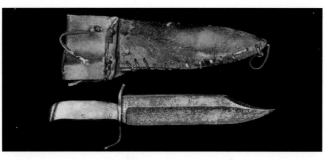

A massive Bowie-type knife and handmade scabbard. 16 inches overall.

A frontier percussion pistol, handmade from available parts, utilizing "J. Henry and Son" treaty rifle lock, the barrel marked with small "U.S." at left breech, plainly and simply fullstocked to the muzzle.

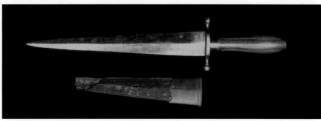

"Arkansas Toothpick" Bowie knife made by J. S. Silver, *ca.* 1860s. 21 inches overall.

Frontier knife with a deer foot handle.

Probably the most perfectly preserved example of a plains rifle by J & S Hawken. Originally purchased about 1840 directly from the St. Louis gunsmiths by Dr. James L. Jones, who according to his descendants, brought the rifle back to Pennsylvania as an important frontier artifact. He preserved it as a pristine example of the most famous and popular rifle of the mountain men. The rifle is 47¾ inches long and .49 caliber.

Flat Heads & Nez Perce, Alfred Jacob Miller watercolor painted *ca.* 1858–1860. 7 by 9 inches. In 1837 Miller went west as the artist on an expedition organized by William Drummond Stewart. Miller was the first artist to travel the Oregon Trail and the only one to experience in person the Rocky Mountains during the height of the fur trade, the rendezvous, and the mountain men.

Chapter 7

THE INDIANS

"The Travelers Meeting with Mandan Indians, Near Fort Clark," showing Prince
Maximilian of Germany and artist Karl Bodmer.

The history of the American Indians is far too complex to even attempt a brief summary of the historical context. It might be easier to summarize the history of the Europeans. That the Indians' treatment by the largely white European settlers is, along with slavery, the darkest part of American history is agreed upon by all. The modern view of the Indians, however, is frequently just as extreme and wrong as the early settlers' view that all Indians were savages and that "the only good Indian is a dead Indian." Many tribes were peaceful, but many others were barbaric in their constant wars with other tribes. It seems that the Indians' relationship to nature is so appealing to many today that their routine enslavement and killing of other Indians is disregarded. While no one disagrees that driving the Indians from the Plains and slaughtering the buffalo were terrible, few seem to be aware that the Indians driven off by the whites in the late 19th century had taken the land earlier in the century from other Indian tribes that had been driven westward from their eastern homelands by white settlers.

Indian artifacts are probably the most available and reasonably priced area of western American history. Indian artifacts have interested people since they began to visit tribes in the early 19th century. There is a very broad market in all price ranges, and very meaningful collections can be formed that represent the very complex cultures of the many very different tribes.

Many of those visiting the Indians did so to convert them to their own religion. A letter signed by twenty-five Christian brothers in Philadelphia, September 18, 1812, is addressed *"To the Chiefs and others of the Seneca Nation of Indians residing at Cattaraugus."* It is typical of the attitude of well-meaning Easterners.

"We often feel our Minds clothed with Love towards you…as you endeavour Daily to please the Great Spirit, who is all Love, and the Author of Love, it will lead you not only to Love one another but to Love all Mankind, and this cannot fail of making you happy…. We wish to see you able to help yourselves, and then you need not depend upon others: — if you will raise Flax and could buy Wool or Cotton to put with it, you might therewith make your own Cloathing…. Being desirous to encourage you to Cultivate the Ground and raise plenty of Grain and Flax, we have concluded to furnish you with two pair of Oxen if they can be procured next Spring without much difficulty…. [W]e Commend you to the Good Spirit, who is able to preserve you through all Difficulties while in this World, and when this Life ends, give you an admittance into His Kingdom, which is a Kingdom of Rest, and Love and Peace."

James Lloyd Breck, a Christian missionary to the Indians and settlers on the Wisconsin and Minnesota frontier, wrote vivid firsthand accounts of Native American life and the trials and rewards of missionary endeavor in 1850:

"And now…I am again on the great Frontier…. I have again come to the very frontier of our rapidly growing country…., already the voice of the Ch[urc]h is heard throughout these parts, &…I felt in a measure that the very formation of an Indian Mission under the Ch[urc]h, was descending upon what impression my words should make upon a people wild indeed but shrewd.

"The very appearance of those Savages was enough to frighten or disgust. Some were half naked, some had knives in their hands & many were painted in the most hideous manner…. They evidently felt much aggrieved by the treatment that they had received from the whites, & were painfully conscious of their darkened state of mind & their own helplessness & repair their gradual but too sure decay as a people."

Trade jewelry. Trade between colonists and Indians was very important for both parties on the frontier. The Indians had pelts, and the colonists manufactured articles and metal products, such as axes and guns. Silver ornaments became important trade items in the 18th century and eventually dominated trade. The average Indian wore much more silver jewelry (see the M'Kenney and Hall illustrations on p. 120) than white men or women did. Most of the early silver jewelry was made by European silversmiths in Montreal, London, and Philadelphia and other American cities.

The Indians began to make their own jewelry around 1800, using coins, primarily Spanish, and tableware for the silver.

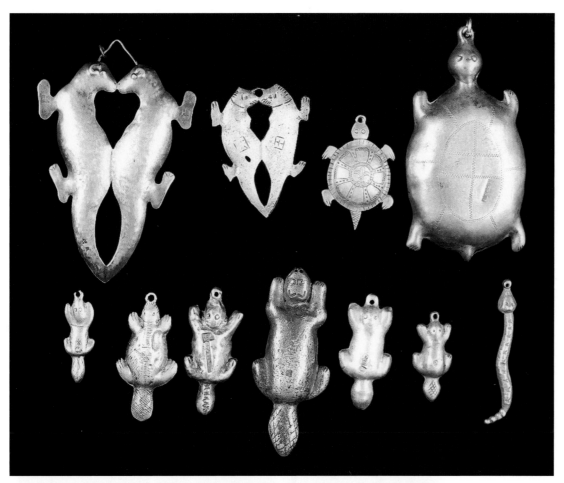

Animal effigies were worn essentially as good luck talismans. Beavers represented wealth and good trading, and the turtles represented longevity. The kissing otters were very popular. These are by various makers, including the Hudson's Bay Company, generally 1750–1800.

Crowns represented social status within tribes. The one on the left was crafted by Ignace Delzenne, Quebec, 1765–1776, the one on the right by Simon Curtius, Montreal, 1797–1801.

Agreement between William Thomson, silversmith, and John Jacob Astor of the American Fur Company to make gorgets ($2.16 each), armbands ($2.75), wristbands ($2.16), brooches (62½ cents), earwheels (86 cents), earbobs (10 cents), crosses (5 cents) and brooches ($3.50), December 23, 1816.

Memorandum of Indian Silver-works to be made by William Thomson N. 718 Wm &c —

Ten Gorgets	First Size	at Two dollars and Sixteen Cents	Each
Ten Do	Second do	at One dollar and Eighty nine cents	Each
Ten Do	Third do	at One dollar and fifty two cents	Each
Ten Do	Fourth do	at One dollar and Forty eight cents	Each
Ten Do	Fifth do	at one dollar and Thirty five cents	Each
Ten Do	Sixth do	at one dollar and Twenty two cents	Each
One hundred Armbands	First do	at Two dollars and Seventy cents	Each
One hundred Do	Second do	at Two dollars and Twenty cents	Each
Fifty pairs Wristbands	First do	at Two dollars and Sixteen cents	for pair
Fifty pairs Do	Second do	at One dollar and fifty two cents	for pair
Fifty Pairs Do	Third do	at one dollar and Twenty two cents	for pair
Seventyfive Emboss'd Broaches	First do	at fifty two and a half cents	Each
Seventyfive Do Do	Second do	at fifty cents	Each
Seventyfive Do Do	Third do	at Thirty Seven and a half cents	Each
Seventyfive Do Do	Fourth do	at Thirty one cents	Each
Seventyfive pairs Earwheels		at Eighty Six Cents	for pair
Twelve thousand pairs Round Earbobs		at Ten Cents	for pair
Three thousand pairs Square Do		at Ten Cents	for pair
Three thousand large Crosses		at Five Cents	Each
One thousand Small Ditto		at Four Cents	Each
Ten thousand Common large Broaches		at Three dollars fifty cents	⅌ Hundred
Five thousand do Small Ditto		at Two dollars and fifty cents	⅌ Hundred

I hereby agree and engage, to make & manufacture all the above articles, agreeable to the patterns, and of the same qualities as those furnished by me last spring, for John Jacob Astor Esq. at the price annexed to each.

And I also hereby bind and obligate myself, to deliver the whole numbers of the different articles, on or before the first day of April One thousand eight hundred and seventeen, to John Jacob Astor Esq. (in the City of New York)

New York December 23 — 1816   William Thomson

Witness
Ram H Crooks

Group of brooches and ornaments by various silversmiths, Philadelphia, Montreal, Quebec, and Hudson's Bay Company, late 18th century.

Large armbands (3½ inches high) by John Thomson of Montreal *ca.* 1799.

Crosses with arms of equal length represented north, south, east and west; when a fire was set for a council meeting four logs were placed in the form of a cross by some Indian groups. The popularity of various forms of crosses in trade jewelry had more to do with the Indians' own beliefs than the Europeans' association of crosses with Christianity.

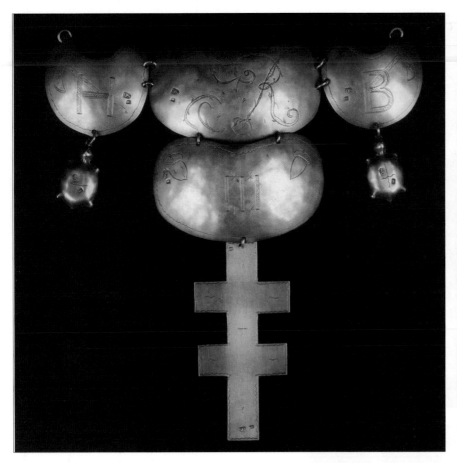

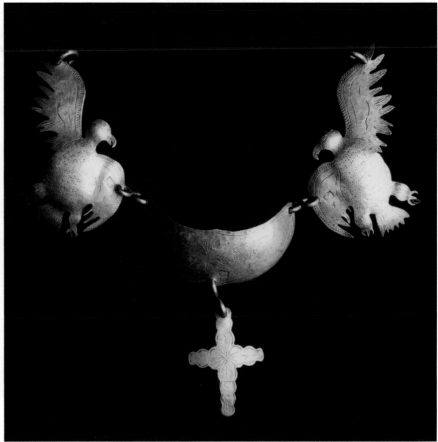

The gorget was worn by colonists as badges of military authority and rank. The shape quickly became popular with the natives as symbolic of the power of the moon. This elaborate neckpiece by Daniel Stoughton of Kingston, Ontario, from about 1800, is engraved with the initials of King George III and the Hudson's Bay Company.

An unusual neckpiece by Simon Curtis, Montreal, 1797–1801, with engraved tomahawks on the gorget.

Articles of Agreement and Convention, made and concluded at the Treaty Ground at Hell Gate in the St. Mary's Valley, this the Sixteenth day of July in the year one thousand eight hundred and fifty five, by and between Isaac I. Stevens Governor and Superintendent of Indian Affairs for the Territory of Washington on the part of the United States, and the undersigned Chiefs head men and delegates of the confederated Tribes of the Flatheads, Kootenays and Upper Pend Oreilles Indians on behalf of and acting for said confederated Tribes, and being duly authorized thereto by them. It being understood and agreed that the said confederated Tribes do hereby constitute a nation under the name of the Flathead Nation, with Victor the Head Chief of the Flathead tribe, as the Head Chief of the said Nation, and that the several Chiefs, head men and delegates, whose names are signed to this treaty, do hereby, in behalf of their respective tribes, recognize Victor as said Head Chief.

Article I. The said confederated tribes of Indians hereby cede, relinquish and convey to the United States all their right, title and interest in and to the country occupied or claimed by them, bounded and described as follows, to wit; Commencing in the main ridge of the Rocky Mountains at the 49th parallel of Latitude, thence westward on that parallel to the divide between the Flat-Bow or Kootenay river and Clark's Fork, thence Southerly and South easterly along said divide to the one hundred and fifteenth degree of Longitude; thence in a South western direction to the divide between the sources of the St. Regis de Borgia and the Cour d'alene river; thence South easterly and southerly along the main ridge of the Bitter root Mountains to the divide between the head waters of the Koos-koos-kee river and of the Southern fork of the St. Mary's river; thence easterly along the divide separating the waters of the several tributaries of the St. Mary's river from the waters flowing into the Salmon and Snake rivers to the main ridge of the Rocky Mountains, thence Northerly along said main ridge to the place of beginning.

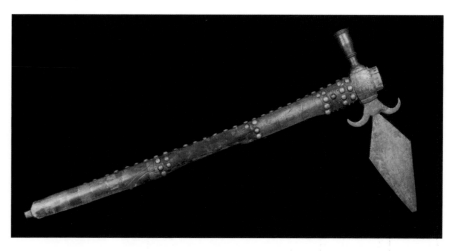

Spontoon blade pipe tomahawk, ca. 1830–1840. The tack-decorated haft is charred in the middle from being left too close to a fire. Pipe tomahawks are more symbolic than functional and were often carried during ceremonies or treaty talks as symbols of power and status.

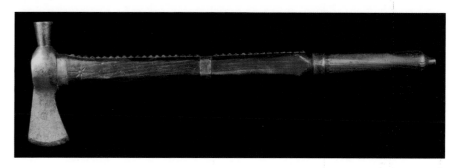

Classic pipe tomahawk with tack-decorated haft.

Flathead Nation. The Treaty of Hell Gate, Bitter Root Valley, July 16, 1855, was concluded between Isaac I. Stevens, governor and superintendent of Indian Affairs for the Territory of Washington, on the part of the United States, and Chief Victor of the Flathead Nation, representing chiefs, head men, and delegates of the con-federated tribes of Flatheads, Kootenays, and Upper Pend d'Oreille Indians. The treaty ceded most of the land the Indians owned in western Montana and northern Idaho to the United States, and retained for them a reservation of 1.3 million acres south of Flathead Lake in Bitterroot Valley, in western Montana.

"The United States agree to pay…in addition to the goods and provisions distributed to them at the time of signing this treaty the sum of one hundred and twenty thousand dollars…to establish…an agricultural and industrial school…one blacksmith shop…a tin and gun shop; one carpenter's shop; one wagon and ploughmaker's shop…. To erect one saw-mill and one flouring-mill…and to employ two millers. To erect a hospital…. The…tribes…promise to be friendly with all citizens…and pledge themselves to commit no depredations upon property…. Nor will they make war on any other tribe…. The said…tribes…[will] exclude from their reservation the use of ardent spirits, and to prevent their people from drinking the same."

Niagara 20th Feby. 1804

Dear Sir

From our former acquaintance and the many civilities I have received from you I am enduced upon this Occasion to request your Assistance

The bearer Mr Norton has in Charge Mr Phelps's Bond, in Order to receive upon it One hundred pounds New York Cury which is to be endorsed upon it and with his receipt will be sufficient for us — when this is compleated I have to request your kindness in taking charge of the Bond and conveying it to me by the first safe conveyance — With sentiments of the greatest esteem I am Dr Sir

Your most Obedt and most humble Sir!

Jos. Brant

T. Morris Esqr &c &c

JOSEPH BRANT, Mohawk chief who led a series of raids against frontier settlements in the western and northern portions of New York during the American Revolution. Letter Signed, Niagara [New York], February 20, 1804.

RED JACKET, chief of the Senecas. Document Signed, Buffalo, New York, June 15, 1824; also signed by ten other chiefs and warriors.

"We the undersigned Chiefs and Warriors of the Seneca Nation do acknowledge to have received by Jasper Parrish Sub-Agent of the United States to the Six nations of Indians Five hundred dollars in full for the Annuity due us."

The Senecas had given up their lands in Western New York, in exchange for this annuity. Along with names like Uncas, King Phillip, and later, Geronimo and Sitting Bull, Red Jacket remains one of the most recognizable figures in the history of American Indians. Known as a great orator, he pursued a policy of friendship with whites, but opposed the cession of Indian lands to the United States and efforts to train Indians in the white man's civilization. Red Jacket became his name because of the richly embroidered scarlet jacket that was presented to him by a British officer shortly after the American Revolution as a reward for his services.

The Crow Indians acknowledge receipt of goods under the Treaty of Fort Laramie. Document Signed, with the "X" marks of Two Face, Rotten Trail, Beard Head, and Horse Guard, August 26, 1856.

The merchandise included blankets of white, green, blue, scarlet, and various other colors; fabric, such as blue and scarlet cloth, calico, checks, stripes and plaids, ticking, unbleached shirting, and blue drill; vermillion; white, blue, ruby, and black beads; flannel and calico shirts; blue cloth coats and pants; packing boxes and cases; brass kettles, tin pans, butcher knives; squaw awls, fishhooks and lines, needles, scissors, weeding hoes, drawing knives, augurs, handsaws, socket chisels, spades, camp kettles, frying pans, axes, hatchets, looking glasses, buttons, basting spoons, tablespoons, tin cups, and sleigh bells; and sugar, coffee, flour, tobacco, bags, and 700 pounds of bread.

Plains pictorial buffalo hide, Northern Cheyenne or Sioux, of unusually large scale, drawn in a classic and refined Cheyenne style, faintly signed in one area, "Kills-Eagle." The pictographs on the hide illustrate a series of episodes from the life of Kills-Eagle (Wan-Bli-Kte). These include confrontations with Crow and scenes of horse capturing, a group of red-painted horses circling the central field, and participation in a particular but unknown exploit. Two of the equestrians are wearing elaborate headdresses, the horses have galloping hooves and elongated necks, and one of the enemies in the confrontation is clad in a cloth kapote.

Kills-Eagle was with the "hostiles" at Rosebud during the Custer campaign. While he did not participate in the Battle of Little Big Horn, his personal account of the events was reported in *The New York Herald,* October 6, 1876.

In his 1992 book, *The Native American Heritage: A Survey of North American Indians,* Evan M. Maurer wrote, *"By the third quarter of the nineteenth century, Plains warrior-artists had become increasingly interested in using more detail in the representation of figures, horses, clothing, and military equipment. They also were developing a style in which they depicted men and animals in full action described by a greater variety of poses and movements."*

Probably collected at Standing Rock Agency, *ca.* 1870s. 100 by 80 inches.

Plains buffalo hide scraper, *ca.* 1880, with unusual brass tack and screw ornamentation. The metal scraper possibly made from an old file that has been sharpened, then wrapped in buffalo hide. Work on buffalo hides was almost exclusively done by women. 12½ inches long.

Buffalo medicine robe, which was hung in a tepee prior to going to war, *ca.* 1870. Approximately 71 by 63 inches. Depicted are two arrows, a bow, a pipe with stem, and a quirt. Also depicted are two morning stars. All of these symbols had great significance to the Indians.

In *Letters and Sketches: With a Narrative of a Year's Residence Among the Indian Tribes of the Rocky Mountains,* 1843, Pierre-Jean De Smet wrote:

"The call of the Rockies was not immediately answered. The Catholic Church and fledgling Jesuit mission and novitiate at the frontier's edge had few men and fewer resources for such a far-flung mission."

Jacqueline Peterson wrote of De Smet in *Sacred Encounters:*

"In 1839…at St. Joseph's mission…at Council Bluffs, they found a man whom the Plains Indians later called 'good-hearted,' a thirty-eight-year-old Flemish Jesuit named Pierre-Jean De Smet. For De Smet, the appeal came as a voice crying from the wilderness. He visited the Salish at the Rocky Mountain Rendezvous of 1840…. The following year…De Smet and his European confreres…set out for the Bitterroot Valley of western Montana…. St. Mary's mission to the Flathead…became for De Smet the imagined heart of an 'empire of Christian Indians,' a wilderness kingdom in the uncontaminated reaches of the Rocky Mountains.

"For a privileged moment in 1841–1842, the mission seemed to prosper. The Salish at St. Mary's settled into a rigorous daily routine of prayer and song, catechism, and agricultural labor…. Missions to the neighboring Coeur d'Alene, Pend Oreille, Colville, Kootenai, and Blackfeet tribes were opened in rapid succession.

"Nonetheless…the Salish resisted Catholic authoritarianism, the concepts of sin and hell, and the imposition of European social, political, and economic values that directly challenged native norms. The Salish wanted Christian power and protection for their own ends, but they weren't interested in farming or making peace with their Blackfeet enemies…. [T]he prayers of the Flathead 'consisted in asking to live a long time, to kill plenty of animals and enemies, and to steal the greatest number of the [enemies'] horses possible.'

"Within scarcely a decade of its founding, St. Mary's mission and the Jesuit missions to the Colville and Blackfeet were closed, their native residents apostatizing due to disease and missionary demands for change far in excess of spiritual conversion….

"After 1847, and for the remainder of his life, De Smet was an advocate for peace…. De Smet lent his charismatic presence as a trusted military and government emissary in treaty negotiations with reluctant or hostile Indian nations, among whom he was well known….

"His most controversial role involved a mission to the camp of Sitting Bull during the Fort Laramie treaty negotiations of 1868. Although he failed to persuade Sitting Bull of the government's good intentions, he brought in a sufficient number of Sitting Bull's people to secure the treaty and diffuse the threat of immediate war. The Fort Laramie treaty was a hollow victory, however. Government promises were broken within less than a decade, and war, however futile, became the only honorable alternative for the Sioux."

A superb Northern Plains beaded and fringed hide woman's dress, probably Blackfoot. Of elegant proportion, constructed of Indian tanned hide, sinew sewn with glass pony beads in white, blue, and black; faceted basket beads in blue and black; Russian trade beads, translucent and blue; white porcelain beads; olivella shells; red, green, and black wool; glass seed beads; red-dyed porcupine quillwork and metal thimbles, with open sleeves and uneven hemline; circle discs and three rows of scalloped beadwork on shoulders; fringe on shoulders and overall.

"This dress was one of several patterns sent by De Smet to Belgian relatives and patrons following the meeting in 1859 between General Harney and Plateau Chiefs at Fort Vancouver. The cut of the yoke, the pony-bead circles at shoulders, and the uneven hem line all suggest Blackfeet manufacture. De Smet may have acquired the dress on his return trip to St. Louis at Fort Benton, on the upper Missouri River." (Jacqueline Peterson, *Sacred Encounters, Father De Smet and the Indians of the Rocky Mountain West*)

This ensemble of war shirt, leggings, and headpiece, *ca.* 1820–1830, belonged to an important Mandan warrior whose exploits and battlefield achievements are chronicled in the remarkable series of painted pictographs. The wash of black paint over the right shoulder and yellow over the left shoulder indicates that the owner while alone, killed and scalped an enemy. The column of early 19th-century pipes represents the number of war parties he led, while the thirteen painted horse quirts show the number of horses stolen and given away. Captured horses are also indicated by the series of parallel lines on the shirt sleeves and leggings. The feat of touching your enemy in battle and living to talk about it was commonly referred to as counting coup. The Mandan people were almost entirely decimated by smallpox in 1837, making material from this group among the rarest of all Native American art.

Arapaho woman's dress from the Central Plains, *ca.* 1840–1850, the hide decorated with extensive beadwork and trade cloth. Very few Arapaho women's dresses are known.

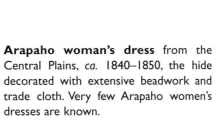

Crow shirt, *ca.* 1870.

Pony-beaded coat of moosehide with beading, probably Iroquois, mid-19th century.

Eastern Apache man's coat, *ca.* 1880. Painted hide with calico and stroud cloth. Extraordinary twisted and dyed fringe with mescal beans, beadwork trim, and brass and silver buttons.

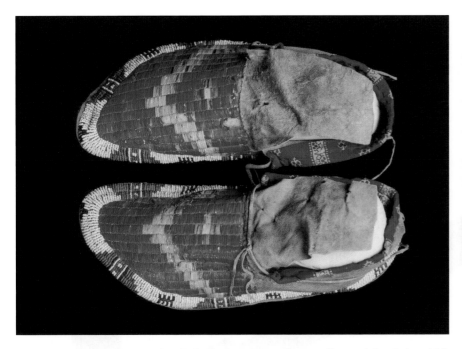

Sioux moccasins decorated with dyed porcupine quills, as well as with beads, late 19th century.

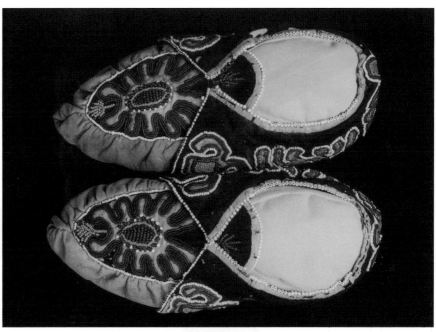

Southeastern beaded hide and cloth moccasins, possibly Cherokee. Constructed of Indian tanned hide, black cloth, and yellow silk, decorated with white, pink, orange, three shades of blue, and two shades of translucent red and green beads, and embellished on top of uppers and on cuffs with stylized elements. 10¾ inches long. Collected by Father Pierre-Jean De Smet.

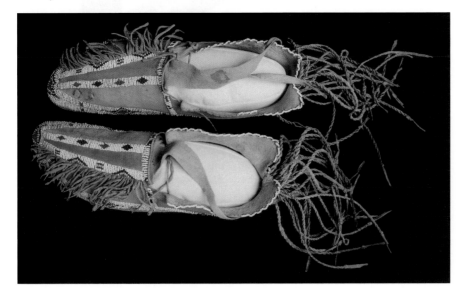

Kiowa Comanche long-fringe moccasins, *ca.* 1860.

Sioux child's moccasins, late 19th century.

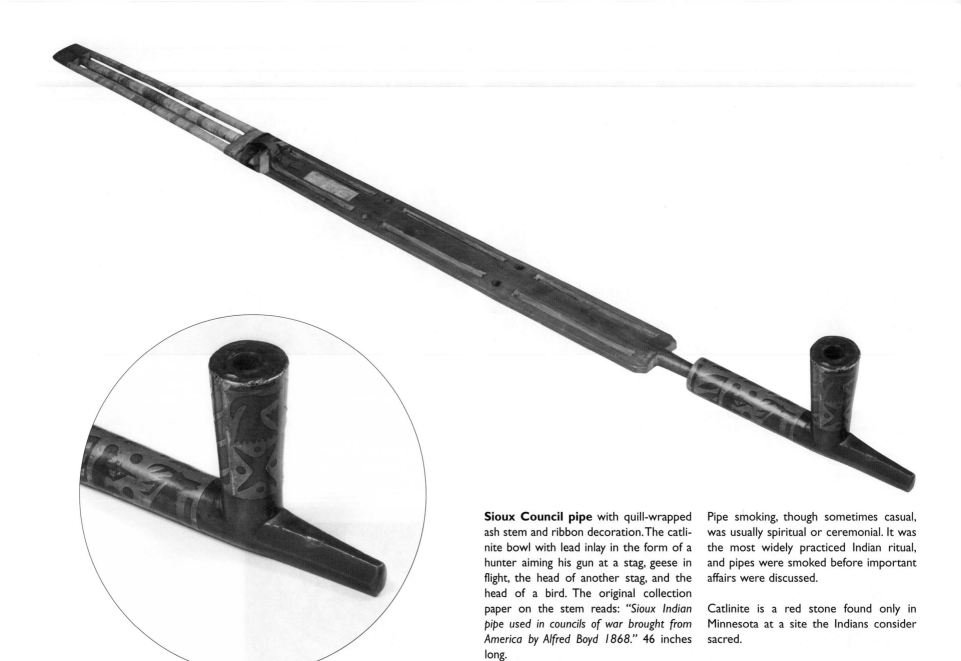

Sioux Council pipe with quill-wrapped ash stem and ribbon decoration. The catlinite bowl with lead inlay in the form of a hunter aiming his gun at a stag, geese in flight, the head of another stag, and the head of a bird. The original collection paper on the stem reads: *"Sioux Indian pipe used in councils of war brought from America by Alfred Boyd 1868."* 46 inches long.

Pipe smoking, though sometimes casual, was usually spiritual or ceremonial. It was the most widely practiced Indian ritual, and pipes were smoked before important affairs were discussed.

Catlinite is a red stone found only in Minnesota at a site the Indians consider sacred.

A Cheyenne beaded hide baby carrier. The sinew-sewn hide carrier is mounted on a wood framework with two projecting forked back slats, each decorated with openwork and metal tacks and stained with deep red pigment. The carrier's white lazy stitched background is decorated with a geometrical motif. Pairs of triangles intersecting at their top points, rectangles, pairs of smaller triangles arranged in a fork-like design, and a narrow band encircling the carrier are rendered in dark blue, bright blue, yellow, green, and translucent red beadwork. 39 inches long.

Laced into the cradleboard, the child could be carried on the mother's back, hooked onto a saddle, or leaned against a tree or tepee. Elaborate cradles were customarily made by the new father's sister.

Winnebago scalloped edge bow, *ca.* 1880.

Lakota Sioux bird effigy spoon made from cow horn, late 19th century. Spoons and bowls were the Indians' principal eating utensils.

A Sioux shot pouch from the upper Missouri River area, made of hide, porcupine quills, glass beads, and commercial cloth. In faint ink on the back of the lower panel is the inscription *"presented to — St. Louis, August 12, 1841 from R J Watson to G Parson 1841 at Ticcadonncaville."*

Shot pouch and powder horn, probably from the upper Missouri, *ca.* 1850. The horn is likely earlier, and came from a cow and not a buffalo. The bandolier is indicative of tribes in the Northern Plains mid-century, notably the Metis; their work is frequently mistaken for that of the Sioux. The Metis inhabited both sides of the Missouri and worked in the fur trade. The pouch designs also indicate a Missouri River tribe, although they reflect a different tradition than that of the strap. They share similar materials and were evidently made at the same time using designs influenced by different Missouri River tribes. The pouch, bandolier, and horn are all most likely Missouri River Metis or Fur Trade, showing the influence of many tribes of the area.

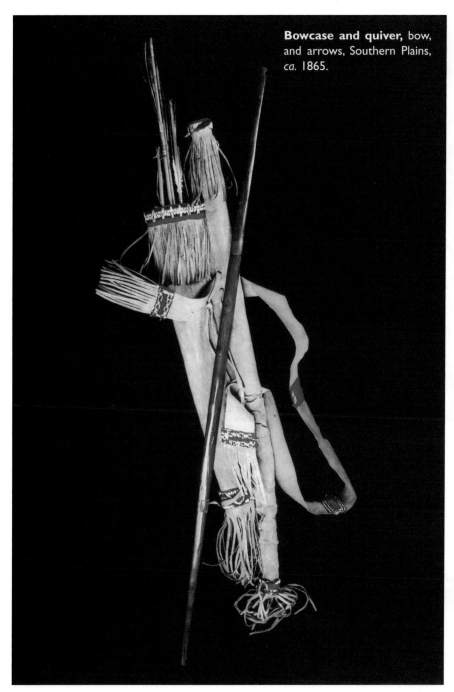

Bowcase and quiver, bow, and arrows, Southern Plains, *ca.* 1865.

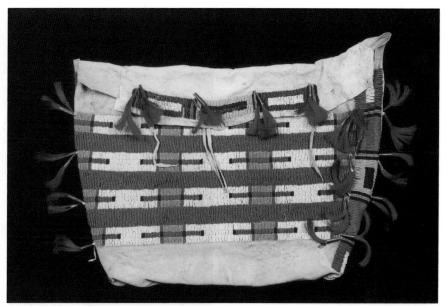

Beaded "possible" bags, such as this, were often tied to a saddle when traveling and at other times hung inside a tepee.

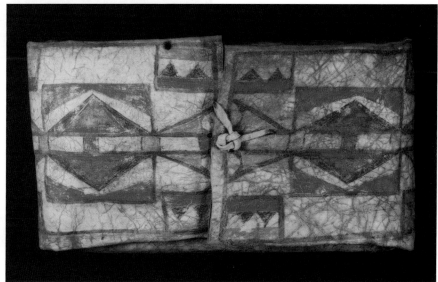

Parfleche, folded rawhide used to carry provisions, especially pemmican, on pack horses or travois. Possibly Plateau area (Idaho-Washington) *ca.* 1870s.

Turtle effigy bustle fetish, Northern Plains, probably Lakota Sioux, *ca.* 1870s. The turtle is finely carved out of catlinite; this stone was considered sacred. It was believed to represent the blood of the earth and was used solely for ceremonial purposes, most notably pipe bowls. The turtle is attached to a rosette of cut feathers and quills, which were attached to a dance bustle.

For many Indian tribes, the turtle symbolized Mother Earth and was associated with the time of Creation. Different tribes had slightly different beliefs but most held a number of them in common. Some referred to the earth as turtle island; the thirteen sections on the turtle's back represented the thirteen moons of the year. Others viewed the world as resting on the back of the Big Turtle and believed that when he got tired and changed position, earthquakes occurred. Because the turtle could breathe air but also lived under the sea, it was thought to be an instrument of the Creator. The turtle was celebrated during dances for its gift of fertility as well.

Blackfoot ermine medicine that belonged to the family of Weasel Tail, a prominent Blackfoot chief, 19th century. The ermines were prized for their pure white color; these are adorned with pieces of cloth, dyed feathers, leather thongs, and brass beads. They were part of a medicine man's bundle and used in ceremonies. The four ermines represent the four directions; the sacred colors were black, white, red, and yellow.

Flintlock Springfield M1807 Carbine (also known as the Indian Carbine). Only two other original examples are known.

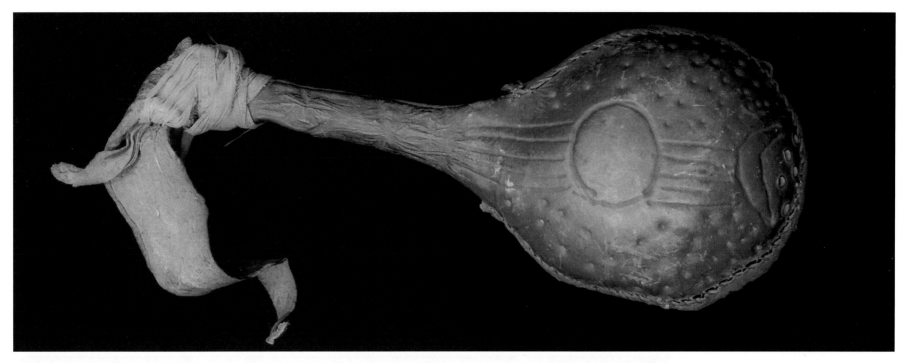

Ceremonial rattle, made of buffalo hide, wood, sinew, pebbles and trade cloth, early 19th century (?).

The origin of this rattle is Suhtai, as indicated by the Hetanehao (Man Power) design and the overall composition. The Suhtaio, an Algonquian tribe linguistically related to the Cheyenne, formed an alliance with the Cheyenne, probably in the early 18th century, but retained many of their own customs. They were mostly absorbed into the larger tribe after the cholera outbreak of 1849.

One side of the rattle's globe has a stylized face. An incised line nearly encompasses this side, with three inward-pointing triangles. Two three-quarter–inch circles indicate the eyes. The center of each circle is also pressed into a concavity; the

pressed areas are matte, while the rest of the hide is shiny smooth. As a result, the eyes appear to have bright irises and dark pupils. At the bottom edge of each eye a zigzag is incised, indicating lightning emerging from the eyes. Two more holes are pierced to indicate nostrils. They are connected across the top by an incised line, which passes through the nostrils and continues down in wavy lines, indicative of the power of breath. These lines frame either side of an incised Man Power design. This design was widely used by the Suhtaio, and is essentially unique to them.

The circle about the face represents hunters closing in on buffalo, aided by lightning — the triangular elements pointing in from three directions represent the flashing eyes of Thunder.

The other side of the globe is a reddish color, and was probably painted with red earth paint. Five "trails" (incised straight lines) lead from the bottom of the gourd to the center, where they are interrupted by a circle. Above the circle, the lines form a crescent. Between the horns of the crescent five holes are pierced. Dots are impressed on either side of this central design, seemingly at random. The five trails represent the paths of the sun and the moon. The circle signifies the sun, and the crescent, the moon. The five holes almost certainly represent the constellation Delphinus, which the Cheyenne call the Beaver. Its heliacal rising near the beginning of April signals the onset of the ceremonial season. This constellation consists of four stars that form a diamond shape, with an additional bright star somewhat to one side — pretty much as

indicated by the pierced holes. The punctate marks represent hailstones — specifically, green hailstones — which were thought by the Cheyenne to fertilize the earth, bringing forth new life and turning the earth green. Conversely, the white stones inside the rattle, which are partly visible through the pierced holes, embody the destructive power of white hailstones, which blight the earth in the fall. This melding of opposites into a unit is entirely typical of Cheyenne art and religion.

At 12 inches in length and 4½ inches in diameter, this is the largest Cheyenne/Suhtai rattle known with the exception of the Buffalo Rite rattle, in the possession of the Northern Cheyenne.

A number of facts indicate that this it is most likely a rattle of Swift Fox warriors.

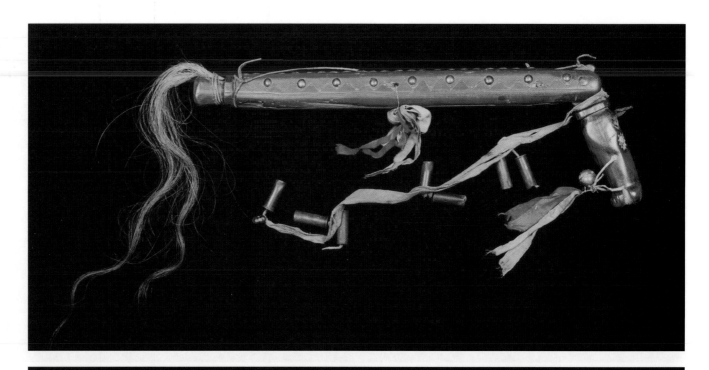

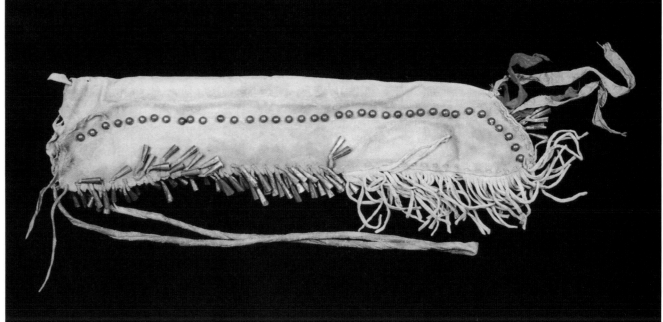

Southern Plains Commanche horse raider's medicine man's bundle composed of a wood "horse stick" with cylindrical shaft, decorated with incised design and brass tacks, in a fringed hide case decorated with brass shoe buttons, ribbons, and tin rattlers, *ca.* 1860–1870.

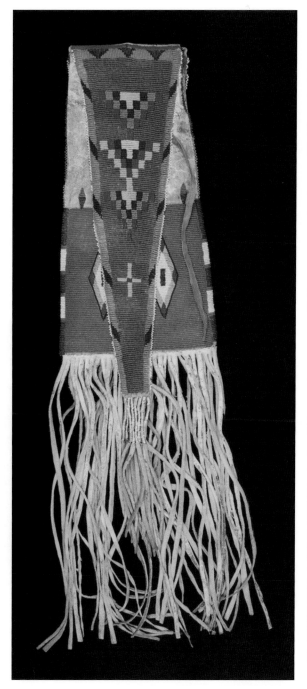

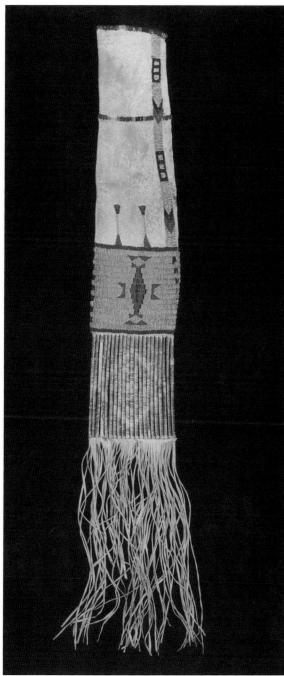

Northern Plains beaded and fringed hide tobacco bag, probably Blackfoot, *ca.* 1875. 52 inches long.

Sioux tobacco bag, *ca.* 1875. Tobacco was sacred to the Indians who mostly smoked it for ceremonial and religious purposes. 40 inches long.

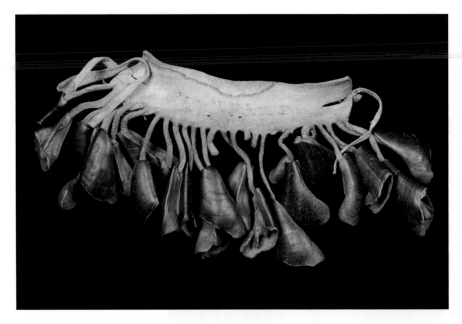

Dance bustle. Two panels of stroud cloth (traded by the English and manufactured in Stroud, Gloucestershire), one red, the other blue, adorned with rows of feathers, attached by leather thongs to the panels. The red and blue panels represent the male and female balance of the Creation. The feathers are symbolic of the power and mystery of the upper regions.

Northern Plains arm/leg band with dewclaw suspensions, *ca.* 1820s–1840s. The rattling of the dewclaws was to remind the wearer of his relationship to the animal world.

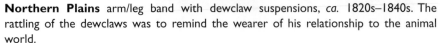

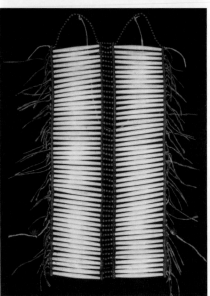

Sioux breastplate made of bone pipes with a center panel of brass trade beads, hawk bell on one side, an 1875 military button on the other, *ca.* 1880.

Jicarilla Apache drum, wood with hide heads, both painted, one with moon and star motifs. Northern New Mexico, *ca.* 1900.

Sioux dance rattle with porcupine quill decoration.

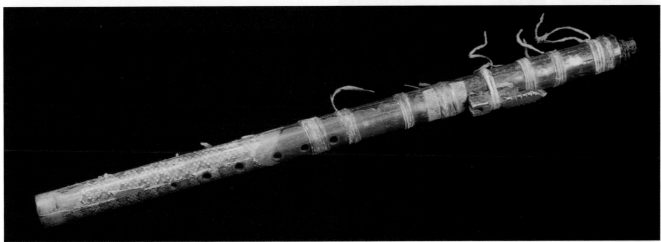

An early courting flute, or flagelot, wrapped with bullsnake skin, *ca.* 1860. The bullsnake was the enemy of the rattlesnake, and the Indians believed it had great powers. Flutes were also used for enjoyment as well as courting rituals.

Northern Plains buffalo hoof rattle, *ca.* mid-19th century, which has been repaired numerous times with various cotton strings and patches of tepee canvas attached to a buffalo tail. This rattle likely played a prominent role in religious ceremonial life.

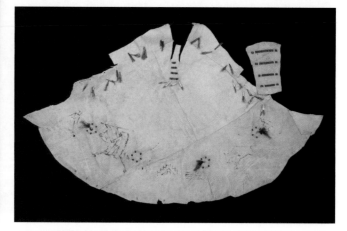

An early Northern Plains doll, *ca.* 1860–1870. Made from buffalo hide, the head adorned with buffalo hair and the face painted. Collected by Father Martin, as written in ink on the right leg.

Classic Plains male doll.

Child's tepee of sinew-sewn buffalo hide, Montana Cheyenne, prior to 1900. Four beaded rings centered with human hair tufts in the style of scalp ornaments on full-size tepees; human hair attachments on wings of smoke vent. Native-pigment–painted figures in pictographic style, including a mounted warrior in full regalia and a buffalo. 40 inches wide.

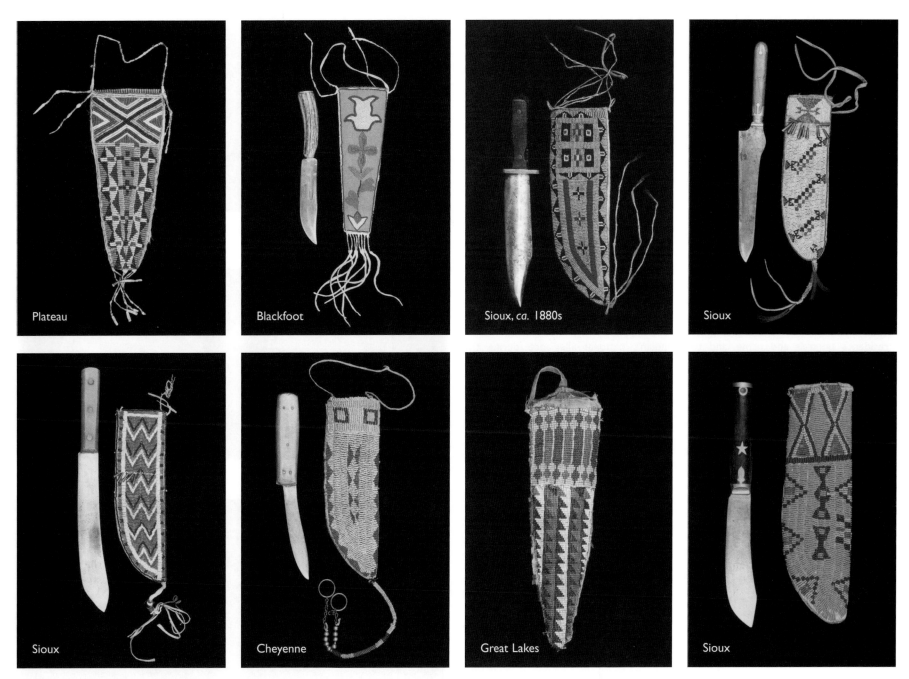

Plateau

Blackfoot

Sioux, *ca.* 1880s

Sioux

Sioux

Cheyenne

Great Lakes

Sioux

Beaded knife sheaths were usually presented as gifts.

Indian Peace Medals. The use of these medals, which were almost always silver, began in the early 18th century, first by England, followed by France and Spain. The medals were seen by the Indians as physical evidence of the alliance and friendship that was declared in the indecipherable treaties they were signing. They were also awarded not only at treaty signings, but also for allegiance to Britain in war and by the Hudson's Bay Company to establish firm commitments in the fur trade.

The United States, beginning with George Washington's administration (see chapter 3), continued the practice, but with a very limited number of medals. Jefferson saw the necessity of medals for the Lewis and Clark expedition (see chapter 5) and began the practice of having Indian Peace Medals with the obverse showing the President's portrait and name, and the reverse engraved with clasped hands, a tomahawk crossing a peace pipe, and the legend "Peace and Friendship." The medals were minted in three sizes through the presidency of Zachary Taylor and, from then until Grant, in two sizes, and finally in one size through the administration of Benjamin Harrison. The large Thomas Jefferson medal, the first produced, was by far the largest (105 mm); the size was reduced by Madison to 76 mm.

The medals were distributed not only at treaty signings, but also at visits to the White House by important Indians, as well as on tours of the Indian Country by important government officials, by expeditions (notably Lewis and Clark's) and later by Indian agents according to a set of regulations drawn up in 1829:

"They will be given to influential persons only. The largest medals will be given to the principal village chiefs, those of the second size will be given to the principal war chiefs and those of the third size to the less distinguished chiefs and warriors. They will be presented with proper formalities and an appropriate speech…. Whenever a foreign medal is worn it will be replaced by an American medal."

The medals carried the full weight of the Indian's national allegiance during the commercial and military wars with England. They were also prized by the Indians as symbols of friendship and are seen being prominently worn particularly in the portraits by Thomas L. M'Kenney and James Hall (see page 120). Many Indians were buried wearing their medals while others passed them down through the generations.

The first English Indian Peace Medal to be widely distributed, the King George I medal in copper.

Louis XVI Indian Peace Medal, 1774, presented to Hakosayee.

George III Medal, the classic design given to Indians, *ca.* 1776–1814. The impressive size (3-inch diameter) of these silver medals was very influential in attracting Indians throughout what is now Canada and North America to the British side and began the tradition of the Indians expecting expensive gifts.

A later George III silver Indian Peace Medal, dated 1814, given to Indians for their support in the War of 1812.

Franklin Pierce Indian Peace Medal with the reverse design changed from the clasped hands and the *"Peace and Friendship"* inscription to one showing the white man and the Indian in front of an American flag with a plow and ax between them and pastoral scenes on either side.

James Monroe. *"Peace and Friendship."*

Abraham Lincoln medal, the reverse showing the advantage of civilized customs over those of the Indian.

Ulysses S. Grant. *"On Earth Peace, Good Will Toward Men."*

Alexander Maximilian, *Reisde in das Innere Nord-America in den Jahren 1832 bis 1834,* 1839–1841.

Prince Maximilian of Germany was already an experienced naturalist and explorer when he began his preparations for his trip to North America, including retaining the skilled artist Karl Bodmer to prepare illustrations of the journey. He arrived in the spring of 1833, and traveled as far upstream as the American Fur Company post of Fort Mackenzie in present-day Montana. He spent the winter at Fort Clark, near the Mandan Indian villages. During this prolonged stay, he and Bodmer had ample opportunity to observe the Indian tribes of the Upper Missouri in their full glory. Bodmer carefully recorded scenes of Indian life in watercolors. In the spring of 1834, they returned to Europe and devoted the next five years to preparing the text and plates for this publication. It is generally considered the greatest and most important color-plate book on the American West.

As a painter, Bodmer was scrupulously realistic, and his portraits of the unspoiled West could never be duplicated. Four years after his trip, half of the Blackfoot and virtually all the Mandan Indians were dead from smallpox.

"Bison Dance of the Mandan Indians."

116

"Moennitari Warrior in the Costume of the Dog Dance."

"Mandan Indians."

In the preface to his *Travels in the Interior of North America, 1832–1834*, Prince Maximilian noted, "*A large portion of [North America] which only a few years ago was covered with an almost uninterrupted primeval forest and a scanty population of rude barbarians has been converted by the influx of immigrants from the Old World into a rich and flourishing state, for the most part civilized and almost as well-known and cultivated as Europe itself. Large and flourishing towns with fine public institutions of every kind have risen rapidly and every year add to their number. Animated commerce, unfettered unlimited industry have caused this astonishing advance of civilization…. The tide of immigration is impelled onwards wave upon wave and it is only the sterility of the Northwest that can check the advancing torrent.*"

"Le-Shaw-Loo-Lah-Le-Hoo, Pawnee." George Catlin pencil sketch, 14 by 10½ inches.

The drawing is inscribed on the reverse *"Pawnee Le-shaw-loo-lah-le-hoo (the Big Elk), a secondary chief, wearing a beautifully ornamented robe, and smoking a long and handsome pipe. His headdress made of War Eagle plumes. As the War Eagle of that country conquers all other varieties of the Eagle Species the Indians set a high value on the tail feathers of that valiant bird, to adorn the heads of the brave, none others are allowed to wear them."*

George Catlin, *North American Indian Portfolio. Hunting Scenes and Amusements of the Rocky Mountains and Prairies of America,* 1844. Large-folio volume containing twenty-five hand-colored lithographs.

George Catlin was the first artist to observe the native tribes of the Plains Indians and to illustrate their habits and customs from firsthand observation. His belief in the noble savage, unspoiled by contact with the outside world, sustained him as he crossed and recrossed the country — from the Mississippi to the Rockies — gathering raw material for his Indian gallery.

In 1844, Catlin published the *Portfolio* as a means of publicizing the cause of the vanishing Indian culture. His tableaux of Indian life demonstrate *"the struggle for survival that was thought to shape the force and independence of savage character."* (Ron Tyler, *Prints of the American West,* p. 31.)

Catlin appealed to his audience with the thrill of the hunt and tribal games and the mystery of Indian ritual. But Catlin's crusade to preserve the "wildness" of the Indians was in vain; within only a few years of his visit in 1832, the Mandan tribe had been wiped out by disease, and the noble savages were no longer untouched by the authority of European civilization.

Wi-Jun-Jon, or the Pigeon's Head Egg, was a young Assiniboine much admired by his tribesman. Catlin met him when Wi-Jun-Jon was on his way to Washington. He painted a portrait of the Indian in his native costume. In Washington, Catlin wrote, *"He travelled a giddy maze and beheld amid the buzzing din of civil life their tricks of art, their handy works and their finery. He visited their principal cities. He saw their forts, their ships, their great guns, steamboats, balloons, etc., and in the spring returned to St. Louis where I joined him…on their way back to their own country."*

Catlin's model for the unspoiled Indian who had lured him to the West was now completely taken over by his experiences on the East Coast. He wore a blue army uniform, the height-crowned beaver hat and carried an umbrella, a large fan, and a small keg of whisky. Wi-Jun-Jon's tales of what he had seen in the East were impossible for his tribesmen to believe and after listening to him for three years, they came to believe that he was an evil wizard, and assassinated him.

"Ki-On-Twog-Ky or Corn Plant, a Seneca Chief."

"Wa-Pel-La, Chief of the Musquakees."

Thomas L. M'Kenney and James Hall, *History of the Indian Tribes of North America, with Biographical Sketches and Anecdotes of the Principal Chiefs....,* Philadelphia, 1836–1844. Published in three large-folio volumes containing 120 hand-colored lithographic plates.

One of the most important 19th-century works on the American Indian and one of the most important color-plate books produced in America in the age of lithography. M'Kenney, the commissioner of Indian Affairs, collaborated with James Hall, the prolific Cincinnati journalist, to produce this work, a series of biographies of leading Indian chiefs, written by Hall, and illustrated by color-plate portraits, based on original oils by Charles Bird King and others. It was the most elaborate color-plate book produced in the United States up to that time.

"A Winnebago."

"Keokuk, Chief of the Sacs and Foxes."

"Ball-Play Dance." From George Catlin's *North American Indian Portfolio. Hunting Scenes and Amusements of the Rocky Mountains and Prairies of America*, 1844.

Chapter 8

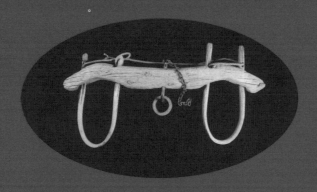

SANTA FE

Josiah Gregg's _Commerce of the Prairies:_ _Or the Journal of a Santa Fe Trader During Eight Expeditions Across the Great Western Prairies, and a Residence of Nearly Nine Years in Northern Mexico,_ 1844, is the best contemporary account of the Santa Fe Trade. Gregg vividly described the scene on the trail:

"'All's set!' is finally heard from some teamster — 'All's set' is directly responded from every quarter. 'Stretch out!' immediately vociferates the captain. The 'heps' of drivers — the cracking of whips — the trampling of feet — the occasional creak of wheels — the rumbling of wagons — form a new scene of exquisite confusion.... 'Fall in!' is heard from headquarters, and the wagons are forthwith strung out upon the long inclined plain."

ounded in 1610, Santa Fe was the first permanent settlement west of the Mississippi River. Unlike Mexico, which had developed because of gold and silver, Santa Fe grew out of the efforts of the Spanish missionaries to convert the natives. Despite generally good relations between the two groups, the Indians sometimes led uprisings against the missionaries and temporarily took control of Santa Fe from them.

By the time of the Lewis and Clark expedition, Americans had started using the Santa Fe Trail. The Mexicans feared these aggressive Americans who were following their destiny across the continent and established a ban on foreigners' trading in New Mexico. In 1810, a group of American traders was jailed for eleven years. Other groups were arrested and their goods taken. Even Zebulon Pike, who had blundered into Santa Fe territory, was arrested and not returned to the United States for some time.

In 1821, a revolt resulted in Mexico's breaking away from Spain, and Santa Fe was open to trade with the Americans. The trail itself was difficult — it was almost entirely desert, and the threat of Indian attack along its entire length was very real. Nevertheless, the Americans came, and the first groups to arrive made enormous profits, as did the Mexicans. In 1824, traders brought a wagon train from Missouri carrying merchandise that cost them $35,000 to Santa Fe and sold it there for $190,000. Soon Mexican traders got into the business and began sending pack trains full of their trade goods north. In the early to mid-1830s the director of customs at Santa Fe charged $500 per wagon.

By 1840, New Mexico feared it would be taken over by the Americans in Texas who claimed Santa Fe and Taos as part of Texas. In response to rumors that the New Mexicans would revolt, the Texans raised an army of 300 to support the

New Mexicans in their revolution. The Texans' information was incorrect. In fact, the New Mexicans were more fearful of the Texans and preferred to remain a part of Mexico. The members of the ill-conceived Texas expedition continued on towards Santa Fe, but being neither properly supplied nor knowing the route, became lost. The Texans were eventually found by the New Mexicans, who arrested them and marched them 2,000 miles to Mexico City and prison. Six years later in 1846, General Stephen Watts Kearny led 1,700 troops to take Santa Fe. The small force of occupation he established before moving on to California was able to quell uprisings in Taos and Santa Fe. The American takeover of New Mexico was the first part of driving the Mexican government south of the present-day border.

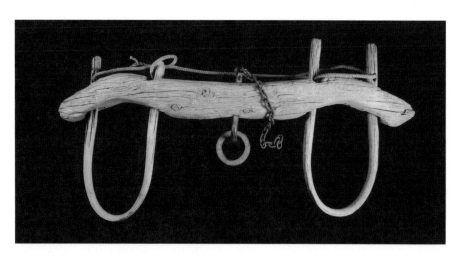

Ox yoke used on the Santa Fe Trail. This type of yoke remained in use in the Santa Fe area until the late 19th century.

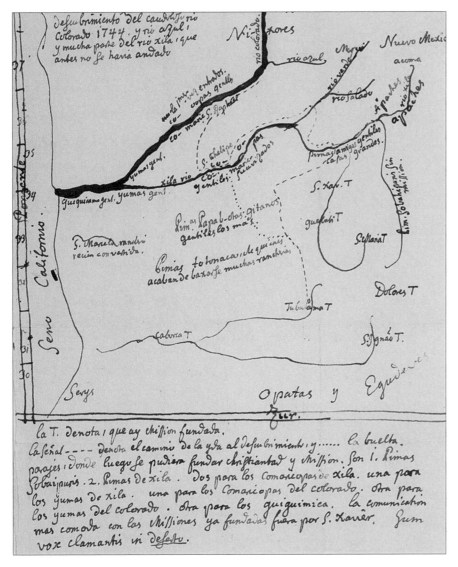

Map of explorations of the Colorado River in New Mexico, with a lengthy letter from the Jesuit missionary Gaspar Estiger, June 6, 1745, to his superior general in Mexico City reporting on the Indians in the area, missions, route, and prospects of spreading the missions further. The map measures 8½ by 7½ inches.

New Mexican hand-wrought iron and brass halberd head, *ca.* late 18th century. 20½ inches high.

127

"Zuni, New Mexico," by H. B. Mollhausen, lithograph, 1858. Mollhausen accompanied the 1853 Pacific Railroad Survey across northern New Mexico and Arizona, and published his plates and account of the journey in 1858.

PABLO LUCERO, provincial mayor of Taos. Document Signed, Taos, August 20, 1830. Concerning disputes between Santa Fe traders.

Carte-de-visite photograph of Kit Carson.

KIT CARSON. Document Signed, March 31, 1859, certifying, as Indian agent, that he has purchased wheat, corn, tobacco, and other supplies at the "lowest market price."

De Witt Peters, a physician on the frontier, in a lengthy letter to Carson written from Fort Davis, Texas in 1860, wrote, *"I am back again in the Army & am the Surgeon of this Post which is 200 miles south of El Paso & about 90 miles from the Rio Grande. I was doing well in New York but not being satisfied with City life I made up my mind to wander out on the frontiers again.*

"Fort Davis where I am at present stationed is on the California Overland Mail Route…

"[H]ow bold the Comanches are here…. The soldiers turned their lead mules around & tied them to the wagon wheel which they also locked & then received the bucks. The Indians charged & the soldiers received them with several volleys from their minnie muskets. Two horses (Indian) were killed & two head Indians were mortally wounded when the red men ran but returned & attacked an ox train behind (loaded with Government supplies). They killed a Mexican Teamster; broke a wagon to pieces & carried off several animals together with such articles selected from the wagon as they fancied. For three weeks every train passing a place called 'Johnson's M…' has had to fight & several have lost all their animals. These Indians have white men & Mexicans with them and are armed to the teeth, even down to Navey sized revolvers. The Mexican spoken of above was killed with this kind of ball as I saw the case & know it to be a fact. For some reason they do not trouble the mail or the mail stations though often, seen by the mail party. We need cavelry in this section very much & no doubt will have some soon as the Mexican affairs on the Rio Grande are being summarily quieted. There was a boy arrived in San Antonio said to have been rescued recently from the Indians of the Plains by you. He came down by the mail in Company with several officers. His Father is a German who lives near Fort Mason & I learned that this pernicious old Father felt very [sad] at having to pay some thing for the boys expenses. The boy liked or at least said he liked living with the Comanches & wished he was back again. The Indians here generally prefer mule meat to that of cattle which they rarely run off, only sometimes killing enough to supply their temporary wants."

Carson became a national hero as John C. Fremont's guide; the reports Fremont wrote publicized his expeditions, himself, and also Carson's abilities in the wilderness. Carson's friend DeWitt Peters wrote a flattering biography of him in 1874.

KIT CARSON'S

LIFE AND ADVENTURES,

FROM FACTS NARRATED BY HIMSELF,

EMBRACING EVENTS IN THE LIFE-TIME OF AMERICA'S

GREATEST HUNTER, TRAPPER, SCOUT AND GUIDE,

INCLUDING

VIVID ACCOUNTS OF THE EVERY DAY LIFE, INNER CHARACTER, AND PECULIAR CUSTOMS OF ALL

INDIAN TRIBES OF THE FAR WEST.

ALSO, AN ACCURATE

DESCRIPTION OF THE COUNTRY,

ITS CONDITION, PROSPECTS, AND RESOURCES; ITS CLIMATE AND SCENERY; ITS MOUNTAINS, RIVERS, VALLEYS, DESERTS AND PLAINS, AND NATURAL WONDERS. TOGETHER WITH A FULL AND COMPLETE HISTORY OF THE

MODOC INDIANS AND THE MODOC WAR.

BY

DEWITT C. PETERS,

BREVET LT.-COLONEL AND SURGEON U. S. A.

HARTFORD, CONN.:

DUSTIN, GILMAN & CO.

QUEEN CITY PUBLISHING CO., CINCINNATI; M. A. PARKER & CO., CHICAGO, ILL.; FRANCIS DEWING & CO., SAN FRANCISCO, CAL.

1874.

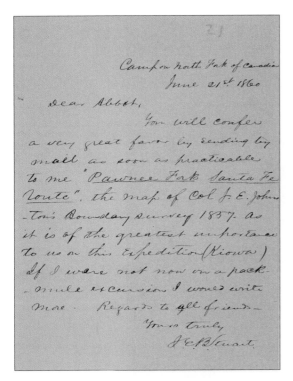

J.E.B. STUART. Civil War Confederate general. Autograph Letter Signed, *Camp on North Fork of Canadia*, June 21, 1860.

"You will confer a very great favor by sending by mail as soon as practicable to me 'Pawnee Fork Santa Fe Route,' the map of Col J. E. Johnston's Boundary survey 1857 as it is of the greatest importance to us in this Expedition (Kiowa). If I were not now on a pack-mule excursion I would write more."

Stuart wrote from the vicinity of the crossing of the Smoky Hill River, where "troops engaged in the campaign against the Kiowas and Comanches under the command of Major John Sedgwick, First Cavalry, camped in 1860. Sedgwick's subaltern, Lieutenant J.E.B. Stuart, noted in his diary that only the 'rocky foundation of the bridge' built in 1857 remained. Flood waters had destroyed the bridge in 1858. Within months of Lt. Stuart's observation, the Page/Lehman Ranche was established, and two other ranches were opened nearby." (Larry and Carolyn Mix, "Smoky Hill River Ranche") At the time, trading ranches, which often served as stage stations, were being established along the many routes of the Santa Fe Trail.

BENJAMIN BONNEVILLE, the Western explorer whom Washington Irving wrote about in the *Adventures of Captain Bonneville*, wrote a lengthy letter to the quartermaster general of the army in November of 1848. He discussed in detail his opinions about the Santa Fe Trail, particularly the problem with Indians and the need for setting up posts at critical points:

"[I]f a post were established on the Canadian River, where the Texas line crosses it; you see at once, the advantage such a post would possess. The Indians and the Texans would each advance their settlements under its protection, & it would become the rallying point for all traders, wishing to participate in the trade of the prairies. It would be supplied with quite as much ease as, Fort Washita has ever been and I think that an Agent for Indians, established here, might readily acquire the happy influence over the Wild Man of the Plains....

"Until New Mexico became ours, I was strongly of opinion, that some day we would be compelled to establish a post...somewhere not far from Bent's Fort, to overawe our Indian population and to give an eye to our trade with Mexico: but, now that Santa Fe is ours — we have in this point, every thing to be desired. I observe...so many plans for a rail road to the Pacific Ocean...no one seriously, will believe, a rail road can be safe, until the route be enveloped by the settlements, at least sufficiently, to secure the track from injury by the Indians. Until this period arrives, we may content ourselves with looking at Santa Fe, as the only true door, to our new territories."

131

"Grand Canyon of Arizona from Hermit Rim Road," by Thomas Moran, 1912. Lithographed 1913 for the Atcheson, Topeka and Santa Fe Railroad. 35 by 26 inches.

Chapter 9

EXPLORATION AND SCIENTIFIC EXPEDITIONS

"An offering before Capt. Cook in the Sandwich [Hawaiian] Islands." From *James Cook, A Voyage to the Pacific Ocean, Undertaken by the Command of His Majesty, for Making Discoveries in the Northern Hemisphere…*, 1784, 3 volumes.

Organized expeditions played a crucial role in America's westward expansion. The quintessential expedition was that of Lewis and Clark, which was organized by Jefferson and paid for by the government. The character of its two leaders and, to varying degrees, every member of the expedition made it successful and, more fundamentally, enabled the party to survive. There were multiple reasons for the expedition, but unlike other expeditions, it depended on two people: Lewis, who focused on Jefferson's scientific goals and inquiries, and Clark, who organized and led a small group of men — and one crucial woman — on a nearly impossible trip.

Earlier organized expeditions, for example Cook and Vancouver, were relatively large-scale naval endeavors. Alexander MacKenzie's expedition was more akin to that of Lewis and Clark. Both had the real goal of finding a water route across North America, and neither could because there isn't one. MacKenzie was the first to cross the continent, but the route is today almost unknown because of its tortured course across very unappealing and difficult terrain.

After the Lewis and Clark expedition, Zebulon Pike and Stehen H. Long led expeditions to the Southwest. Pike was particularly inept as an explorer and managed to be arrested by Santa Fe authorities and led to Mexico. Both explorers described the Southwest as a wasteland and set back enthusiasm for western exploration and expansion for decades. Both created the vision of the "Great American Desert." Long's report, written by Edwin James, called this region "almost wholly unfit for cultivation."

Although John C. Fremont was inept at carrying out the goals of his expeditions, this self-styled "Pathfinder" was of great importance because of the maps produced by his expedition's skilled German cartographer, Charles Preuss.

Fremont's national reputation as an explorer was largely the result of his talent for self-promotion. His romantic reports greatly increased popular interest in the West.

William H. Emory led an important expedition to the Southwest just after the Mexican War and spent six years surveying the new 1,800-mile southern border. His report is a major work on the West and the first reliable information on the border area. By the time of the Civil War, the West was essentially explored and mapped.

The great geographical and geological surveys of the West from the post–Civil War period of 1867 to 1879 include Clarence King's *Report of the Geographical Exploration of the 40th Parallel*. The book contains over 4,000 pages of text and hundreds of plates, illustrations, and maps. It was a landmark publication in American science. Ferdinand Hayden conducted an 1870 survey that explored and documented today's Nebraska, Wyoming, Utah, and Colorado but is perhaps best known for taking along the photographer William Henry Jackson. Jackson produced photographs that gave Americans a sense of the reality of the beauty and scale of the terrain.

The Grand Canyon area remained one of the last geographical mysteries until the 1869 expedition of John Wesley Powell. In the summer of that year, Powell's expedition discovered the canyon's last unknown mountain range, the Henry, and last unknown river, the Escalante. He also studied the Indians he encountered and reported all his findings in his *Canyons of the Colorado*.

All of the expedition reports of this period can be collected, but they range widely in price. Letters are not seen on the market.

ALEXANDER MACKENZIE. Autograph Letter Signed, Fort La Truite, September 3, 1790. Written on the expedition that led him to the Arctic Ocean via the McKenzie River, two years before the voyage of discovery during which he became the first explorer to record crossing the continent. To Alexander Fraser. "*I Expected to have found Some Chipewians…to get Canoes to go to winter to Lac de Carribou. I found Several Campments…. One of my men Lost his woman here going out…. It is supposed that she is among with the Indians…. [O]rder him a three pound Blanke[t]…which he Lent Him 5 years Since at the Beaver River.*"

An Account of the First Transcontinental Overland. Alexander Mackenzie, *Voyages from Montreal, on the River St. Laurence, Through the Continent of North America, to the Frozen and Pacific Oceans; In the Years 1789 and 1793, with a Preliminary Account of the Rise, Progress, and Present State of the Fur Trade of That Country…*, London, 1801.

This classic of North American exploration describes the extraordinary travels of the author in 1789, when he discovered the Mackenzie River, and in 1793, when he crossed the continent to the Pacific Coast of British Columbia and returned. Besides a narrative of his travels, Mackenzie also provided an excellent history of the fur trade in Canada, as well as vocabularies of several Indian languages.

MacKenzie was sent on the expedition to find a water route to the Pacific by the North West Company, which was anxious to supply its fur trading posts from the Pacific rather than from Montreal. MacKenzie's route was too difficult to be commercially useful.

VOYAGES

FROM

MONTREAL,

ON THE RIVER ST. LAURENCE,

THROUGH THE

CONTINENT OF NORTH AMERICA,

TO THE

FROZEN AND PACIFIC OCEANS;

In the Years 1789 and 1793.

WITH A PRELIMINARY ACCOUNT

OF THE RISE, PROGRESS, AND PRESENT STATE OF

THE FUR TRADE

OF THAT COUNTRY.

ILLUSTRATED WITH MAPS.

BY ALEXANDER MACKENZIE, ESQ.

LONDON:

PRINTED FOR T. CADELL, JUN. AND W. DAVIES, STRAND; COBBETT AND MORGAN, PALL-MALL; AND W. CREECH, AT EDINBURGH.

BY R. NOBLE, OLD-BAILEY.

M.DCCC.I.

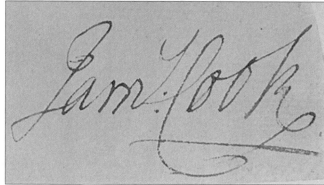

Captain James Cook, the British mariner and explorer, who charted the Pacific Coast of North America and did extensive exploration throughout the Pacific.

Cook was the greatest explorer of the 18th century. The account of his third voyage was based on his journals and those of James King, who succeeded Captain Cook as commander after the renowned explorer's murder in Hawaii. The third voyage was undertaken to continue the British survey of the Pacific, but most particularly to search for a northwest passage from the western side. Sailing in 1776, they discovered the Hawaiian Islands. The expedition then thoroughly explored and charted the Northwest Coast from the Bering Straits along the coast of Alaska and Canada, as far south as present-day Northern California. On returning to Hawaii in 1778, the expedition was at first received warmly by the natives. After the British sailors were forced to return to the island to repair a mast shortly after departure, trouble developed, which led to a tragic series of events in which the great navigator was killed.

"Costumes of the Inhabitants of San Francisco." Jean-Francois La Perouse's
Voyage de la Perouse Autour du Monde... Paris, 1796–1797. The greatest of 18th-century
French voyages to the Pacific. The French navigator made an extensive survey of the
Northwest Coast of America and published detailed maps and descriptions.

"View of San Francisco During Fishing Season." Jean-Francois La Perouse's
Voyage de la Perouse Autour du Monde... Paris, 1796–1797.

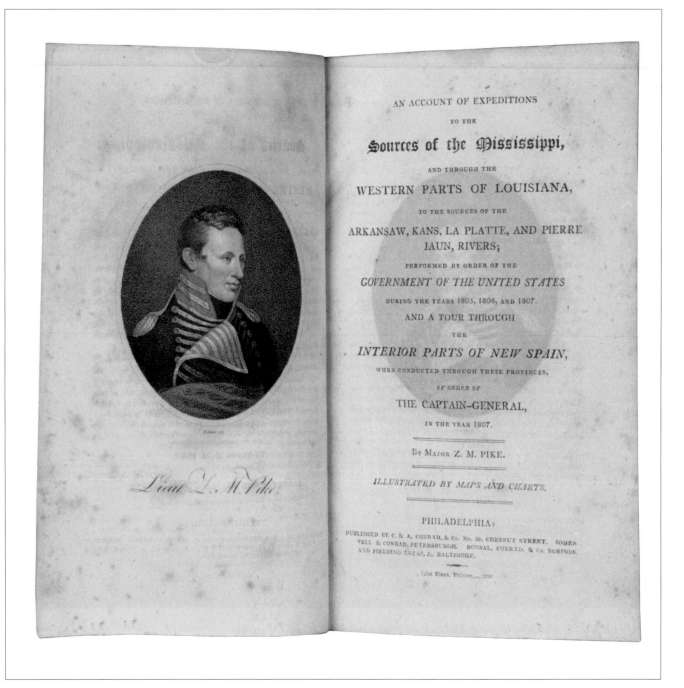

Zebulon M. Pike, *An Account of Expeditions to the Sources of the Mississippi, and Through the Western Parts of Louisiana...,* 1810.

The report of the first United States government expedition to the Southwest, and one of the most important of all American travel narratives. It includes an account of Pike's expedition to explore the headwaters of the Arkansas and Red Rivers, his earlier journey to explore the sources of the Mississippi River, and his visit to the Spanish settlements in New Mexico. The maps that resulted from this expedition were the first to exhibit a geographic knowledge of the Southwest based on firsthand exploration and are considered milestones in the mapping of the American West.

Edwin James, *Account of an Expedition from Pittsburgh to the Rocky Mountains, 1819 and '20...Under the Command of Major Stephen H. Long,* 1823.

This distant view of the Rocky Mountains by Samuel Seymor was the first eyewitness depiction of the West to be published and captured a sense of the immense distances and space.

Long's report of "the Great American Desert" ended government and public interest in the area for some years.

"Junction of the Gila and Colorado Rivers," from *Emory's Notes on a Military Reconnoisance from...Missouri to San Diego...,* 1848, one of the most important government reports on overland travel.

143

Louis Choris, *Voyage Pittoresque…, 1822.*

Louis Choris was a French artist who accompanied the Russian-sponsored Kotzebue expedition in its exploration of the Pacific in 1815–1818, visiting the Northwest Coast, California, and Hawaii and then circumnavigating the globe. This atlas has been called the most important 19th-century color-plate book on the Pacific Ocean, and the segments that relate to the American West make it one of the half-dozen most important illustrated works of the period. The illustrations are beautifully executed and colored, showing scenes of native life, natural history, and artifacts.

The book employed the process of lithography, then in its infancy, as a method of book illustration; this is the first important travel book so produced.

"San Francisco Bay."

"The Presidio of San Francisco."

"The First View of the Great Salt Lake." Howard Stansbury, *Exploration and Survey of the Valley of the Great Salt Lake of Utah Including a Reconnoissance of a New Route Through the Rocky Mountains,* 1852. A report of the first extensive survey of the Great Basin, and a major landmark in the cartography of the American West, based on surveys made by Stansbury in 1849 and 1850.

Chapter 10

Texas

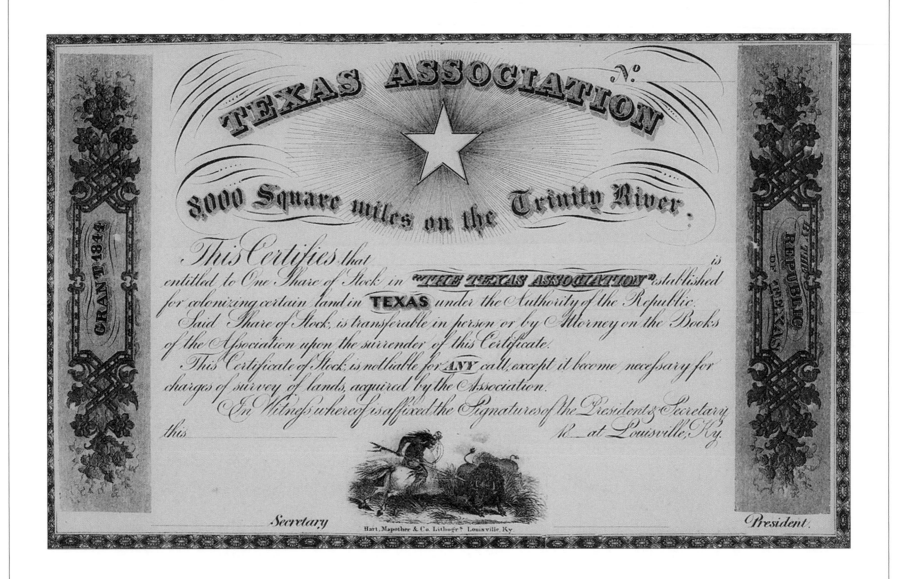

"Texas Association. 8,000 Square Miles on the Trinity River." Stock certificate, Louisville, Ky [1858]. "This certifies that __ is entitled to One Share of Stock in 'The Texas Association' established for colonizing certain land in Texas."

Prompted by the panic of 1819, Moses Austin began the colonization of Texas with 300 families on the grant of 200,000 acres obtained from the Mexican government. When he died in 1821, his son Stephen went to Texas to carry out the project. By 1832, as a result of his unremitting labor, perseverance, foresight, and tactful management, Austin's several colonies had about 8,000 settlers. Other impresarios with similar grants brought the territory's Anglo-American population to about 20,000.

Austin believed in and supported the relationship his colony had with Mexico. A prosperous colony was of great importance to him, and good relations with Mexico were at the heart of his plans. He steadfastly urged his colonists to appreciate their relationship with Mexico, to obey its laws, and to become loyal Mexican citizens.

The Texas colonists, however, saw themselves as Americans and wanted a say in how the colony was governed. The success of the colonies led to more American settlers — more than Austin could handle — and the newcomers were much less tolerant of Mexican rule. By 1832, the Texans had organized a committee that met in San Felipe and presented Mexico with proposals for independent Mexican statehood for Texas.

In 1832, as Santa Anna continued to rise in power, Sam Houston arrived in Texas. A natural military and political leader, he quickly joined the independence movement and played an increasingly important role in the struggle as the Texans' unhappiness with Mexico grew.

Austin showed his skill as a diplomat when he tried to induce the Mexican government to make Texas a separate state in the confederation, so that the American settlers might have the liberty and self-government they considered indispensable. When this attempt failed, he recommended in 1833 the organization of a state without waiting for the consent to the Mexican congress, and was thrown in prison.

Houston urged the Texans to be calm. By mid-1835, Santa Anna had become dictator of Mexico. When the Texans learned of his plan to send a Mexican army on a punitive mission to Texas, they organized resistance and the Texas Revolution began. The Texans defeated the first forces Santa Anna sent. As Houston suspected he would, Santa Anna then sent better troops. In March 1836, he personally led 3,000 troops against the 183 Texans defending the Alamo. Six weeks later, 800 Texans, under Houston's tactical leadership, caught Santa Anna's army of 1,250 and killed or captured all of them.

The Republic of Texas was proclaimed in June 1836; Houston was elected president, defeating Stephen Austin. About 30,000 people had settled in Texas by this time.

Texas.

At home Feb. 12. 1832

Dr Sir

I have rec.d your letter & the maps by Mr Rhoads Fisher who arrived safe with his family, and thank you for your attention –

The affair of Genl. Santana has made no disturbance in Texas, and every thing here is peace and quietness and I think will so remain –

We are very much imposed in this remote corner of the nation to be misled or deceived by false rumors and reports – Such was the case during the whole of last month & the latter part of December Great pains had been taken to impress upon the minds of many here, and on mine, amongst the rest, that the govt. intended to break us up – It was incorrect and I therefore wish you to burn the two last letters I wrote you, one in December & one in January –

I leave in a few days for the seat of govt.

your relation

S.F.A.

T. F. Leaming Esq

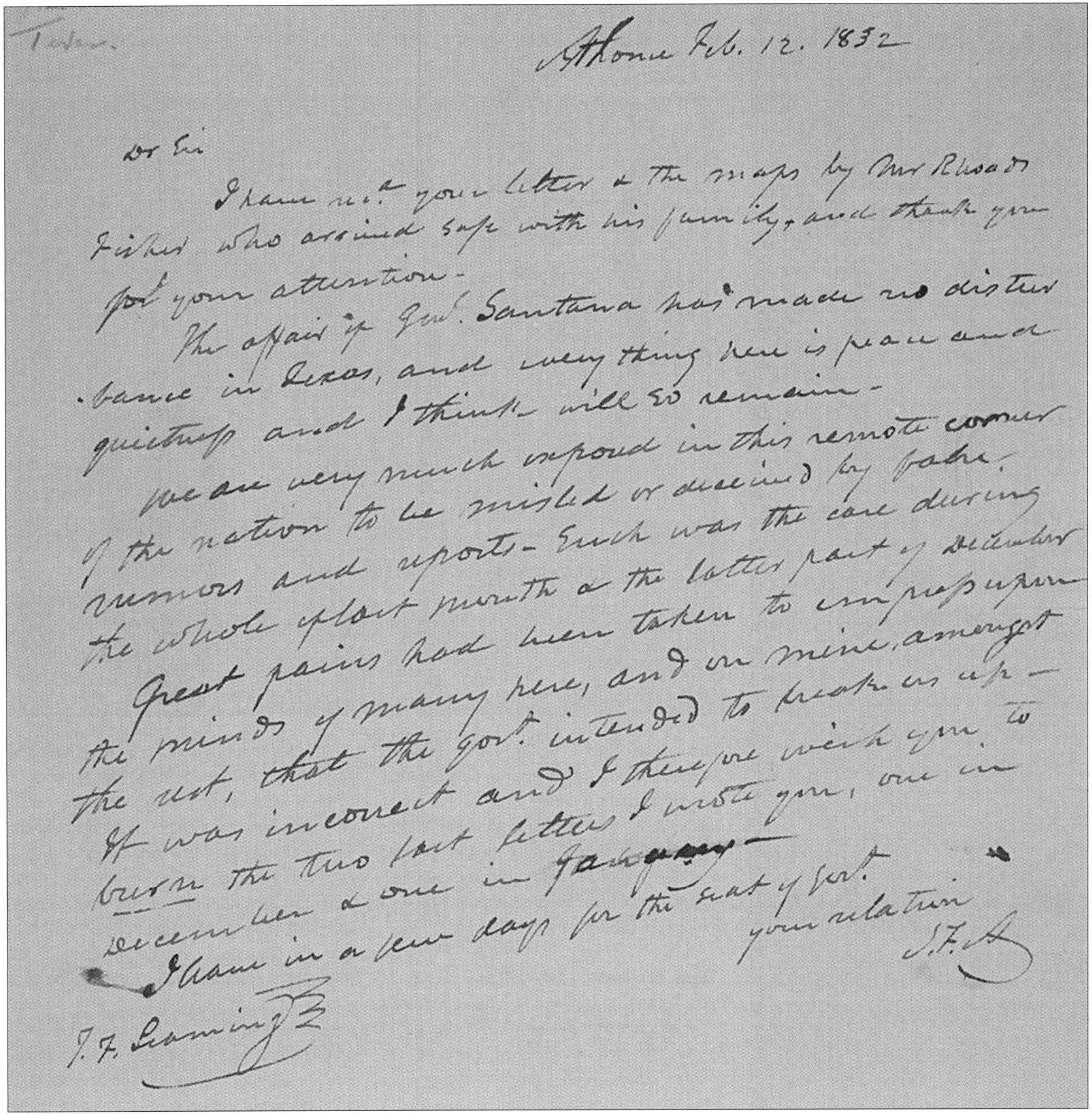

STEPHEN F. AUSTIN was in St. Louis on February 12, 1832, when he wrote:

"I have recd your letter and the maps by Mr. [Rhodes] Fisher who arrived safe with his family.... The affair of Genl Santana [Santa Anna] has made no disturbance in Texas, and every thing here is peace and quietness and I think I will so remain. We are very much imposed in this remote corner of the nation to be misled or deceived by false rumours and reports. Such was the case during the whole of last month or the latter part of December. Great pains had been taken to impress upon the minds of many here, and on mine, amongst the rest, that the govt. intended to break us up — It was incorrect and I therefore wish you to <u>*burn*</u> *the two last letters I wrote you, one in December & one in January — I leave in a few days for the seat of govt."*

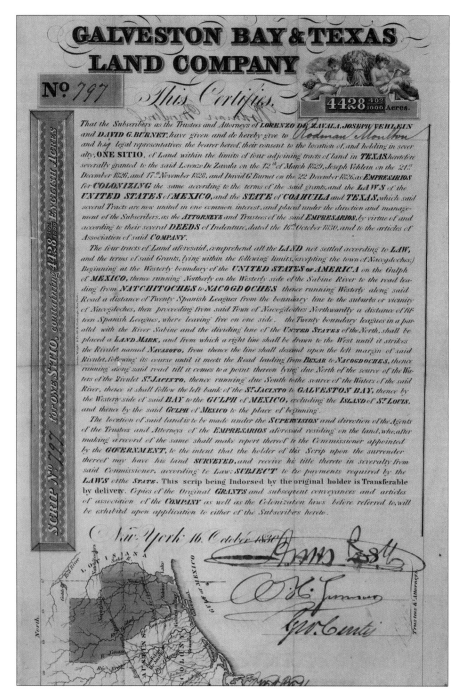

An ornate land grant from the Galveston Bay & Texas Land Company, October 16, 1830, giving 4,428 acres in the area shown on the map, which depicts Austin's colony.

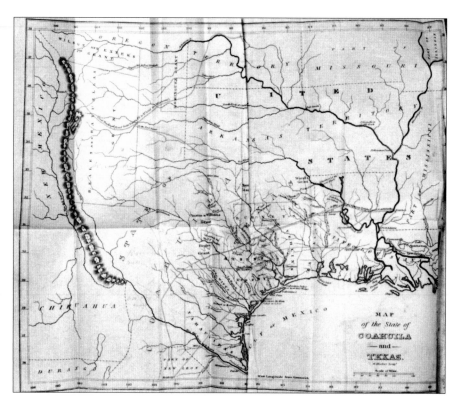

The map from Mary Austin Holley's *Texas. Observations, Historical, Geographical and Descriptive, Written During a Visit to Austin's Colony, with a View to a Permanent Settlement in That Country, in the Autumn of 1831…*, 1833. Written by Stephen Austin's cousin, this is the first book in English devoted entirely to Texas.

"*Texas until within the last few years has been literally a terra-in-cognita…. [T]his is the more remarkable, lying as it does, contiguous to two enlightened nations, the United States…and Mexico…being very easy of access both by land and sea…. A*

report has reached the public here that the country lying west of the Sabine River is a tract of surpassing beauty exceeding even our best western lands in productiveness with a climate perfectly salubrious and of a temperature at all seasons of the year most delightful. The admirers of this new country speaking from actual knowledge…call it a splendid country, an enchanting spot…. All who return from this fairy land are perfect enthusiast in their admiration of it…. It is uncertain how long this extensive and valuable country would have remained unknown and unsettled had not the bold enterprise and perseverance of the Austins torn away the veil that hid it from the view of the world and redeemed it from the wilderness by the settlement of a flourishing colony of North Americans.... With the settlement of this colony a new era has dawned upon Texas. The natural resources of this beautiful province have begun to be unfolded and its charms displayed to the eyes of the admiring adventurers. A new island as it were has been discovered...at our very doors apparently fresh from the hands of its maker and adapted beyond most lands both to delight the senses and enrich the pockets of those who are disposed to accept of its bounties.... Emigration is often undertaken with expectations so vague and preposterous that disappointment if not ruin is the inevitable consequence. Not more unreasonable were the immigrants of the early history of America who expected to find streets paved with gold.... Those individuals of the present day who escaping from confinement in poverty in the northern cities of America or from the slavery and wretchedness of the crowded and oppressed communities of Europe complained of their disappointments in Texas.... Such persons would do well to ask themselves in what part of the world they can get land for nothing, where obtained so many enjoyment with so little labor? What region combines every good?.... A soil that yields the fruits of nearly every latitude almost spontaneously with a climate of perpetual summer must like that of other countries have a seed-time and a harvest. Though the land be literally flowing with milk and honey yet the cows must be milked and the honey must be gathered. Houses must be built and enclosures made. The deer must be hunted and the fish must be caught. From the primeval curse that in the sweat of his brow man shall eat bread though its severity be mollified there is no exemption even here. The immigrants should bear in mind that in a new community labor is the most valuable commodity. He sees about him all the means for supplying not only the necessaries but also the comforts and luxuries of life. It is his part to apply them to his use. He is abundantly furnished with the raw materials but his hands must mold them into the forms of art.

"The inhabitants in general are composed of a class who have been unfortunate in life; as it could hardly be supposed that the fortunate except in a few instances would voluntarily make choice of a country where in they were to encounter such a number of difficulties as the first settlers had to contend with; who in a great measure were banished from the pleasures of life and almost from its necessities, so much so that many of them had to rely upon the precariousness of the chase alone for their first year's support; often times solacing themselves, men women and children on the flesh of a wild horse...without the satisfaction of seasoning it with salt! Although the whole country plentifully abound with that useful article, particularly near the lower waters of the Colorado."

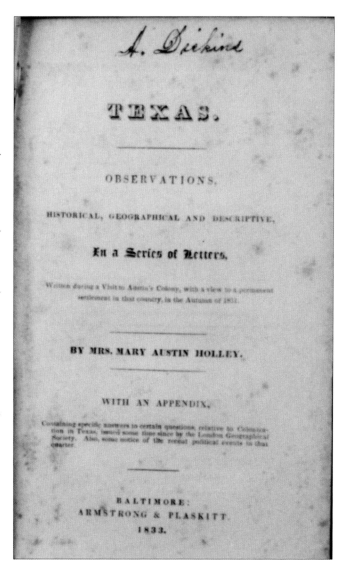

153

David B. Edward's map of Texas published in his book *The History of Texas; or the Emigrant's, Farmer's, and Politician's Guide to the Character, Climate, Soil and Productions of That Country...*, 1836.

Generally considered one of the best works written at the time of the Texas Revolution, the book describes Texas and political events through 1835 through the eyes of a man who was not enamored of the Texans' revolt against the Mexican government.

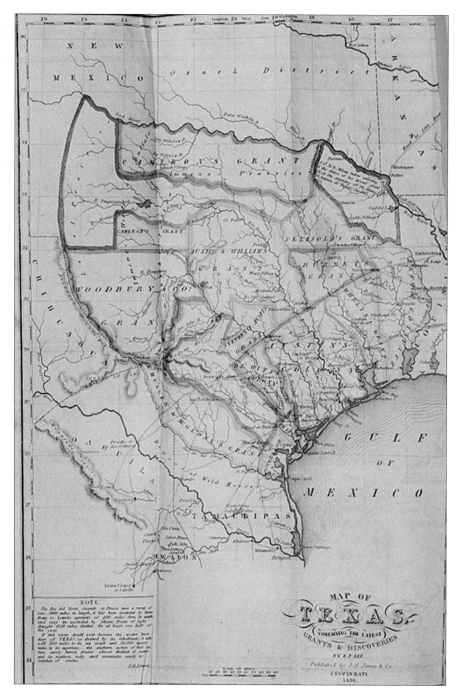

SANTA ANNA, the Mexican dictator who captured the Alamo and led the slaughter of the defending Texans.

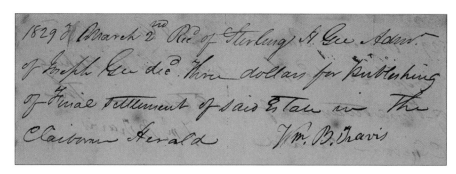

WILLIAM BARRET TRAVIS commanded the Texas garrison at the Alamo. Document Signed [Austin, Texas], April 20, 1834. A petition of Martha Hill regarding the settlement of her late husband's estate.

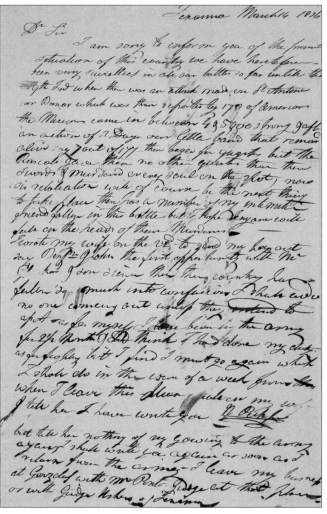

NICHOLAS PICKFORD'S detailed description written in Texoma, Texas, March 14, 1836, of the Battle of the Alamo, eight days earlier.

"The Mexicans came in between 4 & 5000 strong & after an action of 3 Days our little band that remained alive say 7 out of 177, then begged for quarter but the Rascals gave them no other quarter than their swords & murdered every soul on the spot."

In an earlier letter, April 26, 1835, Pickford wrote, "[O]n my arrival here I found the Colony was about being closed for grants for land. I went immediately to the surveyor and entered for a League (say 4440 acres) which is a privalege every man of Famely has. I then made my selection…. It is well wooded & watered & good Cotton Land. I have now been down to War Loop to pay for my League which cost me 55$ & 34$ payable in 6 years. I have also purchased 610 acres of a man that had a fourth of a League joining mine for 6 / Cts pr acre he not being able to pay for it, which makes me out 5050 acres of Land in one Bodey. I have exclusive of that two town Blocks of 48 acres Each one of which I shall build on this fall. I have commenced cutting timber for boards & Shingles & shall calculate to break up from 30 to 40 acres & fence it in by next spring, I shall try hard to get in 20 acres of Cotton the next season if my Sons come out think I can do it…and what is better have done it all myself…and I think there is no better country for a Man to get along in than this, the Inhabitants in this part are mostly Americans from Illonois & Masurie. I am myself agreeably disapointed with the country but still people that are pleased with [Rhode Island] may not like it."

FIRST TEXIAN LOAN SCRIP.

 No. 218. 640 ACRES OF LAND.

CERTIFICATE OF TITLE TO SIX HUNDRED AND FORTY ACRES OF LAND.

Know all Men, That, in consideration of a Loan to the Government of Texas, negotiated by the Commissioners of said Government in New Orleans, on the eleventh day of January, 1836, *Thomas D. Carneal, of Cincinatti Ohio,* is entitled to have and to hold, SIX HUNDRED AND FORTY ACRES OF LAND, of the Public Domain of Texas, according to the terms and conditions of a Contract of Compromise, made and executed on the first day of April 1836, between the Government ad interim of Texas, and the Stockholders in the aforesaid Loan; and of the Act of Congress for fulfilling and carrying into effect the said Contract of Compromise, approved the twenty-fourth day of May, 1838. This Certificate shall be authority for any duly appointed surveyor, to survey, at the expense of the holder hereof, any land, belonging to the Government of Texas, that may be selected by the said holder, at any time after the first Thursday in August next. And should the same be located on any land to which the government of Texas has not the prior right, it may be removed, and laid on other land. When the holder of this Certificate shall file the same, together with the boundaries, or field notes, of the land intended to be covered by it, in the General Land Office, a title or Patent, for the same, shall issue to the said *Thos. D. Carneal,* his heirs or assigns, in the usual form.

In Testimony Whereof, I, **SAM. HOUSTON,** President of the Republic of Texas, have hereunto set my hand, at the **CITY OF HOUSTON,** this *Twentieth* day of *June* in the year of our Lord eighteen hundred and thirty=eight, and of the Independence of Texas the third.

BY THE PRESIDENT

Henry Smith
Secretary of the Treasury.

SAM HOUSTON, president of the Republic of Texas, *"in consideration of a loan to the government of Texas"* gives Thomas Carneal 640 acres of land, June 20, 1838.

Although Sam Houston had evinced an interest in Texas ever since he was a young man — as early as 1822 he had joined a group of investors in applying for a grant of land in Texas, and in 1829, he had been invited by John Wharton to settle there — he apparently did not make his first trip to Texas until December 1832. In the spring of 1829, Houston had resigned the governorship of Tennessee following an acrimonious — and very public — estrangement from his wife. Alone and embittered, he set himself up among his Cherokee friends in the Arkansas Territory as a trader, an occupation he pursued for about four years. In the spring of 1833, he settled in Nacogdoches, where his popularity and character soon elevated him to a position of leadership in the growing agitation against Mexican rule.

Before permanently settling in Texas, he wrote an intimate and lengthy letter to a friend in New York, giving much information on his activities in the months following his retreat to the frontier. Dated from Wigwam Neasho, January 28, 1831, it is the most important Houston letter I have seen.

"I know that since we had parted, the little remaining stock of reputation remaining with me when we parted, since had been assailed by the solemn 'Report of a Committee'…. It was reasonable for me to suppose, that…my friends…might suppose me, only intitled to pity or contempt. Your letter was well calculated to dispel all aprehensions of the kind….You do not know…how often, my heart has recurred to my friends of New York, in which you never fail to be embraced! You are a noble set of souls there, but I cannot be with you and therefore must solace myself with recollections of the past and

hopes of a happy future to you all! I am done with goods, but not with good things I trust. In next month I hope to sell out, close my concern and migrate to some other Theater — say Natchez, and resume my profession, and do whatever else I may as, an honest & honorable man. My original design was to remain in the world as far as possible removed from scenes and circumstance which I believed it my duty to forego, and forget — but the world will not let me rest in quiet or enjoy tranquility — I am assailed when absent and my reputation must suffer too severely, unless I return again, and by proper conduct rally around me proper aids, & after establishing a moral influence such as I can do, repel by my character the assaults, which may be directed, against my reputation. This will disappoint my enemies and gratify my friends! Furthermore mercantile business is not adapted to [my] cast or disposition! Nor if it were possible for me to enjoy all the luxuries of life, could I endure indolence, as a pass time — I must be active, or I would sink, into the horrible gulph of dissipation and debauchery!

"Thus you see a sense of duty to myself and a decent respect for the feelings of my friends shall induce my course, and the things done by me, shall be directed to what I most devoutly believe, will be my countrys Glory, and her good! You speak of our Dear old Chief, and the success of his administration. From my soul, I rejoice in his Glory, and would to God, he had other, and I could add, better aids, to devise and execute his measures — who but a man just as Great as Genl. Jackson, could sustain himself before the American people, with such a weight upon his shoulders as John H. Eaton. He alone is enough to break the Backbone of Atlas; or destroy any other mans moral, and political influence save the old Chiefs! But it

is an evil that must cure its-self and patience must be the remedy, for the disease for any struggle to get rid of the evil, might only produce greater! As to Mr. V[an] B[uren] of your State I know, but little, but deem your remarks…very just, so far as I can judge! So soon as I can get settled, you will be apprised of it."

Within three months of Governor Sam Houston's marriage to Eliza Allen on January 22, 1829, the couple was estranged; on April 16, Mrs. Houston returned to her father's house in Gallatin, Tennessee, and Houston, refusing to discuss the separation, endured five days of public innuendoes before he resigned his governorship and vowed to return to life with the Cherokees. Neither Houston nor his wife ever disclosed the reason for the broken marriage, but historians have since concurred that Houston's hasty condemnation of his young wife's affection for a previous suitor — and the couple's failure to reconcile their differences before they became public — precipitated the crisis. In any event, Houston renounced his promising career and, embittered by the controversy, which his political opponents did much to encourage, set out to live among his Cherokee friends, newly relocated by government treaty to the Arkansas Territory. He settled at Wigwam Neosho, a trading post he built near Cantonment Gibson, just north of present-day Muskogee, Oklahoma, and set up business as a contractor supplying Indian rations. Eager to protect his friends from unscrupulous agents, he traveled to Washington in early 1830 to complain to Secretary of War John Eaton about fraudulent practices in the distribution of supplies. This, as Houston's comment in his letter reflects, provoked a controversy

with the secretary. At the same time, the scandal over the breakup of his marriage continued to rage. In April 1830, a group organized by long-time political foes of Houston's issued a report declaring that Houston's *"unfounded jealousies and his repeated suspicion of her coldness of want of attachment"* were the cause of the separation. The report, which was released to the newspapers, further insinuated that Houston had rebuffed attempts at a reconciliation.

In 1841, John Slocum wrote to a friend in Pennsylvania from Huron County, Ohio, *"[I] travelled through the settled part of Texas. Allmost all kinds of property is plenty in Texas and is worth about the same as here. Government gives evry man that gets thare this year 320 Acres of land by cultivating 10 Acres of the same."*

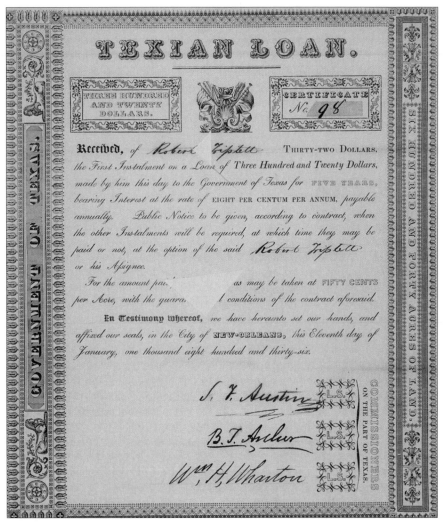

An ornate receipt for the first installment of a $320 loan to the government of Texas, signed by Stephen F. Austin, New Orleans, 1836.

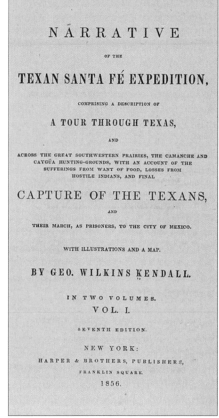

George W. Kendall, *Narrative of the Texan Santa Fe Expedition...Through Texas, and Across the Great Southwestern Prairies, the Comanche and Cayuga Hunting-Grounds, with an Account of the Sufferings from Want of Food, Losses from Hostile Indians, and Final Capture of the Texans, and Their March, as Prisoners, to the City of Mexico, 1844.*

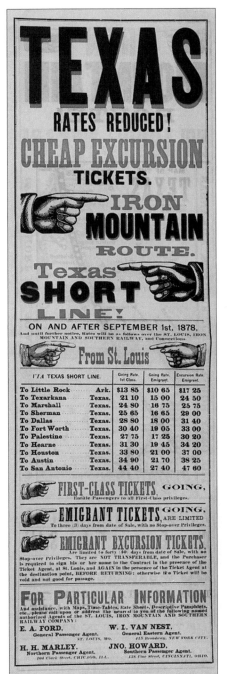

Not everyone thought Texas the ideal place to settle. M. Kennett wrote of his reasons to his mother from Corpus Christi, Texas, on July 16, 1849:

"I shall be on my way for California where I hope after the elapse of a short time to be able to repair my disappointed fortune and make up for lost time in Texas…. The party which I leave with consist of about fifty men well armed and equiped, used to travel through a wild country, tryed soldiers who have fought all through the Revolution in Texas. The distance from here about fifteen or eighteen hundred miles to be undertaken on horseback, and with our experience in a campaign life it will be a mere execution of pleasure."

James Hamilton was enthusiastically involved in the struggle for Texas independence. Having advanced substantial funds of his own to the cause, he was honored by the leaders of Texas with a series of appointments. In 1838, the president of Texas, Mirabeau B. Lamar, made Hamilton commissioner of loans, and in 1839, Hamilton went to Europe as diplomatic agent to France, Great Britain, Belgium, and the Netherlands, where he secured recognition of Texas, as well as favorable commercial treaties. Soon, however, he became a casualty of the austerity that followed Sam Houston's return to the presidency: Texas, in effect, defaulted on $210,000 in gold owed personally to Hamilton. In 1855, he settled permanently in Texas, where he had an enormous land grant, hoping to recoup his debt through land promotion, as well as by political means. That year he wrote a letter full of the same exuberance for the future of Texas that still exists more than a century and a half later:

"[There is] an enterprise in North Eastern Texas which I regard as the most promising operation which is open to the Enterprise of those who have the sagacity & boldness to embrace it. I send you most confidentially a Pamphlet which is yet a sealed Book which I shall not issue until I have made my association with a capitalist or capitalists & made negotiation & selection of Lands. Then I shall transmit it to my friends…to invite them to the lovliest & most fertile region on Earth….

"I send it for your sole & exclusive perusal. I have not the smallest hesitation in avowing, that I can during the ensuing Winter purchase Lands in the Country in question for $1 or $2 pr acre which in five years will certainly & inevitably bring $5 & $10 and after all the capital is replaced with a profit of 50 pCent if one half of the Lands are retained for five years more, the half so retained will sell for $20 pr acre. After you have read my Pamphlet you will oblige me exceedingly if you will go to London & see Mr Peabody. He will show you my Letter detailing the terms & conditions of the association I have proposed the scope an object of which is to raise $100,000 to purchase 100,00 acres in the Region distinctly designated & laid down in the Pamphlet. Rich as Mr. Peabody is the diversion of so large a sum as $100,000 from his Banking business might be inconv[en]ient but it is quite possible he might organise under his influence & lead a Company of ten persons at $10,000 each who would be willing to go into the Enterprise. I know not how it might suit you to take a share but if it did I think I might with safety gu[a]rantee you Fifty thousand in five years for your ten at the lowest possible calculation.

"As the Pacific Rail Road may never be completed to its extreme western terminus yet that it will be build from the Red River indeed from Memphis to the Banks of the Leon in less than five years cannot be doubted which will appreciate the Lands in NoEastern from 500 to 1000 pCent. This Road is already commenced. I have urged prompt action on the part of Mr Peabody as the Season for profitable operation will close in the Spring. As Mr Peabody is but imperfectly acquainted with me you can best inform him who [is] the…man calculated to conduct the proposed Enterprise & to give to it a successful development. Pray oblige an old friend by going to London & seeing Mr Peabody. I have requested him to show you my Letter that you may understand the whole subject….

"In case you do not become a share holder in the proposed association or you do not hand the printed circular to some one who is a member or Mr. Peabody deems the association of impracticable formation then return me the Pamphlet as it might accidently without your knowledge fall into the Possession of some person who might avail himself of information which I have acquired at so much cost & labor."

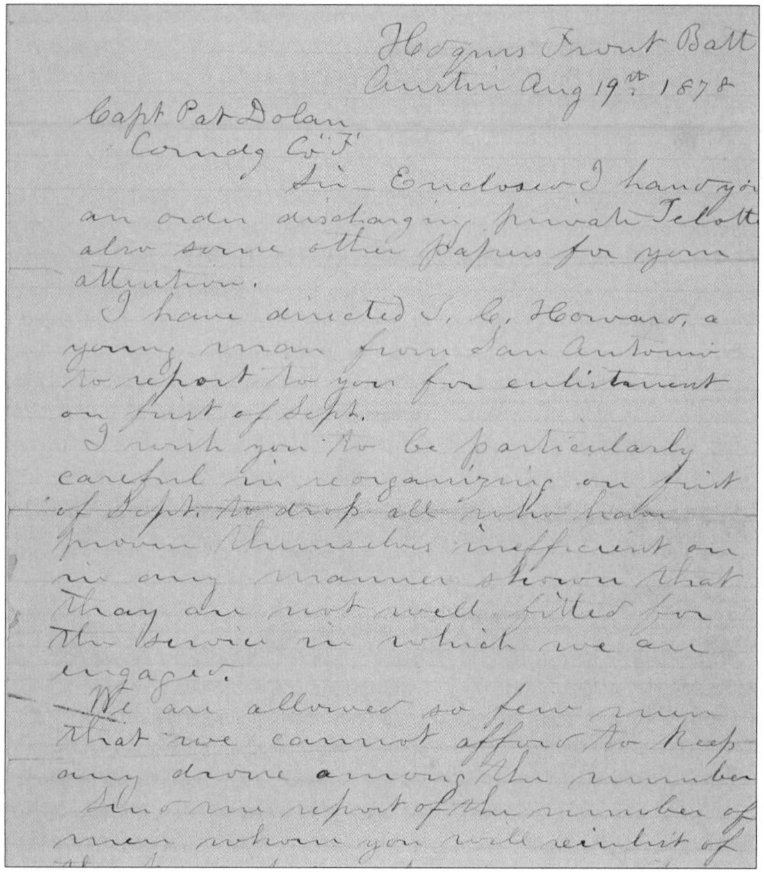

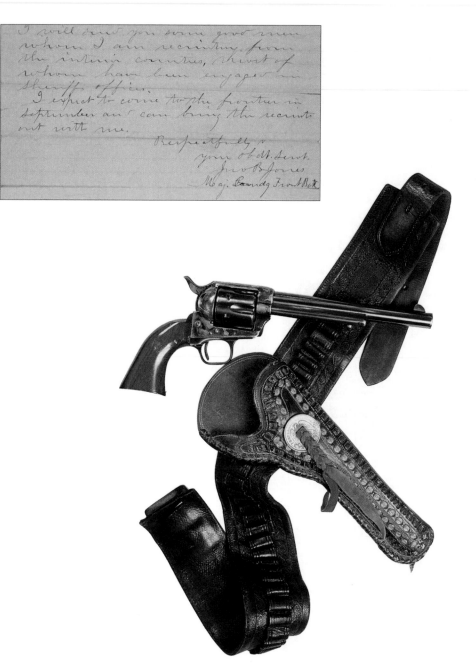

Handwritten letter, left portion:

Hdqrs Front Batt
Austin Aug 19th 1878

Capt Pat Dolan
Comdg Co "F"

Sir— Enclosed I hand you an order discharging private Telott also some other papers for your attention.

I have directed S. G. Howard, a young man from San Antonio to report to you for enlistment on first of Sept.

I wish you to be particularly careful in reorganizing on first of Sept to drop all who have proven themselves inefficient or in any manner shown that they are not well fitted for the service in which we are engaged.

We are allowed so few men that we cannot afford to keep any drone among the number.

Send me report of the number of men whom you will reinlist of

Handwritten letter, right portion:

I will send you some good men whom I am recruiting from the interior counties, most of whom have been engaged in sheriffs' offices.

I expect to come to the frontier in September and can bring the recruits out with me.

Respectfully
your obdt. Servt.
Jno B Jones
Maj. Comdg Front Bat

JOHN B. JONES, commander of the Texas Rangers. Autograph Letter Signed, Austin, August 19, 1878. To Captain Pat Dolan, commanding officer of Ranger Company F. Written exactly a month after his Ranger detachment had tracked down and killed the notorious train robber Sam Bass, Major Jones's letter displays his careful attention to military organization and discipline:

"I wish you to be particularly careful in reorganizing…. [D]rop all who have proven themselves inefficient or in any manner shown that they are not well fitted for the service in which we are engaged. We are allowed so few men that we cannot afford to keep any drone among the number. Send me report of the number of men whom you will reinlist of the present company and if you have not required number I will send you some good men whom I am recruiting from the interior counties, most of whom have been engaged in sherrifs' officers. I expect to come to the frontier in September and can bring the recruits out with me."

Revolver made by Cimmaron, Houston, *ca.* 1892; the holster decorated with a Mexican coin.

THE MEXICAN WAR

America's sense of Manifest Destiny was something Mexico had feared for decades. The Texas Revolution in 1836 strengthened these fears, particularly after the United States annexed Texas in 1845. The United States offered to assume some questionable debts it insisted Mexico owed if the Mexicans would agree to extend Texas's border south to the Rio Grande. The United States also offered to buy California and New Mexico.

The Mexicans rejected these negotiations, and after several thousand American soldiers from Texas invaded Mexico and occupied the land the Texans wanted, Mexico declared war against the United States in April 1846. It was a war Mexico couldn't win, and in seventeen months the Mexicans never won a battle. Mexico City surrendered on August 18, 1847.

The war was very popularly supported in Texas and the Mississippi River Valley. The West got everything it wanted in the Treaty of Guadalupe Hidalgo: The Texas boundary was redrawn, and California and New Mexico were purchased by the United States for $15 million.

George W. Kendall and Carl Nebel, *The War Between the United States and Mexico, Illustrated, Embracing Pictorial Drawings of All the Principal Conflicts…with a Description of Each Battle,* New York and Philadelphia, 1851.

George W. Kendall and Carl Nebel, *The War Between the United States and Mexico, Illustrated, Embracing Pictorial Drawings of All the Principal Conflicts…with a Description of Each Battle,* New York and Philadelphia, 1851. The most important work relating to the Mexican War, the book is illustrated with plates that were executed from drawings made by Nebel at the actual battle sites, and lithographed by Lemercier of Paris. Nebel portrayed a Mexican civilian in the lower left about to hurl a paving stone at the Americans.

Chapter 11

California

Francisco Palóu, *Relacion Historica de la Vida y Apostolicas Tareas del Venerable Padre Fray Junipero Serra, y de las Misiones que Fundo en la California Septentrional, y Nuevos Establecimientos de Monterey…,* Mexico, 1787.

The most important contemporary account of the Spanish colonization of California and the beginning of the mission system that dominated life there until the coming of the Americans. In 1769, the Spanish began to occupy upper California, mainly to forestall any possible incursions by the Russians or English. Father Junipero Serra was the chief figure in the founding of the twenty-one California missions that were a key part of the Spanish government there, and the story of his fifteen years there are a large part of the Spanish effort. The author accompanied Serra to California, and so had firsthand knowledge of many of the events he described.

V. R. DEL V. P. F. JUNIPERO SERRA
hijo de la S.ta Prov.a de N.P.S. Fran.co de la Isla de Mallorca Ex.or de Theol. Comis. del S.to Of. Miss. del Ap.l Col.o de S. Fern.do de Mex.co Fund.or y Presid.te de las Miss.es de la Calif. Septent.l= Murió con gr.e fama de sant.d en la Miss.n de S. Carlos del Rio del N. Monte Rey á 28 de Ag.to de 1784 de edad de 70 a.s Dm.s 4 d.s hab.do gastado la mit.d de su vida en el exerc.o de Mision.o Apost.co

---

Pag. 1.

RELACION HISTORICA,

DE LA VIDA Y APOSTÓLICAS TAREAS

DEL V. P. FRAY JUNIPERO SERRA,

De la Regular Observancia de N. S. P. S. Francisco de la Provincia de Mallorca; Doctor, y ex-Catedrático de Prima de Sagrada Teología en la Universidad Lulliana de dicha Isla; Comisario del Santo Oficio en toda la Nueva España, é Islas adyacentes; Predicador Apostólico del Colegio de Misioneros Apostólicos de Propaganda Fide de San Fernando de México; Presidente y Fundador de las Misiones, y nuevos Establecimientos de la Nueva y Septentrional California y Monterey.

CAPITULO I.

Nacimiento, Patria y Padres del V. P. Junípero: Toma el santo hábito, y exercicios que tuvo en la Provincia antes de pretender salir para la América.

EL infatigable Operario de la Viña del Señor el V. P. Fr. Junípero Serra dió principio á su laboriosa vida el dia 24 de Noviembre del año de 1713 naciendo á la una de la mañana en la Villa de Petra de la Isla de Mallorca: Fueron sus Padres Antonio Serra, y Margarita Ferrer, humildes Labradores, honrados, devotos, y de exemplares costumbres. Como si tuvieran anticipada noticia de lo mucho que el hijo que les acavaba de nacer se habia de afanar á su tiempo para bautizar Gentiles, se afana-

California had always been somewhat neglected by Spain. Only when the Russian fur hunters began to expand to the south from Alaska, did the Spanish begin to establish the chain of missions up the coast. The first mission was San Diego in 1769, and eventually twenty-one were founded as far north as San Francisco. Within fifteen years of Mexican independence, the mission system was in decline, in part because of the expulsion of all Spanish-born missionaries.

By 1846, California was being settled by Americans lured by rich farmland and good weather. Its government was far removed from Mexico, which supplied neither financial support nor an army. The talk of independence was everywhere.

John C. Fremont was in California on an exploring expedition and, knowing of the growing tension with Mexico over negotiations concerning the Texas border, joined the Bear Flag Revolt, aiding an independence group that raised a "grizzly bear" flag in Sonoma on July 4, 1846. Fremont's hopes for sole glory were brief; an American squadron under Commodore John Drake Sloat occupied Monterey, and Fremont had to join forces with him and his successor, Robert F. Stockton, in the conquest of Northern California.

Stockton sent Fremont's men, including Kit Carson, by boat to take Southern California, and by August, San Diego and Los Angeles were occupied. Meanwhile, the troops that had just taken Santa Fe under Stephen Watts Kearny were still making their way to California; west of Santa Fe in September 1846, they met Kit Carson, who was heading east. Carson told them of the conquest of California. At the Colorado River, they received the news that Californios —

the descendants of early settlers from Spain and Mexico — had revolted and recaptured Los Angeles, Santa Barbara, and San Diego. Kearny had to fight his way into California and, reinforced by Stockton's men and American settlers, defeated the Californios at the San Gabriel River on January 8 and 9, 1847. The Americans reoccupied Los Angeles without opposition. The tensions that arose among the occupation forces were largely the result of the traditional army-navy rivalry that continues even today. Stockton refused to recognize Kearny as President Polk's authorized commander and appointed Fremont governor. In February, orders from Washington confirmed Kearny's authority, and Fremont traveled back East, where he was court-martialed for insubordination.

Letters and documents of many of the major figures in pre–gold rush California are fairly available on the market, though none with content concerning these times. Many books are also available, and even though they are collected, prices are still relatively reasonable.

Francisco Palóu, in an autograph manuscript diary, 71 pages in length, entitled Diary of the Expedition by Land Which Was [Done] to Reconnoiter and Discover the Environs of the Port of San Francisco in the Year 1774, gives a day-by-day account of his own expedition from Monterey to San Francisco and back, during a well-equipped and -manned exploration to and around the San Francisco Bay area. It includes extensive and detailed observations on the Native American Indians and their customs, as well as on the terrain, distances, weather, and suitability of various places for the establishment and settlement of missions.

Palóu writes, "Diary…on the voyage… carried out in the month of November 1774 to the environs of the port of San Francisco on the coast of the Pacific Ocean of Northern California, with the purpose of occupying them with new missions entrusted to my Hispanic College of Franciscan missionaries…of Mexico City.

"We encountered…a large settlement of more than 30 houses, well made of grass, and when we approached many Indios came out of them armed with bows and arrows….We called to the Indios, they came nearer, and many of them gave me arrows, which they consider the greatest gesture of peace, and I responded with a string of glass beads.

"The men were completely naked, like all the other heathens, and some of them had a hood of leather or grass to protect their back from the cold down to the waist, leaving the rest of the body uncovered, and the principal, which they had to cover. Some of them are very bearded and most of good size and cor-

pulent. The women are covered with the leather of animals and grass instead of petticoats….

"I made the sign of the cross to them all, who were very attentive to the ceremony, which they did not comprehend, or know what its purpose was. I spoke to them in the language of Monterey some words about God and heaven, and although they were very attentive, I was not satisfied that they understood….

"I…give them a string of beads and a little tobacco…. They went off to smoke…with them the same custom and ceremony as in all the others. The chief was the first to smoke and immediately he passed the pipe on to all the others, and each took a mouthful of smoke while speaking a few words….

"[I] saw the mouth that is like a narrow channel where the great estuary of San Francisco enters the Bay of the Promontories.

"When ships enter via the strait they could anchor behind the island while protecting themselves from the winds, as they would be free from high seas as soon as they entered the strait.

"Standing atop the cliff of the ridge…that forms the narrows or channel of the mouth of the estuary of San Francisco, we had a view of the Bay of the Promontories and…Punta de Reyes and [that] of the Guardian Angel…. This appears to be the Port of San Francisco.

"Inasmuch as this high steep hill is the point of land that forms a wall of this southern range on the strait or channel of the mouth of the estuary of San Francisco…on which

until the present no Spaniard or Christian had set foot, it seemed to us…to be [fitting to] fix on the summit the standard of the Holy Cross."

Palóu's expedition is described by DeNevi and Moholy in their biography of Father Serra, Junípero Serra: "By November of 1774…[Governor] Rivera was ready to undertake the reconnaissance of the San Francisco Bay area preparatory to founding the sixth mission [San Francisco de Asís]. On November 30, sixteen soldiers and Palóu, along with supplies for forty days, headed north. On December 4, Palóu planted a cross on the highest peak overlooking the wide entrance to San Francisco Bay. When the party returned to Monterey on December 13, Palóu presented his diary to the padre presidente, who immediately forwarded it to the viceroy."

In California: An Interpretive History, Walter Bean describes the site where the sixth mission was finally founded on March 29, 1776.

"For the site of the new presidio, Anza chose a point near the northernmost tip of the San Francisco peninsula. Rivera had noted, and it was one of his objections, that the whole northern part of the peninsula consisted largely of sand dunes. About three miles to the southeast of the presidio site, however, Anza found a little oasis on a creek, and here…he marked the site of the mission…. Various obstacles, including some set up by Governor Rivera, delayed the actual founding of the new establishments for several months…. The presidio was formally established…on September 17, and Father Palóu formally opened the mission on October 9."

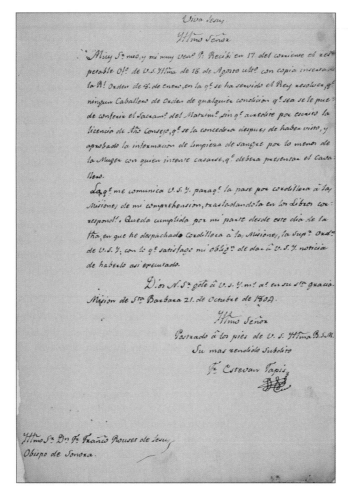

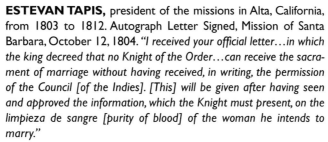

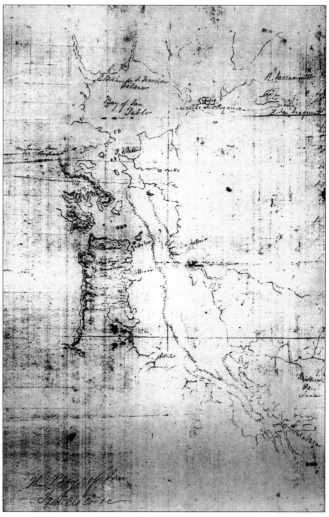

ESTEVAN TAPIS, president of the missions in Alta, California, from 1803 to 1812. Autograph Letter Signed, Mission of Santa Barbara, October 12, 1804. *"I received your official letter…in which the king decreed that no Knight of the Order…can receive the sacrament of marriage without having received, in writing, the permission of the Council [of the Indies]. [This] will be given after having seen and approved the information, which the Knight must present, on the limpieza de sangre [purity of blood] of the woman he intends to marry."*

Map of San Francisco Bay and environs drawn in pencil, 1846, by Edward Kern, who served under J. C. Fremont. The map is lightly sketched with great detail. Place names indicated include Presidio, Mission San Francisco (Mission Dolores), Mission San Jose, Bay of San Pablo, R. (River) Sacramento, R. San Joaquin, and Yerba Buena (island off the shore at Yerba Buena). Kern (1823–1863), a young painter from Philadelphia, joined Fremont's third expedition to the West, serving as artist, topographer, and cartographer. Later, he served with the survey of potential routes for the Pacific Railroad.

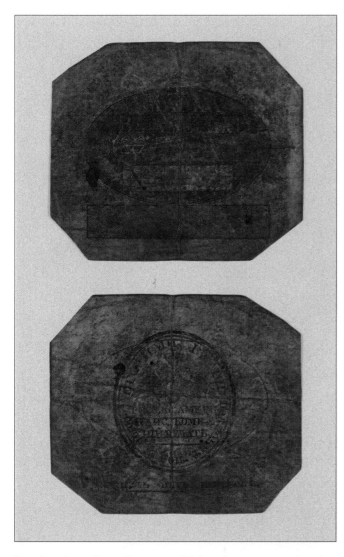

Russian-American Company 25 kopeks currency printed at the Russian Colony, Fort Ross, on the California coast, 65 miles north of San Francisco. Founded in 1812, the settlement was intended to grow food and raise cattle for the mother colony in Alaska. In 1841, the experimental colony was closed and sold to John Sutter on whose land gold would be discovered.

California was described as a paradise in Alfred Robinson's *Life In California*, 1846, an account of his experiences in the 1830s and early 1840s:

"Gold and silver mines have been found in upper California, from which, considerable quantities of ore have been obtained: skillful miners are only required to make them profitable. It is said that coal has recently been discovered; which if true will greatly facilitate the introduction of steam navigation in the Pacific and be the means of making California one of the most important commercial positions on the west coast of America; particularly, if ever a communication should be opened by means of a canal across the isthmus of Panama. That such an event may transpire is not improbable; the day is not far distant, perhaps when it will be realized and one may visit this fertile and interesting country and return to the United States in one-half the time now required for the long and tedious outward navigation. The resources of California, its magnificent harbors climate and abundance of naval stores would make it the rendezvous for all the steamers engaged in the trade between Europe and the East Indies as well as those from the United States; and the facilities for immigration would be such that soon the whole western coast of North America would be settled by immigrants both from this country and Europe."

Addressing the political situation, he writes, *"Why not extend the area of freedom by the annexation of California? Why not plant the banner of liberty there…at the entrance of…the spacious bay of San Francisco? It requires not the far-reaching eye of the statesman nor the wisdom of a contemplative mind to know what would be the result. Soon its immense sheet of water would become enlivened with thousands of vessels and steamboats would ply between the towns which as a matter of course would spring up on its shores while on other locations along the banks of the rivers would be seen manufactories and sawmills. The whole country would be changed and instead of one being deemed wealthy by possessing such extensive tracks as are now held by the farming class he would be rich with one quarter part. Everything would improve; population would increase; consumption would be greater and industry would follow. All this may come to pass; and indeed it must come to pass for the march of immigration is to the west and not will arrest its advance but the mighty ocean."*

In his classic *Two Years Before the Mast*, 1849, Richard Henry Dana described California and its inhabitants in great detail as *"a country embracing four or five hundred miles of seacoast with several good harbors; with fine forests in the north; the waters filled with fish and the plains covered with thousands of herds of cattle; blessed with a climate then which there can be no better in the world; free from all manner of diseases whether epidemic of endemic; and where the soil in which corn yields 70 to 80 fold. In the hands of an enterprising people, what a country this might be! We are ready to say. Yet how long would a people remain so in such a country? The Americans…and Englishmen who are fast filling up the principal towns and getting the trade into their hands are indeed more industrious and effective than the Spaniards; yet their children are brought up Spaniards, in every respect and if the 'California fever' [laziness] spares the first generation it always attacks the second."*

Justus Danckerts, an engraved map, "Recentissima Novi Orbis sive America Septentrionalis et Meridionalis Tabula." Amsterdam [1690]. The earliest printed maps of America all correctly show California as a peninsula. About 1620, a Carmelite friar drew a map, probably based on reports by the Spanish navigators, depicting California as an island. The ship carrying the map to Spain was captured by the Dutch and the chart taken to Amsterdam. Soon thereafter maps representing California as an island began to appear. This map is a reissue of one first drawn by the Dutch cartographer Claes Visscher in 1670 and copied many times afterwards.

Chapter 12

OVERLAND TRAIL

"The Rocky Mountains. Emigrants Crossing the Plains." Currier & Ives lithograph, 1866. 27½ by 20 inches.

The Oregon Trail became possible because of South Pass in Wyoming. This twenty-mile-wide pass is a natural gateway through the Rocky Mountains. The east and west slopes are so gradual it is difficult to realize when you are at the highest point. South Pass was discovered by Robert Stuart in 1812, as he was heading east from Astoria, at the mouth of the Columbia River.

The Oregon Trail began in Independence, Missouri, and went across present-day Kansas and Nebraska and into present-day Wyoming. Fort Laramie was a major stop before crossing the rest of Wyoming and through South Pass. The trail then split into two branches, one leading to the Great Salt Lake, and the other continuing west and later dividing into the California Trail to Sutter's Fort, now Sacramento, and the original route to Oregon.

In the 1830s, immigrants to the West were using the Oregon Trail (in 1836, Narcissa Whitman and Eliza Spaulding became the first white women to travel on it), and during the 1840s, the number if immigrants kept increasing until the news of gold in California set off a tidal wave of people headed to California.

It was important to leave Independence in late spring or early summer to ensure that there would be good grass near the trail (too early and there wasn't grass — too late and the earlier wagon trains would have used all the grass within easy proximity to the trail). To be among the first also meant some chance of hunting game for food. Soon into the season the game was driven far from the trail.

Companies formed at Independence because there was security from Indians in a larger group. Ten wagons was the minimum. Two thousand pounds was the usual load, and east of Fort Laramie the trail side was scattered with furniture that overloaded wagon trains had to dump. The entire trail was marked with graves, an impressive number still visible today.

Depending on the weather, the ability of a group, and luck, the trip to California averaged five months. The Gambrel brothers' letters later in this chapter describe a trip of three months, but as the Gambrels wrote, their trip was exceptional. Twelve miles was the average distance covered in a day.

There were two alternatives to the Overland Trail. The first was to take a boat to Panama, cross the isthmus, and hope for a ship to California. The letters of S. D. King describe the hardship firsthand, as well as the costs. The other alternative was the six-month voyage from the East Coast around Cape Horn to California. Relatively speaking, this could be comfortable. Travelers didn't write of the hardships faced by those crossing Panama to California. Thomas Sherman's journal of his voyage from Boston to California, November 17, 1849 to May 26, 1850, 79 pages, is completely positive and records a pleasant journey around the Horn.

The Santa Fe Trail was almost exclusively for trade caravans, and while the Englishman who wrote the diary at the end of this chapter reached California this way, it was hardly the sensible route.

Despite the number of letters and diaries in the collection quoted here, these represent most of what has come onto the market in forty years. Guidebooks, however, excluding the early ones, are available, and those from the mid-1850s are very reasonably priced.

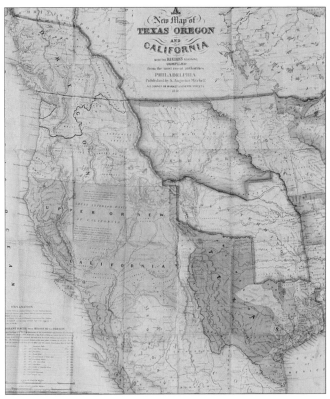

The Personal Narrative of James O. Pattie…*During an Expedition from St. Louis, Through the Vast Regions Between That Place and the Pacific Ocean, and Thence Back Through the City of Mexico to Vera Cruz, 1833.*

One of the classics of Western Americana. The author wandered for six years through the Southwest. His account of his adventures, hardships, and explorations included 22 descriptions of California that encouraged Americans to head west.

S. Augustus Mitchell's detailed "New Map of Texas, Oregon and California with the Regions Adjoining…," 1846, shows the western portion of the United States to the Pacific, with the Indian Territory, Missouri Territory, Iowa, and portions of the states of Missouri, Arkansas, Louisiana, and Wisconsin, as well as northern Mexico and part of British Columbia, illustrating in detail the Transmississippi region on the verge of the Mexican War. Texas is elaborately depicted, with the Rio Grande as its southern border; the Santa Fe Trail and the Oregon Trail are both detailed, the latter with a table of distances published in the lower corner of the map. The map is among the first by a commercial cartographer to utilize the recent explorations, and because of its popularity it exerted great influence.

Zenas Leonard, *Narrative of the Adventures of Zenas Leonard…Who Spent Five Years in Trapping for Furs, Trading with the Indians, &c. &c. of the Rocky Mountains,* 1839.

The author set out for the Rocky Mountains in 1831 and after two years of trapping joined the party under the leadership of Joe Walker; their party made a historic crossing of the Great Basin and the Sierra Nevada, and was the first group of whites to pass through Yosemite and see its marvels. Leonard's narrative is not only a great primary source on the western fur trade, but the first published account of one of the great moments in the exploration of North America and the opening of California. In his narrative, he wrote his thoughts upon first arriving at the Pacific Ocean. *"Most of this vast waste of territory belongs to the Republic of the United States. What a theme to contemplate its settlement and civilization. Will the jurisdiction of the federal government ever succeed in civilizing the thousands of savages now roaming over these plains, and her hearty freeborn population here plant their homes, build their towns and cities and say here shall the arts and sciences of civilization take route and flourish? Yes, here, even in this remote part of the great west before many years will these hills and valley be greeted with the enlivening sound of the workman's hammer and the merry whistle of the plough-boy. But this is left undone by the government and will only be seen when too late to apply the remedy. Spaniards are making inroads to the south — the Russians are encroaching with impunity along the seashore to the north and further northeast the British are pushing their stations into the very heart of our territory…. Our government should be vigilant, she should assert her claim by taking possession of the whole territory as soon as possible — for we have good reason to suppose that the territory west of the mountain will someday be equally as important to a nation as that on the east."*

NARRATIVE

OF THE

ADVENTURES OF

ZENAS LEONARD,

A NATIVE OF CLEARFIELD COUNTY, PA. WHO SPENT FIVE YEARS IN TRAPPING FOR FURS, TRADING WITH THE INDIANS, &c., &c., OF THE ROCKY MOUNTAINS:

WRITTEN BY HIMSELF.

PRINTED AND PUBLISHED
BY D. W. MOORE,

CLEARFIELD, PA.

1839.

ROUTE

ACROSS THE ROCKY MOUNTAINS,

WITH A

DESCRIPTION OF OREGON AND CALIFORNIA;

THEIR

GEOGRAPHICAL FEATURES, THEIR RESOURCES, SOIL,
CLIMATE, PRODUCTIONS, &c., &c.

BY OVERTON JOHNSON AND WM. H. WINTER,
OF THE EMIGRATION OF 1843.

LAFAYETTE, IND:
JOHN B. SEMANS, PRINTER.
1846.

Overton Johnson and William Winter, *Route Across the Rocky Mountains with a Description of Oregon and California...,* 1846.

An important overland guide, one of the earliest issued, and a primary guide book of the first great overland emigrations. Both of the authors went to Oregon in 1843, returning in 1845.

"The climate in Oregon and California is far milder and more agreeable.... As the farmer's stock can live well all winter...he will here possess one advantage that he can never have east of the Rocky Mountains.... [H]e will not be compelled... to labor six months to produce grain and provender to feed out at the expense of another six months labor to his stock.... Another great advantage...paramount to all others is health. Those countries...are...very healthy....They are high dry rolling mountainous and well-watered with the purest springs and streams. When this Province shall have been settled by an industrious and enterprising population disposed to avail themselves of all the advantages which Nature has so bountifully spread out over this country; it will be covered with vast multitudes of stock of all kinds; the upper country will become a manufacturing district and everywhere on and around the extents of Bay of San Francisco, the most active and extensive commercial operations will be constantly going on but no country of which we have any knowledge is so fitted by nature to become one great manufacturing region as the territory of Oregon. It has everywhere over it an abundance of never failing water power sufficient to propel machinery of any kind.... But little is yet known of the minerals of the country. Some lead and iron have been discovered and if an intimate acquaintance with the country shall discover an abundance of the metals then will there be nothing wanting to make Oregon one of the greatest manufacturing countries in the world but the necessary population and capital, both of which time and enterprise of our countrymen will give."

A NEW HI S

OF

OREGON AND CALIFORNIA:

CONTAINING

COMPLETE DESCRIPTIONS OF THOSE COUNTRIES,

TOGETHER WITH THE

OREGON TREATY AND CORRESPONDENCE,

AND A

VAST AMOUNT OF INFORMATION RELATING TO THE SOIL,
CLIMATE, PRODUCTIONS, RIVERS, AND LAKES, AND
THE VARIOUS ROUTS OVER THE

ROCKY MOUNTAINS.

BY

LANSFORD W. HASTINGS,

A RESIDENT OF CALIFORNIA.

CINCINNATI:
PUBLISHED BY GEORGE CONCLIN.
STEREOTYPED BY E. SHEPARD.

1847.

A PARTY OF EMIGRANTS CROSSING THE ROCKY MOUNTAINS.

Lansford W. Hastings, *A New His[tory] of Oregon and California: Containing Complete Descriptions of Those Countries, Together with the Oregon Treaty and Correspondence, and a Vast Amount of Information Relating to the Soil, Climate, Productions, Rivers, and Lakes, and the Various Routs [sic] Over the Rocky Mountains,* Cincinnati, 1847. 160 pages.

The second known and first revised edition of the first guide to the Overland Trail. Hastings was an early promoter of emigration to California. His propagandistic work played on the hopes and ambitions of emigrants, who were lured by the promise of *"as much land as you want"* in California. Hastings has been blamed for contributing to the Donner Party tragedy because of his promotion of a cutoff south of Salt Lake (his error is corrected in the present edition).

Hastings described his own party setting out in May of 1842 *"for the long desired El Dorado of the west…. [A]ll was high glee, jocular hilarity and* happy anticipation as we thus darted forward into the wild expanse of the untrodden regions of the 'western world.' The harmony of feeling the sameness of purpose and the identity of interest which here existed seemed to indicate nothing but continued order, harmony and peace amid all the trying scenes incident to our long and wholesome journey but we had proceeded only a few days travel from our native land of order and security when the 'American character' was fully exhibited. All appeared to be determined to govern but not to be governed."*

Hastings' very detailed description of California and Oregon covers all aspects of life there, a life that he highly recommends: *"A new Era in the improvements of California has commenced. Here as in Oregon foreigners from all countries of the most enterprising and energetic character are annually arriving selecting and improving the most favorable sights for towns and selecting and securing extensive grants of land and the most desirable portions of the country."*

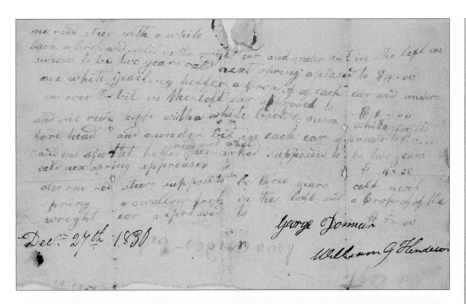

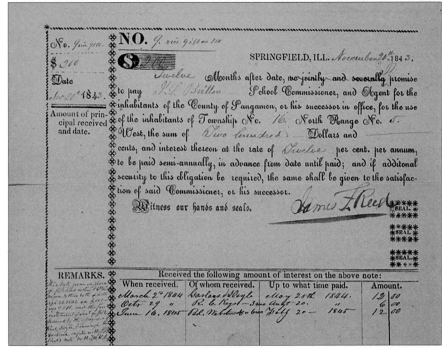

GEORGE DONNER and **JAMES F. REED,** the leaders of the most ill-fated overland party. Documents signed by each, 1830 and 1843.

Francis Parkman, *The California and Oregon Trail: Being Sketches of Prairie and Rocky Mountain Life,* 1849.

Perhaps the piece of Western travel writing most familiar to modern readers, Parkman's narrative describes his experiences on the Oregon Trail and in Wyoming and Colorado in 1846. The exciting adventures of the young Boston Brahmin loose on the plains makes excellent reading, especially his account of life with the Sioux in the Black Hills.

GEORGE BREWERTON

George Brewerton was nineteen when he joined the California Volunteers as a second lieutenant in 1846 and sailed from New York to California around Cape Horn, arriving in San Francisco in March 1847. In January 1848, gold was discovered at Sutter's Mill, and Brewerton was chosen for the job of carrying the news east. He sailed from San Francisco to Los Angeles, where he met Kit Carson, the legendary scout and explorer who was to serve as his guide across the desert and Indian Country. From Los Angeles, they set out with their small party on May 4, 1848, bound for Independence, Missouri, via Santa Fe. This significant journey became known as "Brewerton's Ride," which he later described in a series of three narratives published in *Harper's Monthly:* (1) "A Ride with Kit Carson" (December 1853); (2) "Incidents of Travel in New Mexico" (April 1854); (3) "In the Buffalo Country" (September 1862). The three articles later appeared in book form as *Overland with Kit Carson* (New York: Coward-McMann, 1930).

Brewerton kept no diary of the trip, and the sketches and notes he made were lost during the party's crossing of the Colorado River. Therefore the works he wrote and sketched after the trip were done entirely from his memory, which was prodigious, and his narrative sparkles with

details, as do his sketches. Felled by illness after reaching Santa Fe, Brewerton was forced to remain there while Carson went ahead to Independence; Brewerton followed soon thereafter and joined his regiment in Mississippi.

This important sketchbook records many of Brewerton's images of his momentous trip of 1848. There are several scenes of California, including one of Los Angeles that is one of very few views of the city from this period. The view is similar to the one illustrated in *Harper's* and shows a one-story adobe building with several figures in the foreground.

Of Los Angeles Brewerton wrote, *"The Pueblo of Los Angeles has a population of several hundred souls; and boasts a church, a padre, and three or four American shops; the streets are narrow, and the houses generally not over one story high, built of adobes, the roofs flat and covered with a composition of gravel mixed with a sort of mineral pitch…. In most respects, the town differs but little from other Mexican villages."*

There are very few views of California extant from this period. As Willard O. Waters has noted, *"Accurate and artistic contemporary drawings of scenes from the time of the American conquest to the Gold*

Rush are not common. There were few persons in California, during those years, who had the training or inclination to make a record, with pencil or brush, of what they saw." (Willard O. Waters, *California 1847–1852*, Huntington Library, 1956)

In addition to the California scenes, there are eight views of Texas, two of New Mexico, thirteen of the Rocky Mountains, four of the Great American Desert, and views of New England, New York, and South America. The choice views of Texas are a particularly rare form of documentation; very little artwork of Texas by trained artists in the 19th century is extant. The sketches resemble those published in *Harper's,* although, for obvious reasons, the original sketches are more detailed and highly finished. Brewerton was an inventive and talented artist; he developed a new painting medium during the 1860s in which he combined pastels with oil. His versatility and mastery of medium are evident in the sketches that combine silverpoint, ink, and watercolor. The four loose silverpoint sketches are instructive of Brewerton's technique. He most likely made a silverpoint sketch, then finished and highlighted it with ink and watercolor. The drawings in the album are rendered on a thick, glossy, coated paper, which imparts a luminous quality.

Brewerton probably presented this sketchbook, which includes scenes from all his travels from 1847 until 1860, as a Christmas gift to his father in 1860. Apart from his paintings and published drawings, this sketchbook is the only documentation of "Brewerton's Ride," and records scenes that soon passed into memory, history, and legend.

On the opposite page are a selection from an album of one hundred original silverpoint, pen, ink, and watercolor finished sketches, each measuring approximately 2¼ by 3⅜ inches. Each sketch in the album is identified by Brewerton in ink, indicating location of the scene; most have a year written in ink as well. A remarkable collection of unpublished original artwork.

"Valley near 'Los Angeles,' Cala. 1848."

"The Great American Desert. 1848."

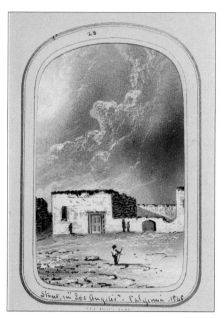

"Street in Los Angeles,' California. 1848."

"Rocky Mt. Camp Winter. 1848."

"The Great Plains. 1848."

"Log Cabin. San Antonio Rd., Texas. 1849."

"Old stone ranche, Texas. 1851."

"Church. Laredo, Texas. 1851."

The first Western letters I acquired for my collection, this series by D. B. Christ begins in Independence, Missouri, March 13, 1849:

"*Independence contains from 16 to 17 hundred inhabitants is within twelve miles of the Indian Teritory, it is a business place on account of the Emigration to California and Origon, then the Sante Fe trade is carried on to a large extent. Mules cost from sixty to Eighty Dollars a piece, oxen sell from fourty to sixty Dollars pr. yoke, waggons from eighty to one hundred and twenty Dollars and with bed and bows. Every thing is high in price; Boarding one Dollar pr. day. Plenty of Indians here. They are a miserable looking set of Beings; I pity them in my soul…. I thought I would make a visit to the Indians; I went twenty four Miles in their Territory and remained four days with them. I have seen many strange things among them, they ware no clothing except what we call leggins and a Blanket now and then. You see some with a few rags tied round his privet part of the body, the squaws the same. The Indian has his head ornimented with different kinds of feathers, the squaw has no covering to her head except her Long Black hair. The squaw has to do all the Laibour such as cutting and gethering wood, fetching water, carry g[r]ain. Their wigwam is made by sticking sticks in the ground and the top of them tied together and then they cover them with Buffalow skins. Their Bed consists of no more than sometimes a skin and some lay on the bare ground on account of having used up their skins for food. Being a hard winter they could get no game; some of them nearly starved. They eate any and everything they can chew and swallow — dogs, Mules, Horses, guts and all….*

"*Now I will give you an account of our state of things and arrangements. In the first place there are six of us in company.*"

This is followed by Christ's description of the equipment and provision he had bought, along with the cost of each item. He continued:

"*I think there will not be Less than twenty thousand people to pass through this place to California this Spring. The reason of our staying here is an account of the grass which we must depend on for food for our animals…. Many hardships dificulty and dangers we have to encounter before we can expect to see the promised land of gold. In the first place we have two thousand miles from this to California; nearly seven hundred miles of this is a prairie or plain where we cant get wood for fire. All we can get in this distance for to cook with is Buffalo Dung. Here it is termed Buffalo Chips. After we cross this plain we will reach the rocky mountain where we will find much dificulty in geting our waggons over many rivers and Creeks. We have to contend with whare I expect to have to Built rafts to cross on by all this I dont mind. But the greatest trouble we will find with the Indians. It is reported that the Indians have a knoledge of this emigration and allready are gethering from all parts of the forest to the route which we have to go. It is not my life that I am afraid of but of their robing us of our animals and provision and if we must starve…. There is not much danger in going among them if you have no property or provision, but it is for property that the[y] will kill, but if all is delivered up they will spare life at least in many cases.*"

From Oregon Canon, Christ wrote this on March 14, 1850:

"I...am in the promised land of gold. After four month and four Days travel we reached a Land inhabited by whites.... Much suffering and hardships we all had to endure during this journey; I suffered most every thing but Death. Thousands have left their Bones on the plains and Rockey Mountains. Many Died from that horrid dissease the Colara and some whare murdered by the Indians and many Died from hardships which were greater than they could endure. It is reported that there is over two thousand souls Died during this Journey last summer...."

"We had much trouble with the Indians. They would steal our Cattle and murder our men... whenever they had an oppertunity, but thank God they did not kill any of our Company as we alwayes stuck close together. They are a cowardly and treacherous Nation; they will not attackt the whites unless they have every advantage of them."

The letter next describes an encounter with the Indians while out hunting which nearly cost him life:

"[W]e was in the Buffalo countrey...after traveling two or three miles I discovered five Indians all mounted on their ponys. I immediately put my spurs to my horse and steared my course for the train. They followed me untill I got in sight of my Company. They got within sixty or seventy yeards of me. In this chase I injured my horse so that he was unable to travel any further so I was obliged to travel the ramainder of the road afoot. This Chase took place on the South Fork of Platt River about six hundred miles from the stateson the plains.... This was the Sioux Tribe that gave me this Chase. There ware some of the whites killed by the Indians, but far more Indians were killed by the whites, as most of those wild Tribes have no other weapon than Bow and arrow and Lance. We had every advantage of them on account of our firearms as we could kill them at a further Distance and had our waggans for to fortify us while they had to take at all times the open plains. Perhaps it would be well to mention here that it is one vast plain Barren Mountains and sandy Desert from the Line of the States untill to California Mountains, with the exception of now and then a few cotten wood trees along some of the streams. But from Fort Hall to the Sink of Humbolt River which is over five hundred miles there is not the sign of a tree.

"Now as I am in California I will fill the rest of my sheet with such matters...[of the gold country]. I have found nothing but a Wild Mountainous Country Inhabited by Indians, Grizzely Bars, Woolfs, Deers and gold Diggers, but we are not much in Danger as the gold Miners are numarous and stick well together and all well armed. Gold is fully as plenty as the reports...if not more so.... Still some have but Little success in their undertaking. Hundreds of miners leave for home with barely anoughp to pay their way home while hundreds is making from two to Eight thousand Dollars a year and a few as high as twenty and thirty thousand a year. In the first place it depends upon luck to strike a rich place and second it takes hard Laibour to Dig it after finding a rich spot, and as many of the men that came here are not used to hard laibour such as Clerks Doctor and Lawyers, therefore many of them find nothing but Disapointment as the[y] thought all they had to do was to pick up the gold. Perhaps you are desirous of knowing of my success. But excuse me as I wish that to remain a seacret."

"I have Built me a Cabin in the fall whare I made my home During the winter. Before I built my Cabin...I had nothing But the wide canapy of Heaven for a covering and the Earth for a bed with the exception of two blanketts.... [In] a few weeks I exspect to Leave my cabin again to rome through the mountains in search of good Digings. The reason for being without Cabins During the summer season is if we find a good diging it will not last more than a few weeks before it is dug out then we have to move our quarters to some other place again. We are all a hard miserable looking set of men in the Mines raged dirty and our faces and heads covered with hair.... I got used so much to hardships and suffering that I dont mind any thing at this time. Nothing is to[o] hard nor nothing to[o] roughp for me at this time."

"I have given you a Breef sketch of matter and things in California which in part may satisfy youre inquiring mind."

The last letter was written from Lewellyn, March 1, 1852:

"[I]t was not gold that induced me to make my first trip across the Rocky Mountains, no it was something more noble, it was that Inquiring mind which my Creator bestowed to me, and I was richly rewarded for all my sufferings in that adventure. But if I did not go for gold then it is not to be supposed, that I cannot go for gold this time, and I do think that I will bring some gold with me when I return, that is if my life is spared. ...I think they have full confidence in me as a leader...or Guide...especially for this trip I have carefully counted the cost before I consented, for I am well aware that we have a Long journy before us, and that we have hardships sufferings and Dangers to encounter. But in all these things I shall act with a firm and determined mind to sustain the character of a man. Fear will find no hiding place in my brest, justice will be my Motto, Love and Friendship shall be my governing principles."

"Emigrants Crossing the Plains," engraving, 1860. 12½ by 11⅛ inches.

"On the Prairie," engraving by Leopold Grozelier, 1860, after a painting by Charles Wiman. 29½ by 22 inches.

Token issued by the trading post at Fort Laramie on the Overland Trail.

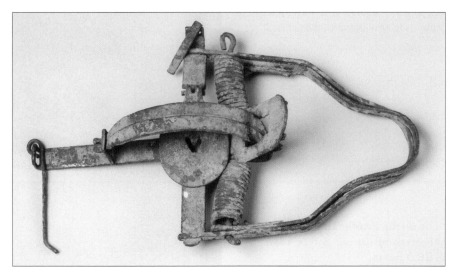

Animal trap found on the Oregon Trail in present-day Wyoming.

Fort Laramie was a major point on the Oregon Trail and an opportunity to send letters back home. David Howe wrote to his wife June 5, 1850, from there: *"There has past thirty five hundred wagons past this fort up to this date. I dont think that is one third that will pas but I am keen to swear that there wont one half the horses get to the mines that is on the road…. [T]his is the porest cuntry I ever seen in time. No grass the bufalo has used the botams so much they have kild the grass out. We seen a company this day right from the mines which give us som incuragement for to procede on. The[y] said they had money enough to doo them and that there was plenty for all So dont think that I am sick of my trip yet. I expect to bee in Sacrimento city by the first day of august."*

Crossing the desert between Salt Lake and the Sierras was the worst part of the journey in the heat of summer, as Jessie Mason wrote his parents on September 15, 1850: *"From St Joseph to the Rocky Mountains we met with no serious diffculties excepting from poisonout springs and alkali water the latter of which was very plentiful. Cattle and horse both would drink this if they had been long without water and causing instant death. The 1st of July we were in the city of the great Salt Lake settled by Mormons.*

"They have plenty of cattle horses &c and raisde large crops of grain and that to where there is not a particle of rain for four or five months. There are thousands of streams running from the mountains however which are made to run over the fields…. The cattle and horses are the fattest that I ever saw. On the 5th we left and on the 12th of Aug we were on the top of the Sierra Nevada mountains at the height of 9,538 feet 3,000 higher

than the top of the White Mountains…. These troubles however were nothing to what we encountered in the Humbolt River…. [I will provide] a short description of the country. Bounded on the North East South & West by high mountains covered with a perpetual Snow the Great Basin as this country is called is entirely shut out from [the] World and [ha]s rivers and lakes of its own. It is 600 miles East and West & about the same North & South. Salt Lake city is on the Eastern side of the Basin. The Springs in this Basin are generally impregnated with sulphur and iron frequently boiling hot. The ground contains much salt and Alkali. It never rains here and the ground is parched the greater part of the year so that nothing except a few insignificant shrubs grow except on the Rivers and creeks which run from the mountains and continually grow smaller until they lose themselves in the sand. It is inhabited by a hostile race of Indians the most degraded perhaps that exists in the world but are not very dangerous as they are extremely cowardly and will run when discovered. They sometimes shoot cattle & horses so that they are obliged to leave them. On the Humbolt River they stole many horses and killed one or two men with arrows. They took two horses f[rom] us."*

At about the same time Charles Treadwell wrote to his sister describing his terrible overland trip: *"[We encountered] the angel of death in the shape of the cholera in its form terrific, following us for 700 miles. Out of 160 of us, 6 weeks after reaching California, every 4th man was dead…. It is said that all men in crossing the plains are more or less insane. We were in constant danger of being attacked by Indians or having our mules stampeded…. For 300 miles west of the Missouri to this place, the country may be considered one vast waste. I could tell you*

of Scotts Bluffs, of the soda springs of ash hollow, the terrible Humbolt valley, winter river mountain cover'd with eternal snows, of the hot springs, of the saleratus ponds, of the Canons of the platte & sweet water Rivers pronounced canyon, of the [sink] of the Humboldt…. California is pretty much moonshine, & those that have started lately will wish such a country never existed."*

The personal toll of the overland journey is described in a series of letters by Alden Putnam to his wife. The earliest letters were written on the Oregon Trail and described the daily difficulties. When he arrived at Sutter's fort he wrote to her on December 3, 1849: *"I find most all the Origon peapol are wiling to return when they make a fortion…. They call it very helthy and a fine farming cuntry…. I shall not leave you to go to California again…. If I had known the feelings from being from my family, Origon and the gold in California would not hav seperated me from you…. You rite you do not know but I think more of gold that I do you or I would not gon to California…. I asure you…I would not swap you for your heft in gold. I would like to make anough to make us in easy sercamstance in life."*

"Life on the Prairie. The Buffalo Hunt." Lithograph by Currier & Ives, 1862, 18½ by 26½ inches.

"M. A. Abrahams/The People's Outfitting Store, Independence, MO." Merchant's token issued by the outfitter at the start of the Oregon Trail, before 1853. Most likely this token represented ten cents and was used by the outfitter to both advertise his business and to substitute for coinage that frequently was scarce on the frontier. Eleven examples are known.

Help in Sight, oil painting by Zeno Schindler, late 19th century. 11 by 16¾ inches.

William Gambrel wrote the first in a series of letters to his mother, "Near St. Joseph," Missouri, May 8, 1849.

"[T]here are more than two thousand persons in this place…bound for California…. I consider our chance for crossing the plains equal to that of any other."

He next wrote from *"On Big Platte 80 miles from Ft. Chile,"* June 4, 184[9].

"We left the mother company on day after our separation and are I suppose 20 miles ahead of them at this time, as the majority of them are too lazy to go to California. For a man who is at all afflicted with laziness, had better change it for the most <u>persevering industry</u>…. [A] lazy man could not place himself more out of his element than by starting on a trip of this kind. My almost entire thoughts are on California and its gold and our journey which, though we have been from home six weeks and traveled nearly 600 miles, is scarcely begun…. I think as we generally travel three miles before any one else leaves camp."

He reached Fort Lamamie on June 17, 1849: *"[I] am still in good health and spirits, and am getting along remarkably well, indeed better than any other ox train that I have see on the route, as we have passed since we left our company near 1500 wagons & 12000 head of stock…. I think we will make the trip in 3½ months."*

He made excellent time across the Overland Trail. He writes from Upper California, October 12, 1849: *"[W]e arrived on the 7th Sept in excellent health after a travel of one hundred and sixteen days. Some of the first waggons however came in in the short space of 90 days….*

Well the reports which we heard in regard to the quantity of gold in this country were not at all exagerated, though the rapidity with which is obtained, was slightly incorrect. We worked about three weeks and made near seven hundred dollars."

He convinced his brothers to head to California and both brothers wrote from Fort Laramie on June 9, 1850: *"[The] 1200 [miles] from California the longest and most difficult end of the road yet before us…. The only Fear we have about getting though is a sufficiency of grass….The ox teems generally look well but the Horse and some of the mule Teems loose very Badly and many are abandoning [them]….When we first started the Horses teems drove by us so fast that I sometimes wished I had have started with Horses but I am of a differant opinion now. Any man could have made an independent Fortune by coming out here and have purchased all the waggons that have been left here & at other places for Sale. I saw waggons sell here for $6 that in the States would command 100 very Readily. I am becoming better satisfied with oxen every day. We are beginning to pass mules & Horses already and we did not expect to outtravel them until we got near the mountains. We have been much troubled about wood for several days. We frequently have to go 4 or 5 miles and then get nothing but cedar shrubs. Notwithstanding our little troubles & inconveniences none of us have thought we have seen any hard times yet. We are all prepared for the worst & will not be disappointed when it comes. An express from Weston overtook us yesterday…told us they had passed 8000 waggons since they left Westport."*

An immigrant's trunk covered with horsehide that has been encased in a buffalo hide by Indians. The trunk contains various animal skins, leaves, and other articles associated with the Pebble Society. There are also lesson books and letters from the Carlisle Indian School and the Omaha Agency.

The route to California via the Isthmus of Panama is described in S.D. King's account. King left from New York in May 1851 and wrote his cousin a 32-page letter, Pacific Ocean, June 4, 1851:

"We came off the mouth of Chargres [Panama]...having made the passage in 8 days & 8 hours....The River is very crooked and its width varied from 100 to 300 feet.... Every kind of tropical tree, plant & vine formed an impervious mass of vegetable matter. From the tallest trees, vines descended like ropes to the ground.... [T]he night being also very dark, we got to what is called an American Hotel about 9 oclock. This part of the trip was extremely unpleasant to such of us as were aware of what might be the consequences, although we were not then aware of the great risk incurred from the numerous snags which threatened our destruction.... [W]e landed about 9 oclock at the great City of Gorgona....The Hotel we stopped at was one of the best in the place, but had all the peculiar comforts to be found only on this route in such rich perfection. Every place was crowded with dirty cots, sometimes a hundred in one long shed. Late as it was, we made some of the arrangements about having mules to start soon the next morning.... [A]fter dinner I started in a hammock, with 3 Indians and one half breed Negro as bearers. They were small and light framed. Picture to yourself a reed or cane as thick as one's leg about 12 ft. long with a Hammock containing his 'Honor' swinging between, with an umbrella to give shade to the face.... [A]bout 2 hours after dark...we reached the place we contemplated remaining at for the night called the 'Ranché Americano.' Owing to the rain, darkness, muddy slippery road this part of the trip was extremely unpleasant. The light went out, & whites, blacks, Indians, mules &c which filled the whole place in hammocks, on boxes, stools & the ground, seemed inclined to rest....

"Of the beauty of the entire land route, winding down ravines, & over hills it is impossible to attempt any account.... The eye was never weary of gazing in every direction. During the afternoon we passed the dividing ridge...and immediately after the character of the growth seemed to change.... [B]efore sun set...we intersected, at 6 miles from Panama, the old Spanish paved road... now most lamentably out of order, being frequently entirely washed away or destroyed for hundreds of feet together....originally.... Deep cuts were made through it on the sides of the hills, & bridges, placed over the permanent streams. The road itself was originally generally 8 ft. wide well paved with good stones and bordered with rows of those of larger size.... About 10 in the morning I arrived at the 'Orleans Hotel' but in such a plight that I took care not to let the ladies see me, not having shaved or changed since the day before leaving the 'Empire City.' I looked more like a grizzly Bear, drawn through a Horse pond than anything else.... The 'Orleans Hotel' is the exact establishment of its kind in the City.... Now every place & hole is occupied, and the main street is obstructed & every house covered with American signs. Hotels, taverns, Restaurants and stores fill every nook, and hundreds upon hundreds of Americans, Jews, mules &c. block up the narrow streets and passages. The place was settled after the destruction of Old Panama situated some 6 or 7 miles distant on the other side of the Bay. All within the walls was originally reserved for the use of persons connected with the Church or the Government offices — the natives and civilians being outside. The house now occupied by the Hotel formerly was occupied by some order of nuns. For a pillow I had something so strange that at times I was tempted to rip it open to discover the hidden mysteries it contained but having made up my mind after close examination of the exterior that it was most probably dried remains of some starved hog or dog, thought it would be best to leave the certainty to be ascertained by some more adventurious lodger than myself.... I was first informed that my trunk...had been stolen.... One of the first consequences of the loss of my trunk was the necessity of purchasing about $50 of clothes to make the necessary changes...it being impossible to get things washed at Panama for less than $5 per day."

The most unusual overland diary in my collection is that of an anonymous Englishman who began his journal on March 1, 1849, as he was departing Liverpool for New York, and it is not initially clear that he knew what his final destination would be.

"Irresolute and undecided as to my future movements chance decided it…. A fellow passenger decided upon starting with an organized party from California. Always possessing a spirit for adventure and new places and new scenes I at once determined upon accompanying him — we set to work making necessary preparation and started a party of sixteen persons on the 9th of April.

The real road and canals got them to Pittsburgh where they boarded an Ohio River steamer for Cincinnati. Despite hardships and problems "we enjoyed the beautiful scenery of Kentucky and Indiana. The further the Ohio River is traversed the more beautiful it becomes…. Never shall I forget the beauty of a moonlit night on the Ohio."

His party encountered many difficulties after crossing the Mississippi, including the death of their leader who was drowned while crossing the Arkansas River. He described passing through Indian Villages:

"[I] visited some of their dwellings and was agreeable surprised to find them so intelligent, well-informed and civilized. The young men tall, good-looking, well-proportioned as are the women. I am told there are more handsome Indians between this and the Pacific."

While the diarist continued to mention the goal of getting to California, his party continued on a southerly route.

"July 1, we have this day entered upon what we consider the first marked accent to the base of the mountains leaving what we at present imagine to be the Great American Desert. The passage across has naturally been uninteresting and worrisome in the extreme. We fully trust the green mountains will soon appear in sight. August 5, five days more have elapsed, still the long expected mountains come not in view."

They were running short on food: "Our biscuits have been divided and perhaps like our days number few. Still I despair not yet."

On August 14 he wrote, "We have seen a white man, a poor shepard who informs us we have but two or three days journey to Santa Fe. This is joyful intelligence to us poor hungry souls."

They continued on, staying at a Mexican village, having been told that Santa Fe was "five days travel and a very poor place…. Encamped within twenty-five miles of Santa Fe where many small companies lay preparing for a final start for San Francisco. The rest will lay down to San Diego on the Pacific Coast. The accounts of Santa Fe are horrible. It appears to be a den of theives and gamblers. Desolation stalks around it…. All kinds of provisions are extraordinarily high-priced. 24th. Started for Santa Fe, arrived early next morning. The accounts concerning this place for me were not at all exaggerated. The town lays in a broad hollow and from the Gallister Road comes suddenly in view presenting most unprepossessing appearance…. The Plaza which is certainly spacious is decorated with sundry pieces of cannon, the American flag being raised in its center. But as to the inhabitants of the place…dozens of unfortunate Californians, who might be said to have gotten themselves into a tarnation

fix having proceeded so far on their weary and dangerous pilgrimage without the means of going further might be seen lounging and milling around the…Plaza…looking for someone to employ them. In a few days the detestable company to which I belonged was scattered in all directions very much to my relief…. The season was now becoming too far advanced to attempt the northern route; to travel four or five months more…on the southern route by the Gila I was determined not to do. I was therefore very glad to avail myself to Capt. Brent's offer to enter the office of his department in which he was Quarter Master."

September was spent in dealing with raids and skirmishes by the Navajos, and then an October 12 entry notes, "Capt. Brent… offered to take me with him to the States. I was nothing but loth to accept it and give up the idea of going to California. My opinion of that country is that the chances of success and safe arrival there are exceedingly doubtful and precarious; should mineral wealth abound as richly as is confidentially reported, California must prove a point of attraction for the whole world during many years to come. It will doubtless improve rapidly in civilization and good institutions. I have been offered a post here for the winter but do not think that my interests lay in such a place as Santa Fe."

Our diarist apparently was very confident in his position with the military, and kept avoiding their efforts to send him east. In January he wrote, "I have…no idea of staying many more weeks in this place but I shall wind my way to the States glad to leave the country in which I have never enjoyed good health and which otherwise possesses not a single attraction."

Finally on February 5, he left with a party of "forty or fifty men well-armed and equipped," noting that "I expect we shall encounter less danger from the red man." Following the Santa Fe Trail back to the States was difficult because of the snow, and their many encounters with Indians, though they had great apprehension, were peaceful. He passed through Fort Levinworth and then to Westport before heading down the Mississippi to New Orleans. Oddly, our diarist, whose name may have been Hough, did not reflect on how differently his American dream would have turned out had he followed the Oregon Trail from Westport in the first place, and not headed south across the prairies accidentally coming upon Santa Fe, a vastly more difficult, if not nearly impossible, route to reach the California gold fields.

Westward Ho! Engraving by T. D.
Booth after a painting by James H. Beard,
1866. 26 by 32¾ inches.

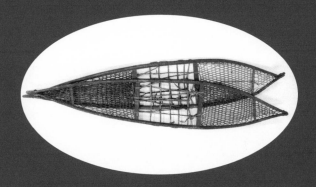

Chapter 13

NORTHWESTERN SETTLEMENT

VANCOUVER'S *VOYAGE*. Henry Humphrys' original watercolor, *View in the Gulph of Georgia NWest America, the Distant Land Being the South Side of Ye Straits of de Fuca.* Aboard HMS *Discovery,* San Juan Islands, June 1792. 11 by 4½ inches. This watercolor is believed to be the only original piece of art created on the Vancouver voyage (1790–1795) remaining in private hands. Although unsigned, it is attributed to Midshipman Henry Humphrys by Commander A. F. C. David, Ministry of Defence. Its dating has been established by the identifying landmarks it portrays (Mount Baker and Guemes Channel in Washington State) and from the entries in the Vancouver (and Humphrys) journals for the time the expedition was in the location depicted.

During the peace negotiations ending the War of 1812, Britain and the United States could not agree on the ownership of Oregon. In 1818, the two countries agreed that citizens of both the United States and Great Britain would have equal rights to trade and settlement for ten years. Hall Kelley's efforts to promote American settlement had an effect, and despite the British domination of trade, American emigrants — primarily missionaries to the Indians — overwhelmed the British traders and Oregon became part of the United States in 1846. By the later 1840s, the Indians had had enough of the missionaries and white men's diseases and went on the warpath. The early settlers Marcus Whitman and his wife were killed, and as can be seen in the letters in this chapter, Indian warfare continued well into the 1850s.

Almost all Oregon and Northwestern-related material is very rare. Vancouver's *Voyage* is probably one of the most available works.

George Vancouver, *A Voyage of Discovery to the North Pacific Ocean, and Round the World...Principally with a View to Ascertain the Existence of Any Navigable Communication Between the North Pacific and North Atlantic Oceans...in the Years 1790 [to] 1795...,* London, 1798. Three volumes; 16 plates.

Vancouver commanded an expedition to the Northwest Coast to determine England's rights under the Nootka Convention of 1790. The ships of the expedition reached the Northwest Coast in 1792 and spent two years in surveying the coastline, resulting in the most precise maps of the Northwest for many years. This is the most important of the 18th-century English voyages to the Northwest because of its superb cartography.

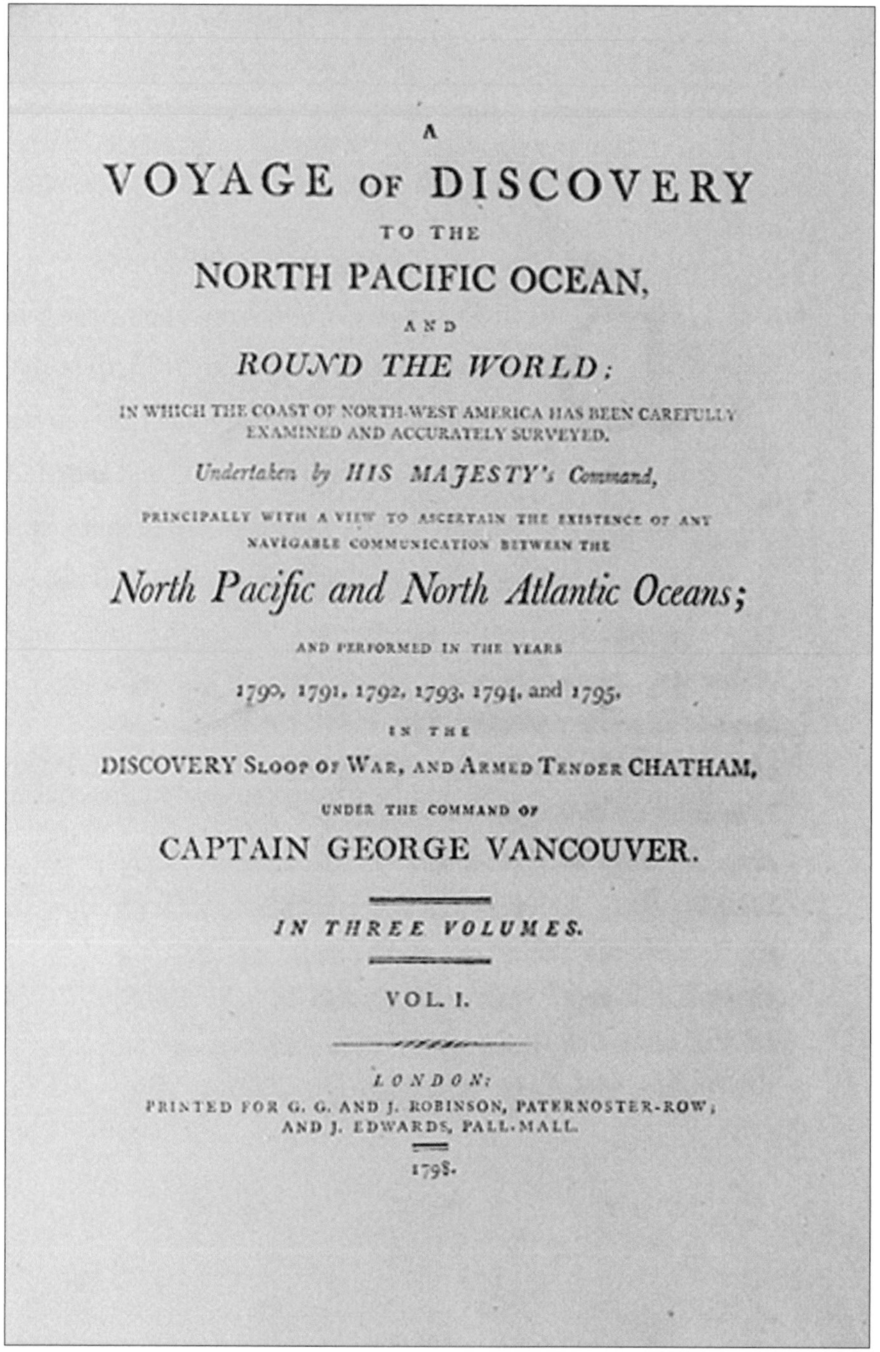

A

VOYAGE OF DISCOVERY

TO THE

NORTH PACIFIC OCEAN,

AND

ROUND THE WORLD;

IN WHICH THE COAST OF NORTH-WEST AMERICA HAS BEEN CAREFULLY
EXAMINED AND ACCURATELY SURVEYED.

Undertaken by HIS MAJESTY's Command,

PRINCIPALLY WITH A VIEW TO ASCERTAIN THE EXISTENCE OF ANY
NAVIGABLE COMMUNICATION BETWEEN THE

North Pacific and North Atlantic Oceans;

AND PERFORMED IN THE YEARS

1790, 1791, 1792, 1793, 1794, and 1795,

IN THE

DISCOVERY SLOOP OF WAR, AND ARMED TENDER CHATHAM,

UNDER THE COMMAND OF

CAPTAIN GEORGE VANCOUVER.

IN THREE VOLUMES.

VOL. I.

LONDON:
PRINTED FOR G. G. AND J. ROBINSON, PATERNOSTER-ROW;
AND J. EDWARDS, PALL-MALL.

1798.

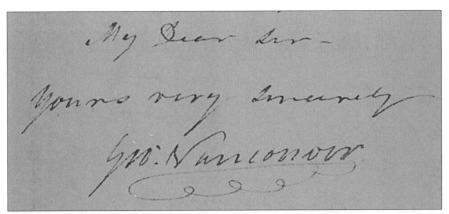

GEORGE VANCOUVER. Signature, on a letter written in 1797 concerning his finances while revising his *Voyage of Discovery.*

"Mount Rainier from the South Part of Admiralty Inlet," from Vancouver's *Voyage of Discovery,* 1798.

197

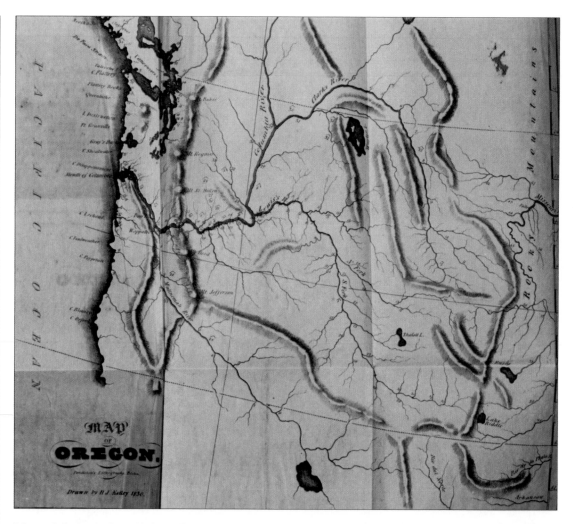

A GEOGRAPHICAL SKETCH

OF THAT

PART OF NORTH AMERICA,

CALLED

OREGON:

CONTAINING

AN ACCOUNT OF THE INDIAN TITLE;—THE NATURE OF A RIGHT
OF SOVEREIGNTY;—THE FIRST DISCOVERIES;—CLIMATE AND
SEASONS;—FACE OF THE COUNTRY AND MOUNTAINS—NATUR-
AL DIVISIONS, PHYSICAL APPEARANCE AND SOIL OF EACH;—
FORESTS AND VEGETABLE PRODUCTIONS;—RIVERS, BAYS, &c.;
ISLANDS, &c.;—ANIMALS;—THE DISPOSITION OF THE INDIANS,
AND THE NUMBER AND SITUATION OF THEIR TRIBES;—TO-
GETHER WITH AN ESSAY ON THE ADVANTAGES RESULTING
FROM A SETTLEMENT OF THE TERRITORY.

TO WHICH IS ATTACHED

A NEW MAP OF THE COUNTRY.

BY HALL J. KELLEY, A. M.

Boston:

PRINTED AND PUBLISHED BY J. HOWE, MERCHANTS ROW.
SOLD BY LINCOLN & EDMANDS, 59, WASHINGTON STREET; A. R. PARKER,
46, NORTH MARKET STREET; AND BY A. BROWN AND
THE PUBLISHER, CHARLESTOWN.

1830.

Map of Oregon from Kelley's *Geographical Sketch,*
1830. *"The settlement of the Oregon country has been
as long contemplated as its paramount advantages of
climate and soil and its local opportunities for trade and
commerce have been known…. No portion of the globe
presents a more fruitful soil or a milder climate or equal
facilities for carrying into effect the great purpose of a
free and enlightened nation, a country so full of those
natural means which best contribute to the comforts and
conveniences of life is worthy the occupation of a people
disposed to support a free representative government
and to establish civil scientific and religious institutions
energized by the mild and vital principles of our republic. Life in that country may be made easy with
comparatively little effort; but it can not be long sustained anywhere without some suffering and laborious
industry. A place where the full sustenance of man is
spontaneously produced would not be desirable for a settlement as it would encourage a propensity for idleness
and idleness is in the soil in which vice can best flourish
and produce its pestiferous fruit."*

Hall J. Kelley, *A Geographical Sketch of That Part of North America
Called Oregon…*, Boston, 1830.

Kelley was a one-man organizing office for immigration to Oregon.
This is his first work, describing Oregon and promoting American
settlement there.

No. *78*

This certifies that

    has paid *Twenty Dollars to the* AMERICAN SOCIETY FOR ENCOURAGING THE SETTLEMENT OF THE OREGON TERRITORY, *as a pledge for the faithful performance of obligations, to be stipulated and defined by Covenant between him and the said Society.*

                                         President.

                 Secretary.

    N. B. The following are the principal conditions and stipulations of the Covenant, viz: that the emigrant shall give oath or affirmation to obey and support all just and equal laws and regulations made and provided for the settlement by the Society, the same not being repugnant to the Constitution and Laws of the United States of America.

    That all the common and public property and revenues of the settlement shall be held liable to the payment of all debts that may be incurred on account of said settlement; and that, in all other respects he shall truly and faithfully demean himself a peaceable and worthy member of the Oregon community.

    That the Society shall defray all expenses of the first expedition from St. Louis, excepting arms, knapsacks, clothing and blankets, which are to be supplyed by the emigrants respectively.

    That the Society allow to each emigrant, agreeable to the terms of their first Circular, a lot of seaport land, or 200 acres of farming land, *provided* he or his assigns continues to occupy it, two years from the time of receiving said lot; the Society will guarantee and maintain his or her right to a free enjoyment of religious and civil freedom, and an equal participation in all the privileges and immunities of a member of the Oregon settlement.

The American Society for Encouraging the Settlement of Oregon Territory. Document Signed, by the president and the secretary [1831]. An unissued certificate, stating that the bearer has paid $20 to the society.

"The emigrant shall give oath of affirmation to obey and support all just and equal laws…provided for the settlement by the Society…shall be held liable…. In all… respects he shall truly and faithfully demean himself a peaceable and worthy member of the Oregon community…. The Society shall defray all expenses of the first expedition from St. Louis, excepting arms, knapsacks, clothing and blankets…. The Society allow to each emigrant…a lot of seaport land, or 200 acres of farming land, provided he continues to occupy it two years…. The Society will guarantee and maintain his or her right to free enjoyment of religious and civil freedom, and an equal participation in all the privileges and immunities of a member of the Oregon settlement."

Henry Warre, *Sketches in North America and the Oregon Territory,* London [1848]. 20 handcolored lithographs on 16 sheets.

One of the rarest and most beautiful of Western books. In 1845, Captain Warre was sent by the British government to the Oregon Territory, at the height of the dispute with the United States over its ownership, to scout out the country in case British troops were brought into Oregon. He traveled overland across Canada to the Pacific Northwest, visiting present-day Oregon, Washington, and British Columbia. By the time he returned the political crisis had been resolved. Warre, an accomplished artist, executed these illustrations on the spot, and published them upon his return to London.

"Fort Vancouver."

"Source of the Columbia River."

"The American Village."

"Valley of the Willamette River."

The conflict with Indians seems to have dominated life in Oregon in the 1850s, at least as reflected in my collection. Robert Atherton wrote from Scots Valley, 1853: "*I arrived here a few days ago from the Klammuth River, the Indians having commenced killing the whites in the vicinity has brought on a general war between them, and renders it dangerous for small parties to be out. The whites have all assembled at Rogues River Valley and built a Fort for protection all the farms in that vicinity have been abandoned as well as the mines. The Indians have declared their intention of driving the whites from that section of the country; expresses are daily arriving from them for aid, but the[re] are hardly people enough here to protect themselves and are very poorly armed; about two hundred Indians have assembled within ten miles of us, all well armed but have said that they do not intend to fight unless attacked — we place very little faith in what they say and expect them to make a break on us.*"

The following year, A. P. Thayer wrote from Corvallis: "*[W]e succeeded in reaching Salem the Capital of this Territory on the 1st day of September...1853.... We both enjoyed good health...but we were unfortunate in loosing our Cattle.... My farm consists of about 250 acres of good dry prairie & the balance timber, it is well watered with a running stream running acrost it.... [T]he grass grows green & fresh all winter hence it must be the best grazing country in the world.... The soil is very productive & natural for wheat. Our prairie here can be broken with a pair of horses. The first time, oats potatoes & barley together with all kinds of vegetables grow in abundance here.... Were I to cross the plains again I would take mules & bring no freight whatever except what clothing I wanted on the* road & 100 lbs of provision to a person. But it is far better to come by water, it costs less & far safer. The indians have been very hostile to the Immigrants this last summer. A good many have been killed, I crossed the Cascade Mts this fall with a neighbor who had heard that his brother had been killed. We did not know but that he had been left wounded. We found when we met the train that he was with at the time, that he had been shot dead.*"

A year later, on November 22, 1855, J. A. Nicholson wrote from Fort Kelly, Umatilla River, Cayuse County, to his brother in Portland: "*[O]ur little Fort, built by us in two days, in the very heart of the Enemy's Country, surrounded by hostile bands on every side and within.... This camp was thrown into confusion by the arrival of an express bringing the news of the occupancy of Ft. Walla Walla, our destination, but the great chief...the Yellow Bird with 100 Indians.... We went to work built a picket 100 ft. square, 7 ft. high, and since then have been working at block houses. We are well fortified, and can hold this place against 3000 Indians. Scouts have daily skirmishes with Indians & wolves, but as yet none of our command have been wounded...we hope for some hard fighting. I for one want to get a scalp.*"

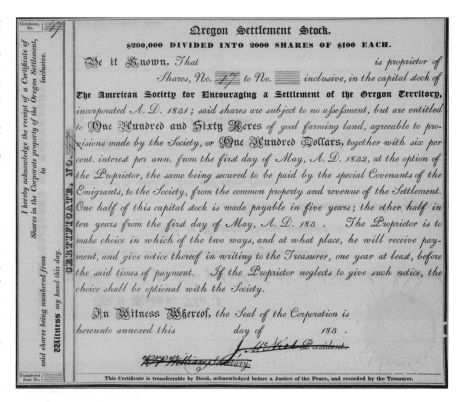

The American Society for Encouraging the Settlement of Oregon Territory. Document Signed, 1830s, acknowledging ownership of 160 acres of good farming land.

Oregon, like all of the Northwest, had a barter economy of beaver pelts and wheat. With the discovery of gold, two thirds of the inhabitants left for California. In early January 1849, $400,000 in gold dust reached Oregon, creating the same problems of disputes over the weight and fineness as in California. That year, a private group was formed — the Oregon Exchange Company. They minted $5 and $10 coins, both denominations containing more gold than their face value. Consequently they were melted down, and there are only thirteen to sixteen known examples of this $10 coin.

"Miners Cabin, Oregon."

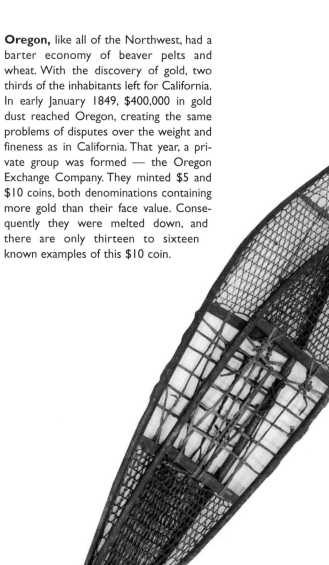

Snowshoes from the Northwest Coast, *ca.* late 19th century.

Mount Hood, oil painting by H. Francks,
ca. 1900. 9½ by 13½ inches.

Chapter 14

THE MORMONS

"Mormon Family, Great Salt Lake Valley."

T he Mormon migration is one of the greatest Western stories, showing the power of religious belief combined with hard work and ingenuity. The letters of Brigham Young in the collection quoted here tell the Mormon story firsthand.

207

BRIGHAM YOUNG. Letter Signed, Nauvoo, Illinois, April 30, 1845, as president. Also signed by the Mormon trustees, N. K. Whitney and George Miller.

This is one of the letters that Brigham Young wrote seeking a new home for the Mormons, less than a year after the murder of Joseph Smith.

"Suffer us…in behalf of a disfranchised and long afflicted people to pr[of]fer a few suggestions for your serious consideration in hope of a friendly and unequivocal re[s]ponse…. It is not our present design to detail the multiplied and aggravated wrongs that we have received in the midst of a nation that gave us birth…. *[W]e are a disfranchised people. We are privately told by the highest authorities of this state, that it is neither prudent or safe for us…. [T]he blood of our best men has been shed, both in Missouri, and the state of Illinois with impunity….*

"But…the startling attitude recently assumed by the state of Illinois…has already used the military of the State…to coerce and surrender up our best men to unparalleled murder…. [T]he murderers of Joseph Smith are suffered to roam at large, watching for further prey…. [I]f we continue passive and nonresistant, we much certainly expect to perish, for our enemies have sworn it….

"[W]ill you express your views concerning what is called the Great Western Measure, of colonising the Latter Day Saints in Oregon, the Northwestern Territory, or some location remote from the states, where the hand of oppression shall not crush every noble principle and extinguish every patriotic feeling?"

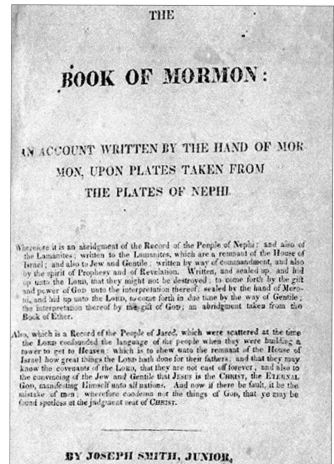

JOSEPH SMITH, the founder of the Mormon Church. Document Signed, Nauvoo, Illinois, April 1, 1840. A contract for the sale of *"a lot in the town of Nauvoo."*

Smith and his followers had just arrived in Nauvoo the preceding summer after they were forced out of Missouri by religious persecution. Within three years, Nauvoo had become the tenth-largest city in the United States. In 1844, Joseph Smith and his brother were assassinated and the Mormons were forced to evacuate the city in 1846. The Mormon temple was burned that year.

The Book of Mormon: An Account Written by the Hand of Mormon, Upon Plates Taken from the Plates of Nephi..., Palmyra [NY]. Printed by E. B. Grandin, for the author, 1830.

First edition of one of the most influential publications issued in America in the 19th century. The founding work of the most important religious sect in the American West.

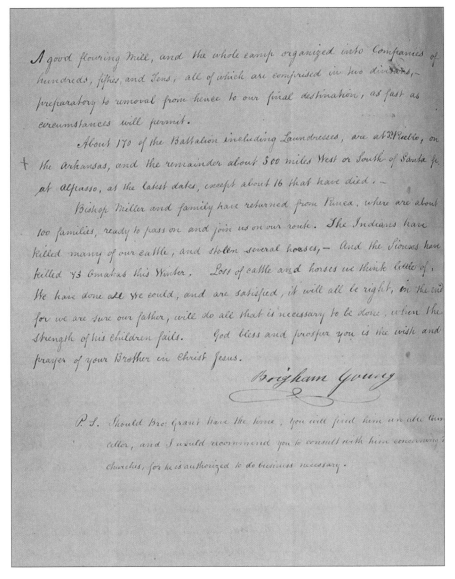

BRIGHAM YOUNG. Letter Signed, from Winter Quarters [Nebraska], February 26, 1847, to Elder J. C. Little, describing the great Mormon migration.

"I expect to start for the mountains before you arrive, as it is necessary for a Pioneer Company to be on the way, as early as possible, to ensure crops a-head, and I know of no better way than for me to go with the Company : and if the Brethren love me as I them, they will not be long behind. I feel like a father with a great family of children around me in a winter storm, and I am looking with calmness, confidence, and patience for the clouds to break, and the sun to shine, so that I can run out and plant and sow and gather in the corn, and wheat, and say children, Come home. Winter is approaching again and I have houses, and wood, and flour and meal, and meat, and potatoes, and squashes, and onions, and cabbages, and all things in abundance, and I am ready to kill the fatted calf, and make a joyful feast, so all who will come and partake : come on then Bro Little; you need not stop at Washington to transact any business for the Camp, for we have made all necessary arrangements with our friend, Colonel Kane, through Bro. Grant, and if you do not arrive at Winter Quarters before I leave, We will say, all is right, We shall only loose each other's society for a few days : you will come on in the next company, and a taste of the mountain air together will be sweet to us.

"Set the churches in order, and leave everything just as it should be : and if you are meek and lowly in heart, and watch continually the whisperings of the Spirit : — the still small voice, you will not look for wisdom and knowledge, and you will prosper in all you put your hands unto, and the Saints will be blessed by your labors. You will select some good efficient Elder on whom you will confer your local office and calling, to seek the best interest of the children of the kingdom, and counsel them with a fathers care.

"We now have a survey of 41 Blocks, of 820 Lots, 700 Houses, 22 Woods, with Bishop & Counsellors and municipal high Council all happy & prosperous. A good flouring mill, and the whole camp organized into companies of hundreds, fifties, and Tens, all of which are comprised in two divisions : — preparatory to removal from hence to our final destination, as fast as circumstances will permit.

"About 170 of the Battalion including Laundresses, are at Ft. Pueblo, on the Arkansas, and the remainder about 300 miles West or South of Santa fe at Alpasso, at the latest dates, except about 16 that have died.

"Bishop Miller and family have returned from Punea, where are about 100 families, ready to pass on and join us on our route. The Indians have killed many of our cattle, and stolen several horses, — And the Siouxs have killed 43 Omahas this Winter. Loss of cattle and horses we think little of. We have done all we could, and are satisfied it will all be right, in the end for we are sure our father, will do all that is necessary to be done, when the strength of his children fails. God bless and prosper you is the wish and prayer of your Brother in Christ Jesus."

James Marshall, who discovered gold at Sutter's Mill, was a Mormon, as were many of the original miners. When gold dust was brought back to Salt Lake City, Brigham Young conceived the idea of producing Mormon coins. The obverse depicts the emblem of the Mormon priesthood, the three-pointed Phrygian crown above the all-seeing eye. "HOLINESS TO THE LORD" appears around the edge. The reverse is engraved with clasped hands representing friendship, and "GSLCPG" (Great Salt Lake City Pure Gold) — though the gold was from California and the coins overvalued by fifteen percent. Issued in $2½, $5, and $10, as well as in the $20 shown here — all were mass melted because of the overvaluation.

A year after Young wrote his letter, Martha Haven described the Mormon westward movement from Winter Quarters, Omaha Nation, January 1848.

"[T]hese Western moves are hard...on the people. You can have but a faint idea of it....

We can never know how to value any thing until we are once deprived of it....We shall probably have to go without many things that would add greatly to our comfort....You know but little, Mother, of a Western life....We are not going to a remote corner of the earth to hide ourselves. Far from it."

The Mormons issued a different coin — made from Colorado gold and worth $5 — in 1860. The Lion of Judah is depicted on one side. The beehive, the symbol of Mormon productivity, on the other side, is protected by an American eagle.

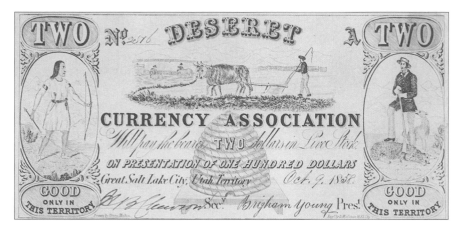

Currency issued by the Mormons, 1858. Payable in livestock and *"Good only in this territory."*

Four printed bills in the amounts of 50¢, $1, $2, and $3, signed by Heber C. Kimball, Thomas Bullock, and Brigham Young. The bills bear the inscription *"G.S.L. City, Jan. 20, 1849,"* and the embossed seal with the miter and eye device.

The burgeoning Mormon settlements in the Salt Lake Valley soon felt the need for a convenient medium of exchange. Gold dust was used at first, but the loss resulting from repeated weighings led Brigham Young to order the printing of paper currency in 1849. Using a small handpress, which had been brought overland in a covered wagon, the Mormon leaders issued bills that are the earliest known specimens of Utah printing.

JIM BRIDGER is forced to sell his Green River ferry to Mormon interests as a prelude to their takeover of Fort Bridger and establishment of a monopoly on the emigrants' business. Document, Bridger's Fort, May 21, 1853.

"This agreement…between Wm. J. Hawley, I.S. Thompson and John McDonald of the first part and Jas Bridger and Louis Vasques of the second part…whereas the parties of the first part have obtained from the Legislature of Utah a good and lawful license for keeping a ferry on Green River, and as the parties of the second part have already two good and sufficient Boats, with Ropes to run them on said River, Now the parties of the first part do covenant and agree with the parties of the second part, that if they will furnish said Boats and Ropes and men to work them on the Ferry known as Bridgers on the lower Ferry on Green River that they the parties of the first part will share and divide equally with them, the parties of the second part, all money's, stock or anything else which may be taken in at said Ferry in payment for crossing said River."

"Great Salt Lake City in 1853," James Linforth, *Route from Liverpool to Great Salt Lake Valley…Together with a Geographical and Historical Description of Utah…Also, an Authentic History of the Latter-Day Saints' Emigration from Europe…,* 1855.

One of the most important publications devoted to the Mormon emigration to Utah, and a landmark in the artistic depiction of western scenes. On one level it is a guidebook for Mormon emigrants, following the usual formula of overland guides except with elaborate illustrations. Beyond this, it depicts many of the significant places of Mormon history.

BRIGHAM YOUNG. The retained draft signed by Young, 1852, of a petition to the U.S. Congress for an appropriation for a fledgling school system. It also discusses the problem of land given to Utah by the United States — land that was unusable because it was under Indian title.

"Your memorialists — feeling a deep interest in the promotion of a general system of education and the general diffusion of knowledge among all classes, and laboring under the difficulties incident to the settlement of all new territories, & especially those so far removed from the confines of civilization, and feeling grateful to the general government for the valuable library furnished our territory, as also for the appropriation of two sections of land in each township when the same shall have been surveyed & brought into market, & which lands will eventually, in some cases, prove beneficial in promoting the object for which they are granted, but, at present, they are wholly unavailable…as your honorable body must readily perceive, owing to the fact that the Indian title has, in no instance, been extinguished in any part of said territory… & having no resources on which to base the establishment of a school fund."

Brigham Young wrote in December 1856 to the president of the British and Scandinavian missions:

"The last train of hand carts arrived on last Sunday — many of them with frozen feet but greatly improving in health since they were met by the assisting companies. They were met at the upper crossing of the Plate where they had been encamped in a storm which they could not travel in for nine days. The ox trains, or so called 'Independent companies,'…have not yet arrived.… [T]hey are probably at Bridger by this time where they will also receive sufficient assistance to bring them in. We learn that they are generally well. We wrote you last mail that no company must hereafter leave the Missouri later than the first day of August, upon further consideration we have fixed upon the first of July as the latest that any emigrating company should be permitted to leave the Missouri River.

"The wagons are good this year and we suggest that they hereafter be of the same kind with the following exceptions — let them be made to track five feet, shoulder boxes 4¼ and point boxes 3 inches in diameter in the clear,… hub 1 inch thicker — the braces that go from the hind axle to the reach should be 12 inches longer and be set one inch nearer to the forward hubs than they now do, the iron strap on the tongue should be straight & be as heavy again as it now is; wagon boxes or beds should be enlarged in proportion to the increased width of track; in other respects they will answer as heretofore made, except that all the timber must be of the very best quality, or we do not want them."

Young wrote Horace Eldredge, an early and important member of the Mormon Church and from 1852, the immigration agent for the Mormon Church in St. Louis, on May 29, 1857:

"Some few have grown weary of their continued privations, disappointed hopes, and the stern realities connected with living as saints should live, and building up the Kingdom of God. They could not build themselves up, and a tenth of their substance and labor, shook them, but the consecration of their all, they could not endure."

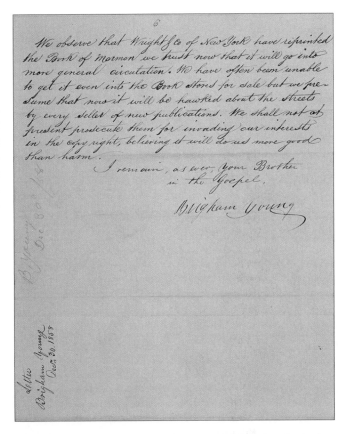

Young wrote again to Eldredge from Salt Lake City, December 30, 1858. This extraordinary letter, written after Young's removal as governor of Utah, concerns the government intervention and the possible statehood of Utah, relations with President Buchanan and his administration, a new edition of the *Book of Mormon,* the mail service, courts, the new governor, and a clique of bitter enemies of the Mormon church.

Washington Mousley described to his family the Mormon Miracle, writing from Great Salt Lake in November 1857:

"It is a pleasure…to inform you of our good health and prosperous Journey to these peaceful vales of the mountains of Eaphrem…over 1300 miles with ox team. I have sawe & converse with the red man of the forest I have slept where wolf howled & buffalo roam I have saw the red antelope and deer in his native air & all was a pleasure to me…. I never saw so handsome a site as is presented to our view when emergine from the canion to Salt Lake Valey….The farmes are not so scattered as they are in the states…. I have been some 60 or 70 miles from the city and I believe I never pasd through a country that there was one quarter as much wheat raised in one year. There is enough grain in Utah to serve the population for 3 years…. I can accumulate more property in this country in 5 years under present prospects, than I could in the east in 25 years….

"We are well and never had the chance to do as well in our lives…[a]tmosphere is purer, and but little if at all tainted with gentile putrefaction, or apostate discontent. The earth seems to revolve as formerly, all these affairs notwithstanding, for we found on our return…our eyes feasting on the city of white houses, peaceful homes and verdant gardens, here still it stands, lovely when seen by the clear beams of silver light now shed nightly upon it from the fair moon. Where is it equal? Where do the cooling streams of melted snow water every tree-shaded street as here? Where the same am[oun]t of peace, faith, power? Nowhere at present, not even in Washington! and most assuredly neither in St. Louis nor New Orleans!!! I learn…are very much opposed to the settling of any portion of the Indian lands, because the Indian claims are not yet bartered for! and they cannot give away even by mail contract what they have neither bo[ugh]t nor paid for! If we should defer our way side settlements till they had arranged these matters righteously with the 'natives,' how long should we wait? We do not mean to put it into the power of Gov[ernmen]t to refuse our making settlements, neither do we design to make much noise in our ceaseless labors to benefit the human family, & ourselves. How long should we have waited here for a home, had we waited until U.S. extinguished the Indian claim here? Instead of a reply, Echo, answers — 'How long'? I trust we shall he[ar] from you, of an increase of means having enabled you to do what was necessary, and that as formerly you can accomplish what you want to."

Currier & Ives lithograph of Salt Lake
City, undated. 15¼ by 11⅛ inches.

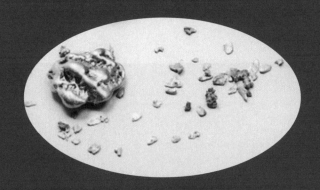

Chapter 15

CALIFORNIA GOLD RUSH

AUTOGRAPH OF

Ja's W. Marshall

OLD SUTTER MILL.

THE DISCOVERER OF GOLD IN CALIFORNIA

January 19th, 1848.

The letters of the forty-niners and later prospectors describe life during the California gold rush very eloquently, if phonetically, and tell the story firsthand. James Marshall, who was in charge of building a sawmill for John Sutter, who had arrived in California in 1839, discovered gold in the American River, as he notes on his card on January 19, 1848. Neither benefited — in fact Sutter was ruined. Those already in California in 1848 overran his land and paid no attention to who owned it if there was gold on it. It is ironic and tragic that this Swiss émigré, whose interest was in building the infrastructure for settlement, was ruined because the stampede for gold could not be incorporated into his vision for California.

Others like Collis Huntington and Mark Hopkins quickly saw that the best chance of making money was not in pursuing gold directly in the rivers and mines but in selling the prospectors the tools they needed. The two partners were in the hardware business and went on to finance the Central Pacific Railroad with Charles Crocker and Leland Stanford. In all but a few areas of California, the days of panning for gold in the rivers and streams were over quickly and were replaced by the rocker or sluice, which would process more gravel but still could sometimes be handled by one man but was usually run by a small group. By 1853, this method had been superseded by the practice of digging mine shafts to follow the veins of gold underground and shooting high-pressure jets of water that would tear apart mountainsides to get at gold — several of the later letters describe the destruction of the landscape.

The California gold rush is one of the most collectible areas of the American West. Letters and guidebooks are frequently available and, less often, illustrated letter sheets.

JOHN A. SUTTER, pioneer in California who founded his colony on the site of what is now Sacramento; after gold was discovered on his property (1848), he went bankrupt, as his workmen deserted him, his sheep and cattle were stolen, and his land was occupied by squatters. Autograph Letter Signed, April 5, 1866. To Edward E. Dunbar, who was soon to publish *The Romance of the Age: or, the Discovery of Gold in California.*

"[Your] narration…attending the Discovery of Gold by Marshall at my saw mill in February 1848…is…correct….The account of this great discovery in…the 'Encyclopedia Americana,' is quite incorrect…especially where it states that the first gold was picked up by a little daughter of Marshall's…Feb. 9, 1848. Marshall never had a daughter….The account is also incorrect when it states that a party of three Americans, two of them Mormons, collected in January 1848 a large amount of gold on Mormon Island, Sacramento. Gold diggings were not discovered at the Saw Mill by Marshall. I never heard of Mormons connected with the Army or of Mexicans & Indians having gathered gold on the banks of the streams in California during the years of the Mexican war."

Many groups formed companies in which each argonaut had a share, or in which financial backers who stayed home shared ownership with the miners. In the papers of Samuel Allen there is a printed charter for a mutual aid corporation in which the members could pool resources in order to get to the mines. Signed by all fifteen members of the company, the agreement required the men to act jointly in the interest of the whole, stating they would not "engage in, or be concerned with, any game of chance or skill, by which money may be lost or won; neither shall he use intoxicating liquors…neither shall any work be engaged in on the Sabbath."

In the diggings, Allen's early optimism quickly became informed skepticism: "I find that it is all a lottery in the diggings, some make thousands in a week but they are rare while others make but a bare living…. Dollars here take the place of cents at home, a man wont look at any thing less than a dollar…. Those of us who work steady can make 6 dollars a day in the best of the season. Our living, port, break, and flour costs about $1.50 a day a man and if we should go into the luxurys…such as onions and potatoes…would take all to live…. I would not advise any one to come here."

"Miners Improved Gold Scale manufactured expressely for California."

Knife with blade inscribed "California Gold seeker protector."

Document wherein a forty-niner agrees to share equally what gold he finds with his backer, who is staking him to his trip to California from Missouri, 1849.

Many gold rush ventures started with reading a guide to the California gold fields, such as Sherwood's published in 1849. The preface is certainly encouraging: "To assist the increase of those preparing to immigrate to the rich and inviting regions of California — to embody in a condensed form all the valuable and trustworthy information in regard to the location extent and character of its mineral wealth, particularly its gold whether in mines or scattered upon the varied surface of its soil or intermingled with the sands of its rivers — to furnish a clear succinct and full account of its climate, its native and immigrant population, its agricultural resources, its commercial prospects and advantages — and also aid to supply facts — facts in regard to the best cheapest and most expedious modes of reaching this newly opened and richly developing country is the design of this pamphlet."

It also contains over twenty-five pages of very interesting advertisements addressed "To California gold diggers, exploring parties and other," offering everything necessary for the overland voyage and the finding of gold in comfort.

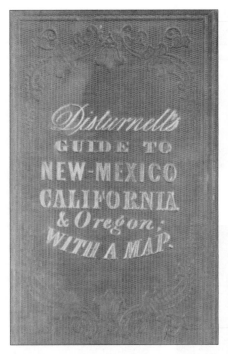

John Disturnell, *The Emigrant's Guide to New Mexico, California, and Oregon; Giving the Different Overland and Sea Routes...,* 1849.

This emigrant's guide, most notable for its map, was one of the best of the West generally available at the onset of the gold rush.

"This painting is the likeness of 'Daniel' 'Trip,' and Henry 'Eldridge,' Taken in California, at the gold mines in 1849. The right hand is 'Henry' 'Eldridge.'" Signed C. T. Allen. 9¾ by 6½ inches.

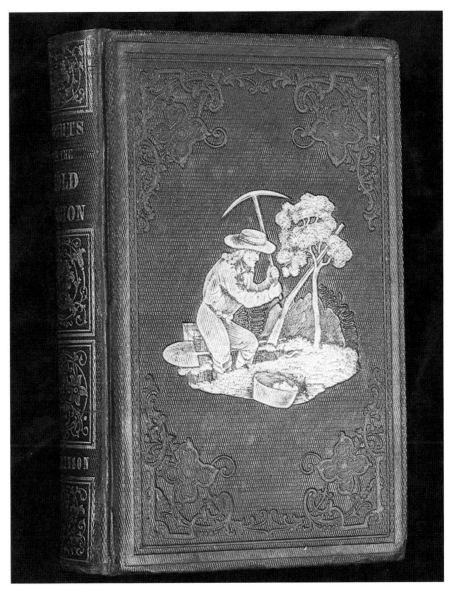

Theodore T. Johnson, *Sights in the Gold Region and Scenes by the Way,* 1849. One of the earliest published accounts of the gold fields, and one of the most popular descriptions of the gold rush.

Studio ferrotype of three miners wearing sourdough hats and dressed in work clothes, the first holding a double barrel shotgun.

San Francisco in 1849 was described by George Payne in terms of property values:

"A large fire occurred last week, by which a large amount of property was destroyed... but in order to understand the loss which parties have sustained it is necessary to know something about the amount for which the buildings rented.... The largest building — a hotel, rented for $14,000 per month, the house originally cost $100,000. The next two — occupied as eating houses and gambling houses — rented for $10,000 per month each. Then there were about twenty five small buildings & stores that rented for about $2,000 per month each — & must have cost an average of $5,000 each to build them."

Another fire is briefly mentioned by Edward Allyn in a letter in June, 1850:

"A fire the Friday before we came in I should think it burnt one third of the Citty. [T]here is nearly as many folks live in tents as there is in houses."

Allyn then turns to a general description of San Francisco:

"[T]he best buildings are used for the lowest and mos wanton purposes, the first floor of such house is for gambling, they are furnished in the most costly style.... [T]he Churches are about the poores buildings in the Citty Women attract about as much attention when they promenade the Streets as a Carrivan would to home. Murder is only an honorable way of Settling disputes.... [T]he Streetes are full to a jam with human beings of all collers, and Countrys under heaven.... Pork, 30 cents a pund Chees .50 to one dollar Butter one dollar Onions one dollar Coffee .60 fresh beef. 18 Tea one dollar...molasses two dollar a gallon.... [A] rugged woman can make fifty dollars a week washing...if she can git the water herself without buying it. [W]ater is .25 bts a pail full...pails two to 3 dollars each, brooms two dollars apice.... [I]t was not an uncommon thing for a person to get stuck in the mud, so he could not git out without helpe, which would cost him two dollars, with regard to crime.... Stealling and the punishment is quite severe. If a person steals the smallest thing and is catchd it is a job on the chain gang for thirty days, that is he has to work with a large iron ball chained to his leg, but if a large amount their life is the forfeit....[T]here is some five hundred buildings now in progress and it is possible that before this letter reaches you they may be in ashes."

The Golden Gate and San Francisco in 1849. Watercolor.

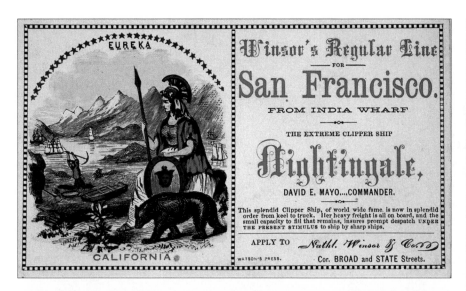

Clipper ship advertising cards for ships sailing to San Francisco from Boston or New York.

225

SS *Central America* treasure — gold bars and placer nuggets recovered from the shipwreck, shown with a miner's scale.

The SS *Central America* was a passenger ship carrying passengers and cargo from San Francisco that transferred at Panama en route to New York when a hurricane struck the Atlantic, and the ship was sunk off North Carolina, September 12, 1857. There were 153 survivors; about 425 passengers and crew were lost.

Also lost was all of the gold the ship was carrying. In 1986, modern technology led to the recovery, in 8,000 feet of ocean, of much of the gold.

Large gold amalgam ball, the result of one of the oldest means of separating gold dust from the surrounding detritus. The recovered material is mixed with mercury. This attracts, indeed assimilates, the gold; the pasty mass is washed to remove the valueless concentrates and then the remaining material is placed within a tightly woven fabric or chamois and the mercury is squeezed out (leaving the outer surface pattern); finally the ball must have the remaining mercury burned off. One method frequently used by prospectors was to halve a potato, scoop a hollow out of the center, place the ball within, rejoin the halves, and "bake" it for three quarters of an hour in the campfire. This removed the remaining mercury, leaving a ball of nearly pure gold. Recovered from the SS *Central America.*

A gold pan holding a large gold concretion, recovered from the SS *Central America,* of irregular form, containing a mixture of various types of placer gold, including flour gold, dust, nuggets, grains, and flakes; the bottom of the formation contains fragments of wood, apparently from the box containing the gold. Several large nuggets found in California during the gold rush are at the left.

The California pictorial letter sheets provide the best visual chronicle of the California gold rush. Imprinted on sheets of writing paper were views of mining camps, argonauts panning for gold, pioneers pushing their way across the continent, terrifying city fires, vigilance committees in San Francisco streets, and California's spectacular natural wonders.

Most were double sheets, 8½ by 10½ inches when folded, and gave the writer two-plus pages for writing (when folded smaller they required no envelope as the final space left by the writer was the address panel). While historians have called them forerunners of picture post cards, they may also be compared to printed greeting cards — it was easier to have someone else tell the story of your everyday life. Few surviving examples, however, were used for letter writing and most were saved for their pictorial qualities. They are a unique record of lives and scenes from the gold rush.

"Crossing the Plains to California."

"The Miner's Ten Commandments."

"The Mining Business in Four Pictures, Going Into It, Making Something, Making Nothing, Going Out of It."

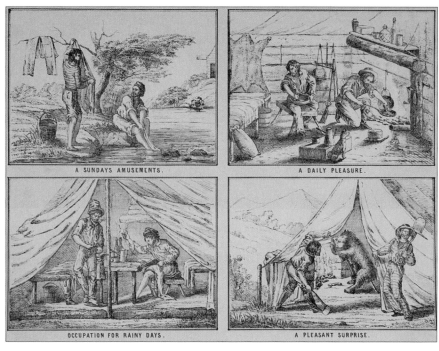

"Sundry Amusements in the Mines: A Sundays Amusements. A Daily Pleasure. Occupation for Rainy Days. A Pleasant Surprise."

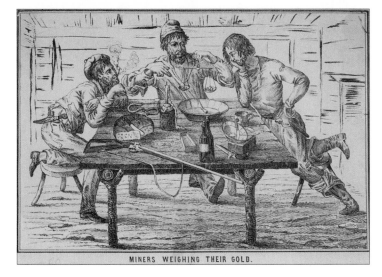

"Miners Weighing Their Gold."

In 1848 the military governor of California sent 230 ounces of gold bullion to the secretary of war, who instructed the Philadelphia mint to have the gold coined into specially marked $2½ gold coins (total of 1,389) each with "CAL" above the eagle.

The Pacific Company was most probably founded in Boston early in 1849 with thirty-seven members contributing $1,000 each towards the purchase of a ship and equipment for the gold fields. They are believed to have sold the coinage dies they brought with them in the fall of 1849. The new owners struck $5 and $10 coins by sledgehammers. This $1 gold coin is unique.

Private coinage firms met the demand for lower denomination coins by merchants, but there was always the question of whether they contained their face value in bullion. The first firm whose members' names are known was Norris, Gregg & Norris. They minted this $5 coin in 1849.

Baldwin & Co. started in San Francisco as jewelers and watchmakers. In 1850, they added private coining and produced this horseman design. When the coin was found to be three percent overvalued, the company was forced out of California and their coins melted down for bullion.

Private coiners were constantly accused of minting coins whose bullion value was less than the face value, as a result of both its substandard fineness and being underweight. Some coins were twenty-five percent overvalued. Moffat & Co. was the great exception and its reputation was unimpeachable. This $16 ingot was produced in 1849; its weight corresponds to a Latin American doubloon.

Wass, Molitor & Co. shared a reputation similar to Moffat's for honesty. The delay in opening the San Francisco branch mint caused a severe coin shortage as private coiners had stopped operating and most coins had been melted down in anticipation of the federal coins. Local bankers convinced Wass, Molitor to resume minting, and in 1855, they produced $10 and $20 coins as well as this $50 coin. All private coinage ended in 1856, when the new branch mint was fully operational.

Less than a year after the discovery of gold, miners who were being flagrantly underpaid for their ore, merchants who were desperate for an accurate medium of money, and the general public petitioned the military governor for a state assay office. In September 1850, a federal assay office was approved by Congress. In 1851, $50 gold coins were minted and, in 1852–1853, both $20 and $10.

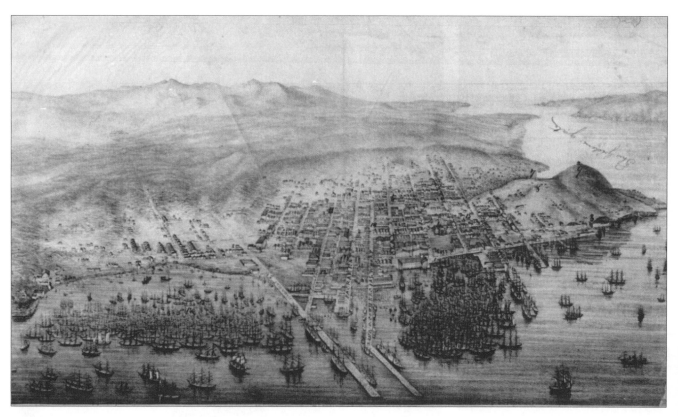

Bird's-eye view of San Francisco from *Miriam's Model & Nature July 1852*. Lithograph by Cookes Le Count, 1852, with contemporary annotations.

"Compliments of Diamond Lil, Good for One Piece, Barbary Coast, San Francisco."

The 1851 $5 coin produced by Schultz and Co. is known only in ten to twelve examples because when assayed they contained only $4.87 in gold. This was sufficient reason for the public to reject them and they were melted into bullion.

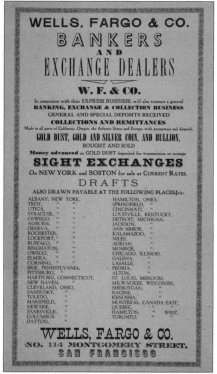

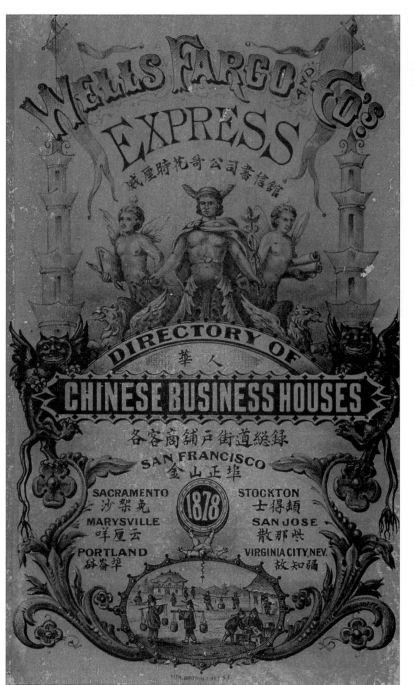

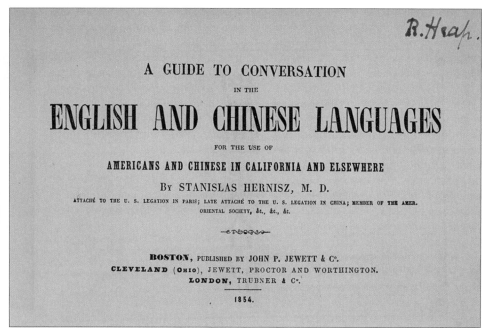

A Guide to Conversation in the English and Chinese Languages..., by Stanislas Hernisz, 1854. *Please* and *thanks* don't appear in the dictionary.

The Chinese population of California was unable to file many claims, because of the widespread discrimination against them, but became invaluable when the Central Pacific Railroad began to employ the Chinese in large numbers to build the railroad across the Sierra Nevada. The work ethic of the extraordinarily industrious Chinese was the key element in the success of Stanford's, Crocker's, and Huntington's efforts to get their track laid over the mountains.

Just like their letters on the Overland Trail, the Gambrel brothers' letters from California provided their family with interesting observations about life in California. The first on November 30, 1849, notes:

"We have realised nearly 1000$ since, laid in our winter provision and are comfortably fixed in a splendid (not exactly house) but log cabin of our own manufacture. Our furniture is not however of as costly a kind as the nobility of some countries might be expected to use. For example our dining Table is constructed of a pine puncheon, the surface of which has been hewn with a hatchet and is somewhat narrow. Owing to this we sometimes upset our 'tea things' but being of tin they seldom sustain any serious injury. Our chairs are all three legged stall, as our floor is quite uneven we are unable to use any other kind. The last though not least that I will mention are our Bedsteads & Bedding, but when I look at them I am compelled to acknowledge my incompetency to describe them and will only say that a repose on them is far more luxurious than on the best Feather bed in Missouri.

"Our fare with some would not be considered of the most dainty kind, meat & bread & bread & meat are daily cooked up by we cooks, Jno and myself, sometimes we indulge in the luxury of Coffee. Though notwithstanding our tough mode of living, we are perhaps far better contented than whilst in Randolph we have become thoroughly accustomed to this way of living and it suits us better than any other. We rise in the morning from our beds of slumber in time to prepare breakfast by day light. As soon as this is over we put out for the diggings and work hard all day, and return home at night, as our diggings are about one mile from camp — all as merry as larks being

conscious of having made from 20$ to 60$ a piece that day, all cash in hand and no Credit. This is what renders a life of this kind so agreeable. Hard work and a change of climate has wrought quite a change in the appearance of my corporeal frame... I have become more avaricious since my arrival here than I had ever before been. I want 25 or 30,000$ before I start home, which amt I can accumulate....

"This is also one of the most enjoyable climates in America and I have no doubt as healthy as any part of the Globe."

"A Scene in the Gold Fields," by Henry H. Mallory, 1850s. 17½ by 26 inches.

April 12, 1850:

"You need give yourself no uneasiness on a/c of my dissipated habits of which you spoke as my habits shall be preserved inviolate…. The prospects at present are very gloomy for the mines though we can easily…26 to 30$ pr any during the summer."

September 22, 1850:

"We have done but little in the way of mining as yet & will not be able to do much until the Rainy Season comes on as all the claimes convenient to water are taken up. We think as soon as the Rain commences we will be able to make ten or twelve Dollars pr day. We are carrying our dirt about 300 yards to water $ make 3 or 4 dollar pr day…. The country suites me very well and particularly so in one respect, money does not make Gods of men here.

"There are more discouraged men & long faces here than I ever saw in my life. Every Boat that leaves the City is crowded with persons returning, a number have returned who crossed this year.

"You wished to know how we got along on the plains &c. Well we had an awful time I assure you but I did not have as hard time as I expect on our trip was a pleasure compared to a good many others if we had not had a good deal more than an average team."

September 22, 1850:

"[A]s there are thousands just arrived who are working for just enough to take them home, having become utterly disgusted with the country, already particularly men who have left families behind. They are realizing all those feelings which I predicted to you

and a thousand others — nearly all the married men from Randolph intend returning this fall & winter — those who have enough money will leave immediately, the balance this winter & next spring.

"The Situation of California has undergone a complete Revolution. Several of the most important Streams in C[alifornia] have almost proved a most complete failure & thousands have lost every cent realize by the hardest labour last fall. The little spot selected by us last fall for our opportunity is completely overrun by people. There is a town building up in the diggings — which will excel in population Glasgow & Huntsville combined. All the emigrants from Randolph flocked directly here — those who are working are making from 2$ to 12$ pr day. They are nearly all dissatisfied and wish themselves back home…

"Though notwithstanding all this a young man can [earn] two or three times as much as he can at home. During my last trip to Sacramento City I was offered 150$ pr month to Clerk."

December 9, 1850:

"Last year…every Body seemed to be satisfied but men who had left families — but this year it is every Body & I expect there is no country in the world where there are so many dissatisfied People congregated together & no Prospect to become Reconciled but it will be a lesson learned by experience long to be Remembered by young & old Rich & poor When they are doing tolerably well to let first rate alone."

Double barrel shotgun made by A. J. Plate, San Francisco, 1850s.

May 16, 1851:

"They have commenced a new description of mining near us, that is washing the dirt on the surface of the hill....To obviate this difficulty a large company has been found, and are bringing by means of a canal a stream called dirt creek over their rich hills at a cost of ab[ou]t $20,000....The Company pay from five to six dollars pr day for hands."

July 17, 1851:

"Things are coming to a [frightful mess] in California at present so far as crime of every description is concerned as we are daily apprised of the perpetration of some murder or robbery. The people are commencing to take the law in their own hands, as the civil law seems to be perfectly disregarded. If a man is caught stealing the slightest thing he is immediately taken out and swung on the nearest tree. There have been four men condemned to death in the last 3 or 4 days for robbing our mare.... Notwithstanding there seems to be no abatement of crime. Two or three men have been stopped lately in the public roads not one mile from our House and robbed of large am[oun]ts of money, and what is worse many who have been detected in committing thefts &c were recognized as being men of respectability and good standing at home. Such as the affects of Cal[ifornia] on poor Human nature.

"This is no doubt the most contaminating Country in its influence on the character of youngmen of any other in the known world, here every species of vice and immorality is practiced openly and above board and in such a manner as to decoy young men, who have naturally, a disposition to morality and virtue, but who are in a measure devoid of self government."

May 27, 1852:

"[O]ne of the greatest countrys as Regards its mineral advantages and climate — which are not surpassed if equaled by any country in the world — but the labour it requires to obtain the gold of this Country is proba[b]ly Greater than you Imagine or Requires a strong constitution to engage in mining successfully for any length of time, and also requires some considerable capitol as the largest body of mining is now done by Capitalists or least that which is done profitably. Laboring hands in this Country are worth from $4 to $5 pr day."

September 20, 1854:

"When I last heard from them, they had gone down about ninety feet, and had found earth that would pay them $1.00 to every 50 lbs. This would not pay them for working them."

April 16, 1859:

"I am getting very tired of a California life, and that of an old Bachelor, although there are many more inducements at present in this country for one to remain than in former times, yet I cannot reconcile myself to its customs yet. We have many young Ladies and many Grass widows in our new and flourishing place, the latter particularly, are very numerous."

December 25, 1860:

"Los Angeles was the capitol of California under Mexican Government, and is yet quite a novel city. It yet has its ancient churches and Forts, erected more than 200 years ago, and the country generally contains relics of old missions, which are great curiosities to an American. The climate is unsurpassed, and while you are now almost freezing with severe cold, oranges, Figs, & Grapes are ripening, and are quite cheap and abundant in the market."

The Colt .44 Third Model Dragoon was very popular on the frontier in the early 1850s. It was John C. Fremont's choice for a pistol.

Pepperbox revolver by Allen and Thurber, popular in the gold fields.

A very ornate certificate of membership in the Committee of Vigilance of San Francisco, which was *"reorganized...1856 for the mutual protection of life and property."* Signed by William Coleman as president and the other officials, and bearing the embossed blind seal of the Committee, *"Be Just and Fear Not...Self-Preservation, The First Law."* 19½ by 15 inches.

The discovery of gold attracted men who were willing to work as well as those who intended to make their fortunes at the expense of others. The mining camps that sprang up overnight were soon confronted with incidents of lawlessness, and miners' courts, organized by committees of vigilance, were set up in many camps to administer justice. Most observers were impressed by the fairness of the miners' courts. Bayard Taylor, whose travel narrative, *Eldorado* (1850), did much to popularize California and who spent six months touring the mining camps as correspondent for the *New York Tribune*, wrote, "Regulations [were] established as near as possible in accordance with the existing laws of the country.... Nothing in California seemed more miraculous to me than this spontaneous evolution of social order from the worst elements of anarchy." It was a lesson worth even more than the gold.

In 1856 the Constitution of the Committee of Vigilance was published:

"Whereas it has become apparent to the citizens of San Francisco, that there is no security for life and property, either under the regulations of society as it at present exists, or under the laws as now administered, and that by the association together of bad characters, our ballot-boxes have been stolen...or stuffed with votes that were never polled...our dearest rights violated, and no other method left by which the will of the people can be manifested: Therefore, the citizens whose names are...attached...unite themselves into an association for the maintenance of the peace and good order of society — the prevention and punishment of crime — the preservation of our lives and property, and to ensure that our ballot boxes shall hereafter express the actual and unforged will of the majority of our citizens.... We are determined that no thief, burglar, incendiary, assassin, ballot-box stuffer, or other disturbers of the peace, shall escape punishment.... The name... of this association shall be the Committee of Vigilance.

"Great public emergencies demand prompt and vigorous remedies. The People — long suffering under an organized despotism which has invaded their liberties...have... arisen in virtue of their inherent right and power.... For years they have patiently waited and striven, in a peaceable manner...to reform the abuses which have made our city a by-word. Fraud and violence have foiled every effort, and the laws to which the people looked for protection...have been used as a powerful engine to fasten upon us tyranny and misrule.... Organized gangs of bad men...have parceled out...offices among themselves, or sold them to the highest bidders [and] have employed bullies and professional fighters to destroy tally-lists by force, and prevent peaceable citizens from ascertaining...the true number of votes polled at our elections and have used cunningly contrived ballot-boxes, with false sides and bottoms.... Felons...and unconvicted criminals...have thus controlled public funds and property....The Jury-box has been tampered with...to shield the hundreds of murderers whose red hands have cemented this tyranny, and silenced with the Bowie-knife and the pistol, not only the free voice of an indignant press, but the shuddering rebuke of the outraged citizen.... Our single, heartfelt aim is the public good.... We... shall spare no effort to avoid bloodshed or civil war; but undeterred by threats or opposing organizations, shall continue peaceably if we can, forcibly, if we must, this work of reform, to which we have pledged our lives, our fortunes and our sacred honor."

Some remained optimistic and retained the sense of adventure. James Lum wrote his brother from "The 'Ends' of the Earth":

"My reasons for going to California I need not state, suffice it to say, that I do not feel an inclination to get married and settle down, but, on the contrary I feel an impulse urging me to romantic adventures and I wish to gratify my desire to see distant countries, and further, I can probably make more money in that country. I have waited patiently since the discovery of gold in California to see what future developments would bring forth, and I am satisfied that the gold is inexhaustible."

By 1854, there were few if any opportunities for individuals, and letters are usually pessimistic. Josiah Boucher did not encourage his brother:

"I say to all yong men who have no intrest in that cuntry and would like to stay here five years, and not care wheather they ever got away they will do well by comeing. Men who have famileys and interests at home and wishing to come to this country and make A fortune and return home withen A year. I say they had better cut there throts. Then theyr friends can attribute the act to inanity and honor them with A decent burial. It is not the man who works but the man who manoevers he gets the money and the man who econemises he saves it."

Underground mining was not what those who went to California had in mind but by the mid-1850s a large number of those who went to California could find work only in these mines. P. J. Norton wrote to his son Charles on July 13, 1856:

"[Y]ou will find that your study in Book keeping will Be of use to you in enny kind of Bisness that you may engage in. You Say that you have not give up the notion of going to Anopilus which I was glad to heare that is if it is your Minde to go thare for it is A place that A young Man has a chance to improve and Make himself A Big Name and Be useful to his Country But Charles it cante Be done withoute A Grate Menny hardships and trobles…. We have Ben having Some Sony warm weather for the Laste Month But it has not Afected Me Much for I have Ben Working in A Tunnel Nigh[t]s and Sleeping Day times and it is vary harde worke for it is all vary hard Rock and I have to Blaste it all and to give you Some eideas of how hard it is take two of us Aboute three Hours steady

Drilliing to Sink A hole one foot Deape and working Day and nigh[t] we are Able to Make from 2 to 4 ft A weake in Length of tunnel."

Despite the new mining methods, there was still hope. In early 1858, Dan wrote to Jane from Drytown:

"It is dangerous for a person to venture out of town at night, from the fact that the miners have lit[er]ally gutted the Earth, and co[n]sequently left holes sticking out all over the count[r]y — some of them a hundred feet deep…. Men sometimes work for a whole month on a claim, which does not pay their bord — others make a fortune in a day, thus uncertain is Gold Digging."

Eight years after the gold rush had started, Joseph Seavy described a very different California. He wrote from Mission Dolores in 1857:

"California is an excellent state. Vegetable productions attain the highest degree of perfection both in size and flavour. Here is a field for obtaining wealth for young active enterprising men. Yet all do not get rich here. Many destroy themselves by intemperance. In San Francisco there are but a very few persons that were there six years ago — many are dead — many have left the state. It is a great city for one only about seven years old, containing 60 of 70 thousand inhabitants. I live three miles from the city but it is thickly settled all the way and two lines of omnibuses are constantly running starting once in about 20 minutes — fare to the city eight cents."

In a manuscript entitled "California Sketches, from Crane's Flat, Head of Yosemite Trail," written for *The Republican*

Journal, Lawrence, Kansas, E. Z. Gore gives a fascinating report of a stagecoach traveler following the Yosemite Trail in the period after the California gold rush. He describes his journey through deserted mining camps:

"[E]verywhere we saw where the 'whirlwind' had passed over — the ground all turned over or deeply dub into deep quarries or pits — all vestiges of the original surface lost and oftentimes for miles on our path nothing left but a desolate wilderness of rocks below us on either side, probably now showing very much the appearance they originally presented…before the sand, gravel and gold had been washed and filtered." He notes that the towns are *"melancholy to look upon — so weather-beaten and dilapidated"* with the *"loafers lounging around the liquor saloons."*

He finds it *"difficult to imagine the noisy activity, the dashing, reckless prosperity which must have pervaded them in the 'flush' days of California gold digging."*

He pities a *"gang of Chinamen, perhaps washing over the gravel that had been washed a dozen times already and making two to four bits a day from it and a good living for them at that, except when they try a faster method of getting gold by robbing their neighbors sluices at night."*

"**Kinney, Goodridge and Ingram's Steam Saw Mill, Eureka, Sierra Col, California 1857.**" Pencil and paper sketch, 12 by 15½ inches.

Chapter 16

CROSSING THE CONTINENT

Classic Concord Western stagecoach made by Abbot & Downing in 1874. This stagecoach was made for Sealy and Wright, who ran the route between Tucson and San Diego. It was then sold to Pioneer Stage Line and ran between Los Angeles and San Francisco. Virtually all of the stagecoach parts are original and have not been replaced or restored. The "red plush" upholstery over horsehair specified in the original order (in the Abbot & Downing Archives) is tattered but there. Of the approximately fifteen Western Concord stagecoaches surviving, it is one of the few not restored.

STAGECOACH

The start of stagecoach service from St. Louis to San Francisco via Tucson and Los Angeles on September 15, 1858, inaugurated a dramatic ability to cross the continent. This much longer southern route was forced on the stage line by Southern politicians who controlled the mail subsidy that the stage line needed in order to operate. This route averaged twenty-five days and cost $200. The Concord Coaches cost $1,500, featured leather "springs" that created a rocking effect, and weighed over 2,000 pounds. They carried up to twenty passengers crammed inside and on the roof on a first-come basis. These expensive coaches were initially used only on the better roads.

Steamboats with flat bottoms were the major means of transportation into the West before stagecoach routes were established. This illustration of the Yellowstone River is by Karl Bodmer, 1833.

"Clipper Ship *Sweepstakes*," lithograph by N. Currier, 1853. 16 by 23 inches. Clipper ships regularly competed for the fastest times from New York to San Francisco around Cape Horn. The establishment of regular stagecoach service across the country took away the clipper ship's passenger traffic.

Nine-passenger "Mud Wagon" Coach, the body painted red with yellow pinstriping and yellow and green lettering reading, *"Wells Fargo & Co./U.S. Mail/Sacramento/Folsom/and Placerville."* Originally used on this route through the gold area. The name *mud wagon* reflected its lighter weight compared to that of the Concord Coach, which could get bogged down on muddy roads of the West. This wagon was restored by M. P. Henderson in the early part of the 20th century in Stockton, California. It later appeared in various movies, including *Wells Fargo* in 1939.

The Establishment of the Overland Mail. President James Buchanan. Autograph Manuscript Signed [Washington, October 9, 1858].

"A glorious triump[h] for civilisation & the Union. Settlements will soon follow the course of the road & the East & the West will be bound together by a chain of living Americans which can never be broken."

On the verso, A. R. Corbin, Ulysses S. Grant's brother-in-law, wrote an explanation for Buchanan's statement:

"The within draft of the reply to the telegraphic despatch from John Butterfield (announcing the arrival of the first overland mail at St. Louis from San Francisco in 23 days and four hours) was written…October 9, 1858."

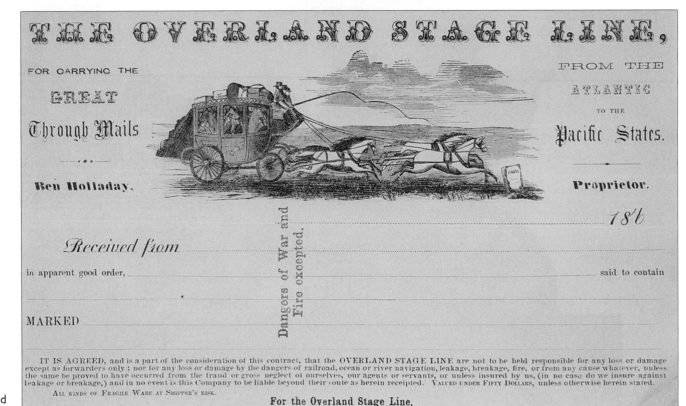

Receipt form for Ben Holladay's Overland Stage Line, 1860s.

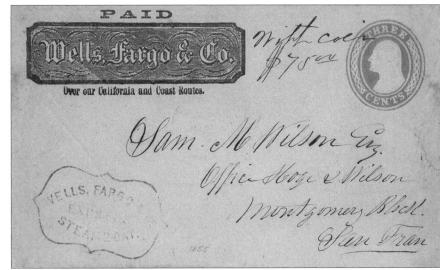

Envelopes bearing imprints of different companies that carried the mail across the country before the transcontinental railroad in 1869.

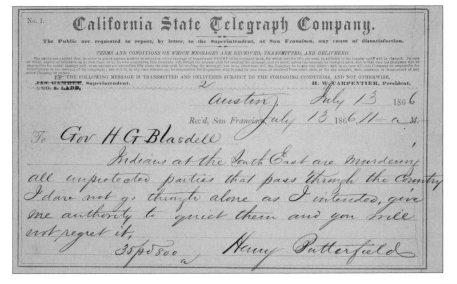

HENRY BUTTERFIELD. Autograph Telegram, received in San Francisco, July 13, 1866, from Austin, Texas, to Governor H. G. Blasdell.

"Indians at the South East are murdering all unprotected parties that pass through the country. I dare not go through alone as I intended, give me authority to quiet them and you will not regret it."

247

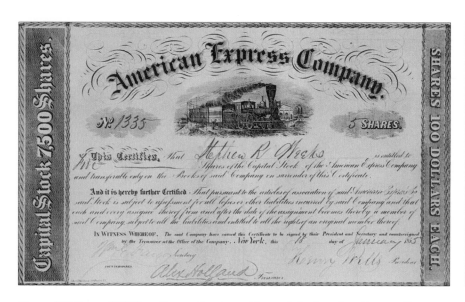

Henry Wells and William Fargo. Stock certificate of the American Express Company signed by the two founders, 1855.

Wells Fargo strong box in original condition with the original padlock. 20 inches long, 10 inches high, 12 inches wide.

BEN HOLLADAY, pioneer of the overland express business. Autograph Letter Signed [June 15, 1861]. To J. B. Judge.

"I must have $2,500 Monday morning for 30 or 60 days. I can look to no one but you to help me."

Colt 1849 pocket revolver, .31 caliber, issued to Wells Fargo.

Stage Robbed!

The up stage from Milton to Sonora was robbed at 2 P. M., Friday, August 3d, 1877, by three masked men, and Wells, Fargo & Co.'s box robbed of about $600 in silver coin and $200 in gold coin. Two of the robbers were armed with shot guns, and the other with a six shooter. A passenger gives the following description:

No. 1.—A stout, well built man; 5 feet 8 or 10 inches high; weight probably 160 pounds; short, thick hands; nails stubby and short; did not look like a working man's hands; one eye blue, the other white with a film over it, may be blind; spoke good English; wore an old dark coat; dark pants; black hat; common every-day boots; probably a middle aged man; black mask.

No. 2.—Slim man; weight probably 130 to 140 pounds; very small, delicate hands; the left hand covered with a nice fitting blue cotton glove, with border around the wrist; long slim fingers and nails; small feet; fine, very high heeled boots; heels standing well under; blue eyes; wore rust colored pants or overalls; blue cotton jumper; did considerable talking; voice smooth and pleasant; used good English and no profanity.

No. 3.—Did not speak; smallest man of the three; fine high heeled boots; foot short and stubby; hands dark, as a Mexican; wore rather high black hat with black cord and two small tassels. Armed with pistol.

☞ There is a liberal reward offered by the State and Wells, Fargo & Co. for such offenders. For particulars see Wells, Fargo & Co.'s

"STANDING REWARD"

Posters of March 1st, 1876.

J. B. HUME,

Special Officer Wells, Fargo & Co.

Stockton, August 15th, 1877.

[Don't post this but hand to officers.]

[Agents of WELLS, FARGO & CO. will please place this in the hands of local Officers and Business Men, and preserve a copy in Office. ☞ DO NOT POST. ☜]

$1200 REWARD.

ARREST STAGE ROBBERS.

The stage from Sonora, Tuolumne Co., to Milton, Calaveras Co., was stopped by two men, armed with shot guns, about 5 o'clock Monday morning, February 2nd, 1885, at a point about four miles east from Copperopolis. They broke open the iron safe in the stage, and rifled Wells, Fargo & Co's Express of Coin and Gold Dust, valued at about $2,000. Both men are believed to be Americans; the taller one speaks fair Spanish.

There is a liberal reward offered by the State and Wells, Fargo & Co., for the arrest and conviction of each offender. For particulars, see Wells, Fargo & Co's "Standing Reward" poster of March 1st, 1877.

Among the Treasure taken are the following described articles:

1 Sealed Bag, addressed D. Meyer, San Francisco, containing one lot of 2oz. and $2. amalgam, value $17.50; one lot 5oz. Gold pounded out of quartz, value $18 per oz; one lot 1oz. and $11.25 Placer Gold; one lot 12oz. Gold pounded out of quartz, value $18.50 per oz.; and about $18 in mixed Gold.

1 Sealed Bag, addressed to Selby Smelting & L. Co., San Francisco, containing one piece Retorted Gold, 38 oz.

1 Sealed Bag, addressed to Wells Fargo & Co's Bank, San Francisco, value $160.—No other description.

1 Sealed Bag, addressed to Bank of California, S. F., value $20.—No other description.

Also, Sundry Packages, etc., of Coin, aggregating $694.20, and $35 Currency.

Parties making arrest of, or obtaining clue to said robbers, will please communicate by wire with B. K. Thorne, Sheriff Calaveras County, San Andreas, or with the undersigned, at San Francisco.

Gold Dust Buyers, Bankers and Assayers are especially requested to keep a sharp lookout. Any person giving the undersigned information that leads to the arrest and conviction of robber or recovery of treasure will be suitably rewarded.

JAMES B. HUME,

Special Officer W. F. & Co.

San Francisco, February 11, 1885.

Stockton, California, August 15, 1877.   **San Francisco,** February 11, 1885.

Double barrel shotgun with an inlaid badge, *"Wells Fargo & Co Stage Depot."*

PONY EXPRESS

The Pony Express was romantic from the first day riders headed east from San Francisco and west from St. Joseph, Missouri, on April 3, 1860. Crowds in both cities realized the historical significance of the start of this ten-day mail service across the central route of the continent that was fifteen days faster than the Overland Stagecoach, which went by a much longer southern route.

The approximately 1,800-mile route had way stations about every ten miles, where riders changed horses. In its eighteen months of operation, before staggering costs, lack of a government mail subsidy, and the telegraph put it out of business, the Pony Express carried 34,753 pieces of mail.

A former Pony Express rider, Walter Crowninshield, wrote from Dayton, Nevada, in 1885:

"[T]o give you a history of the Pony Express from its inception with its incidents, accidents and adventures, even those only with which I was acquainted would fill a book.... Yet it is well worth preserving. If you should attempt it I hope you will do it in a more reliable manner than was done some years ago in a sketch that I saw in 'Harper's Monthly.' The author made us ride each horse sixty miles without changing. I did not care for myself but sympathized with the poor horses.

"In 1858, Buchanan, then president, sent an army to Salt Lake. General Floyd was Secretary of War and gave a contract to forward army supplies to Messrs. Russel and Majors, one of them being the relative of the Secretary. Of course they made a few millions out of the contract and as the war proved a fiasco they made a few more by buying the army equipment for little or nothing and selling to the 'saints' at a high figure.... What has that to do with the Pony Express? A great deal. In 1858 a daily mail contract was lett by the superintendent to take the mail overland by stage. It was taken by the so-called 'ox bow' route — down through lower California, Arizona, etc. and took something over thirty days.... Russell and Majors saw at once that the time could be beaten by at least ten days on this central route but the 'powers that be' in Washington did not believe it could get over the mountains in winter. To prove that it could, they...started the Pony Express as their own venture in the spring of 1860. Showing beyond a doubt that ten days could be saved on this route, summer or winter. Meanwhile Lincoln was elected letting out Mr. Floyd and his friends but the fact had been demonstrated and the Overland Stage was removed from the southern to the central route.

"The 'pony' had become too great a pet on the Pacific Coast to be dropped and with some assistance from the government was continued until the telegraph was finished in the fall of 1861 when the famous 'little horse' was killed by its lightening. The riders rode from 50 to 70 miles each four trips a week, two each way, using from four to six horses each — that is changing every ten or fifteen miles according to stations, water, etc. On Lincoln's election, 1860 we made the trip between the telegraph at St. Jo, Mississippi and Carson City, Nevada in five days, eighteen hours. Our quickest trip having double relief, that is an extra horse midway between stations.... We truly saw some rough times between the Indians and the jealous Mormons."

Letter sent from San Francisco via Pony Express to New York, with the original printed envelope of Wells Fargo & Co., with ten-cent U.S. postage seal, and one-dollar Pony Express stamp. It has cancellations at San Francisco, September 5, 1861, and Atchison, Kansas, October 9, 1861. The long time it took this letter to arrive is explained by the "MISSENT & FORWARDED" stamp.

Woodcut showing a Pony Express rider, undated [late 19th century]. 40½ by 27½ inches.

Two-dollar Pony Express stamp on an envelope of a letter sent from San Francisco, May 25, 1860, arriving in St. Joseph, Missouri, June 6. The oval Pony Express cancellation is in the upper center.

One-dollar Pony Express stamp sent from San Francisco, August 15, 1861, to New York City.

TELEGRAPH

At the start of the Civil War, there was a strong commercial incentive to construct a telegraph line across the western plains, linking the two coasts. Many companies, however, believed the line would be impossible to build and maintain. In June 1860, Congress passed and President James Buchanan signed *An Act to Facilitate Communication Between the Atlantic and Pacific States by Electric Telegraph* and authorized the secretary of the treasury to advertise for builders of the line, which was to be completed within two years. Hiram Sibley, the only bidder, then undertook on the construction of the line on his own, running it from Missouri to San Francisco, and completing it to the government's satisfaction in 1861. The Pacific Telegraph Company had been organized for the purpose of building the eastern section of the line from Omaha to Salt Lake City. Sibley sent Jeptha H. Wade to California, where he consolidated the small local companies into the California State Telegraph Company. This entity then organized the Overland Telegraph Company, which handled construction eastward from Carson City, Nevada, joining the existing California lines to the Pacific Telegraph Company.

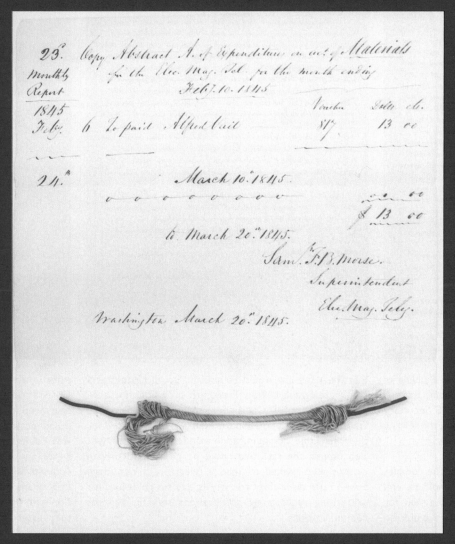

A section of the copper wire from Morse's first telegraph line, seven inches in length, about five inches of it wrapped in cotton insulation, together with an explanatory note by William Penn Vail:

"Piece of the wire used by Prof. Morse and Alfred Vail, in the 1st trial of the Magnetic Telegraph, over a long wire, on Jan. 6th, 1838, at Speedwell, Morris County, New Jersey. Length of wire used was three miles."

In New York, on September 2, 1837, Alfred Vail saw Morse give a demonstration of his "electronic telegraph" over one third of a mile of wire coiled around a room. Fascinated, he *"persuaded his father and brother at Speedwell to help him provide Morse with all the necessary assistance…advice, a workshop with tools and the money to perfect the telegraph…. On September 23…an agreement was signed between Morse and Alfred in which the latter promised to construct by January 1, 1838, 'at his own proper cost and expense' a model of the telegraph to exhibit before officials in Washington. The Vails were also to pay for all incidental expenses including the cost of the patent. In return Alfred [and his brother George, as silent partner, would received one fourth of the rights]. At about the same time, Dr. Leonard Gale became a partner with another one-fourth interest. That left Morse with one-half rights and an agreement that legally entitled him to the major share of the credit.'"*

The Federal Government Approves the Building of the Telegraph "Between the Atlantic and Pacific States." Document Signed, November 11, 1861, by U.S. Secretary of Treasury Salmon P. Chase and Hiram Sibley, the leading American promoter of the telegraph industry.

In this historic document, dated shortly after the completion of the line, the federal government upheld its end of the deal, promising to pay Sibley $40,000 a year for the priority use of the line for ten years, with the proviso that the same line would be available to all citizens at a regular telegraph charge. There are provisions for connecting military bases, and complimentary service to the Smithsonian Institution and the National Observatory for their scientific communication needs. The government also capped the rate that could be charged to private citizens who wished to send a telegraph at not more than $3 per dispatch of ten words, and set guidelines for prioritizing requests by corporations sending business communications.

After Hiram Sibley formed an association with Ezra Cornell to found the Western Union Telegraph Company, chartered in 1856, with Sibley as president for ten years, he advocated a transcontinental telegraph line. When it was completed, the telegraph became one of the most important factors in the development of the social and commercial life of America. It not only ended the usefulness of the Pony Express, but also facilitated communication with the army's western forces and generally opened the western frontier to huge potential growth.

TRANSCONTINENTAL RAILROAD

The dream of a transcontinental railroad stirred the imaginations of many Americans during the early part of the 19th century. Merchants interested in Pacific trade, gold seekers, and people simply seeking a new home in the West all yearned for a better way of reaching the Pacific Coast. As early as 1838, the daguerreotypist John Plumbe had petitioned Congress to fund a transcontinental railroad route survey, but to no avail. Three surveying parties were sent out by the government in 1853–1854 to determine the best route to the Pacific. Each of the proposed routes — the northern, the central, and the southern — had the strong support of the politicians representing the eastern starting points. Stephen A. Douglas of Illinois favored the northern route, Thomas Hart Benton of Missouri the central, and Jefferson Davis, then the secretary of war, the southern. It became a purely sectional issue.

The Civil War settled the selection process and in 1862 Lincoln signed the Pacific Railway Act, the first step toward a transcontinental railroad.

Work began in the West by the Central Pacific Railroad, which had discovered the work ethic of the large population of Chinese immigrants in San Francisco and hired them to build the railroad across the Sierras. In the East the Union Pacific hired mostly Civil War veterans, many of them Irish, to build the route across the plains.

On May 10, 1869, the two lines met at Promontory, Utah. Two years later it was possible to cross the continent in six days.

The three competing railroad surveys of northern, central, and southern routes were published in 1855–1860 in thirteen volumes. Profusely illustrated with maps, colored lithographed plates, profiles, and drawings, they are the most important and massive compilation of exploration reports and data about the Transmississippi West published in the era of exploration. The Pacific Railroad survey in two years increased the contemporary knowledge of the geography, topography, geology, and natural history of the West by a quantum leap. The illustrative material (engraved and lithographed views, specimens of birds, fish, and other animals, etc.) is of the highest quality. The project represents the greatest printing of illustrative material undertaken in the United States up to that time.

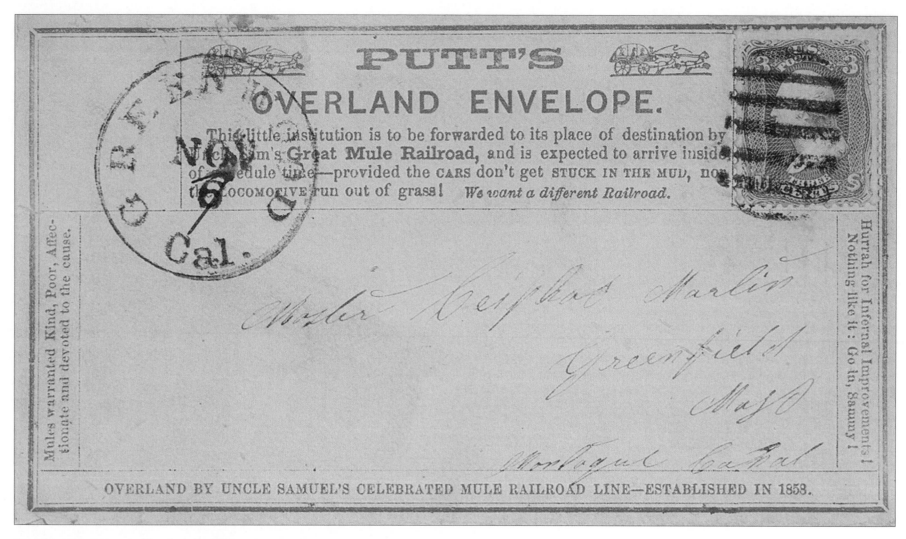

Envelope used for overland mail, 1858, with an imprint urging a transcontinental railroad:

"This little institution is to be forwarded to its place of destination by Uncle Sam's Great Mule Railroad, and is expected to arrive inside of schedule time — provided the cars don't get stuck in the mud, nor locomotive run out of grass! We want a different railroad."

The first proposal for a transcontinental railroad. Asa Whitney, *A Project for a Railroad to the Pacific...*, New York, 1849. He addressed the preface, *To the people of the United States.*

"For yourselves, for your children, for your country, for the destitute over population of Europe without food and without homes — for the heathen, the barbarian and the savage on who the blessings and lights of civilization and Christianity have never shown — for the Chinese who for the want of food must destroy their offspring — for the aged and infirmed who deliberately go out and die because custom, education and duty will not permit them to consume the food required to sustain the more youthful vigorous and useful — and for all the human family and not for myself do I ask you to examine this subject, read and examine it.... I do consider this subject of vast and vital importance to the many interests and objects I have enumerated and I do hope for those interests, for the glory of our country and for the preservation of our union to the Pacific that the whole subject may be examined by the people. There is no time for delay for the land the only means will soon be no longer available.... Will you allow me to take these wastelands and from their settlement build this great thoroughfare for all mankind, the construction of which can not under any plan advance faster than the settlement of the country on its line? By connecting the two together the facilities which the road would afford for settlement would furnish means and facilities for the advancement of the work quite as rapidly as is possible from any other source or means."

A

PROJECT

FOR

A RAILROAD TO THE PACIFIC.

BY ASA WHITNEY, OF NEW YORK.

WITH REPORTS OF COMMITTEES OF CONGRESS, RESOLUTIONS OF STATE
LEGISLATURES, ETC., WITH OTHER FACTS RELATING THERETO.

NEW YORK:
PRINTED BY GEORGE W. WOOD, NO. 15 SPRUCE STREET.
1849.

"Central Pacific Railroad Bloomer Cut 63 Feet Deep."

"Central Pacific Railroad, Cape Horn."

257

Leland Stanford's certification that the Central Pacific Railroad has completed the first ninety-two miles of track in its historic journey to meet the Union Pacific at Ogden, Utah, three years later. Document Signed, Sacramento, December 18, 1866.

"[I]n accordance with…the Act of Congress, entitled 'An Act to aid in the Construction of a railroad and telegraph line from the Missouri River to the Pacific Ocean….' Said Company is authorised to issue its bonds to the extent of One hundred miles in advance of a continuous completed line of construction… ($8.422.000)."

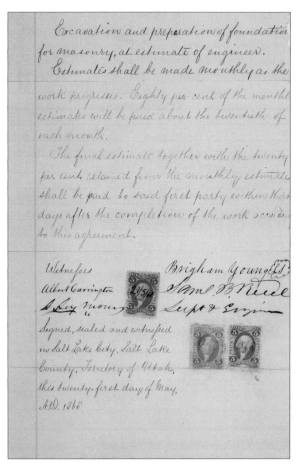

JACK CASEMENT, chief of construction for the Union Pacific Railroad. Autograph Letter Signed, Cheyenne, April 29, 1868. To his wife:

"I came from the end of track this evening.... We have got the track clear over the Black Hills and hope now to push along three miles per day. The Indians shot two conductors at Sidney today. They scalped one of them; they will probably both die."

Brigham Young's contract with the Union Pacific Railroad to construct the transcontinental railroad around Salt Lake. Document Signed, Salt Lake City, May 20, 1868.

"East End of Tunnel, Weber Canon."

When Brigham Young signed this document, his Mormon domain was shrinking. One of the signs of the fading frontier was the approach of the transcontinental railroad. Newell Bringhurst discusses Young's role in the railroad's development in *Brigham Young and the Expanding American Frontier*:

"As with mining, Young viewed this development with mixed feelings of hope and anxiety. On the one hand, he welcomed the railroad. As early as 1853, he had petitioned Congress for the construction of a transcontinental railroad to link the Great Basin with the East Coast, making it easier for East Coast-European Mormons to migrate west. Young was so anxious for a transcontinental railroad that he had paid the entire cost of the first two-year survey made by the Union Pacific Railroad prior to actual construction. And he attempted to influence the proposed route by recommending its construction along the North Platt, over the hills to the Sweetwater, to South Pass, and from that point to the Green River, and ultimately to Echo Canyon down the Weber River into the Great Basin. In the end, Young's proposal was almost identical to the actual route followed by the Union Pacific. By 1868, as the railroad reached present-day Wyoming, Young secured a contract to grade, bridge, and tunnel for the Union Pacific and enlisted the services of several thousand Mormon workers. The Mormon leader viewed the contract a godsend for helping to pull the region out of a severe economic slump...."

"Finally, on May 10, 1869, construction on the transcontinental railroad was completed.... Brigham Young wasted little time utilizing the railroad for the benefit of himself and his followers. He organized his own enterprise, the Utah Central Railroad Company, which connected Salt Lake City with Ogden and the transcontinental route. Completion of this line in January, 1870, meant that the days of Mormon pioneer travel across the plains by wagon, horseback, or on foot were over forever.... Young also pushed the building of additional railroad lines, running both south of Salt Lake and north of Ogden, designed to establish closer transportation links throughout the territory. Although the transcontinental railroad benefited the Mormons, Young worried about its negative effects. There was an increased influx of non-Mormons into the Great Basin, which forced the Mormons to confront more and more a non-Mormon population whose practices and beliefs ran counter to their own. The railroad also contributed to increased dissension within the ranks of Mormonism itself."

"Citadel Rock, Green River Valley" from Ferdinand Hayden's *Sun Pictures of Rocky Mountain Scenery...Containing...Photographic Views Along the Line of the Pacific Railroad*, 1870. This photograph by Andrew J. Russell illustrates the Union Pacific Railroad's method of erecting temporary bridges out of timber, shown on the right with the locomotive crossing it, while on the left the time-consuming job of building a permanent bridge of stone goes on.

Andrew J. Russell, *The Great West Illustrated in a Series of Photographic Views Across the Continent; Taken Along the Line of the Union Pacific Railroad, West from Omaha, Nebraska* [New York: Published by the Authority of the Union Pacific Railroad Company, 1869]. Fifty original albumen photographs depicting scenes along the railroad.

A legendary rarity among photographic books on the West, *The Great West Illustrated* contains some of the earliest and most beautiful photographs of the 19th-century western landscape. These images document the great project of the transcontinental railroad, including scenes of dramatic rock formations, coal mining towns, railroad engines, bridges, Laramie, Salt Lake City, the Mormon Tabernacle, Brigham Young's house, a Mormon family, and the like.

In 1868, the Union Pacific called on Andrew J. Russell to take photographs of their part of the line. During three trips on the railroad route (one in 1868 and two in 1869), Russell was able to produce the present remarkable photographs of bridges, locomotives, rocky landscapes, and mining towns.

This elaborate photographic book was evidently issued in a very small edition, for distribution to the prominent men who helped finance the transcontinental railroad. Probably fewer than a dozen copies exist today, and most of these are in institutional collections.

"Supply Trains."

"Dale Creek Bridge, From Above."

Buffalo hunters were employed by the railroad advancing west to feed the work crews. Typical equipment illustrated against a large buffalo hide are skinning knives, sled, snowshoes, buffalo skin winter mittens and Sharps, Spencer, and Winchester rifles.

The Golden Spike ceremony joining the Central Pacific and the Union Pacific Railroads, Promontory, Utah, 1869. Photo by Savage & Ottinger, Salt Lake City.

Executives of the Union Pacific gather at Promontory, Utah, for the joining of the east and west rails, 1869. Photo by A. J. Russell.

"The Route to California. Truckee River, Sierra Nevada." Lithograph, Currier & Ives, 1871. 8 by 12 inches.

"Through to the Pacific." Lithograph, Currier & Ives, 1872. 8 by 12 inches.

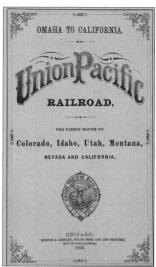

Omaha to California. The Union Pacific Railroad's schedule, 1868.

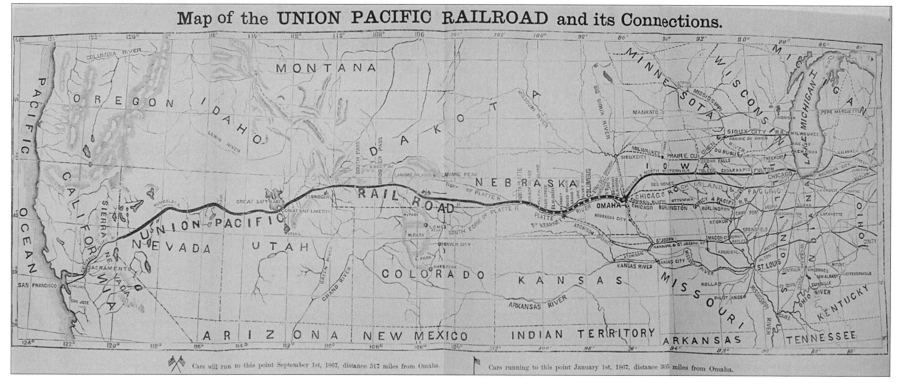

An 1867 map of the Union Pacific route to the Pacific.

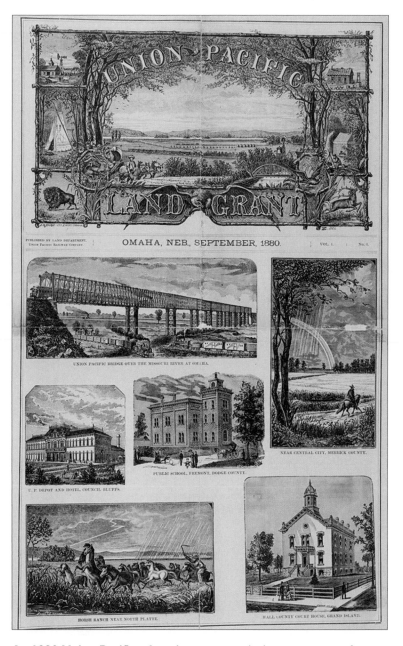

NORTHERN PACIFIC RAILROAD
AND
Benton Line Steamers.

JOINT THROUGH FREIGHT TARIFF
Via BISMARCK, D. T.
ALSO SPECIAL RATES TO BISMARCK.
— Taking Effect April 1st, 1878. —

FROM ST. PAUL, MINNEAPOLIS or DULUTH to HELENA, M. T.

Groceries and all Heavy Goods,	$3.70 per 100 lbs.
Dry Goods & Knock-down Furniture, and medium bulky goods,	4.70 " "
Household Goods, Furniture, Carriages, &c.,	5.70 " "

FROM ST. PAUL, MINNEAPOLIS AND DULUTH TO	Per 100 lbs. 1st Class.	Per 100 lbs. 2d Class.	Per 100 lbs. 3d Class.	Per 100 lbs. 4th Class.	Rates of Insurance on River, Per $100 Valua'n.
Standing Rock,	1.50	1.40	1.30	1.20	.25
Fort Rice,	1.50	1.40	1.30	1.20	.25
Fort Stevenson,	1.50	1.40	1.30	1.20	.25
Fort Buford,	1.70	1.60	1.50	1.40	.50
Fort Peck,	2.00	1.90	1.80	1.70	.50
Carroll,	2.00	2.00	1.90	1.80	.50
Cow Island,	2.00	2.00	1.90	1.80	.50
Fort Benton,	2.00	2.00	2.00	1.95	.75

All goods via the above Line, and for the above points, should be marked } **BENTON LINE.**

Shippers desiring River Insurance should send Duplicate Bills of Lading to St. Paul Fire and Marine Insurance Company, St. Paul, Minn., or H. I. Bodley & Co., St. Louis, Mo.

Freight consigned to Deadwood, St. Paul to Bismarck. }	Regardless of classification, $1.00 per 100 lbs. And in car load lots, - - .80 " " "			
Local, St. Paul, Minneapolis & Duluth, to Bismarck.	1.25	1.20	1.10	1.05
do. In Car Load lots, to one consignee,	1.00	1.00	1.00	1.00

The Northern Pacific Railroad Company will give Through Rates and Bills of Lading in connection with the Northwestern Express, Stage and Transportation Company, to Deadwood. Also Through Bills of Lading, via Benton Line, to Helena, M. T.

H. E. SARGENT,
General Manager, N. P. R. R., ST. PAUL.

G. G. SANBORN,
Gen'l Frt. Agent, N. P. R. R., ST. PAUL.

T. C. POWER,
Gen'l Manager, Benton Line Steamers, 83 Market Street, CHICAGO.

The transcontinental route of the Northern Pacific Railroad opened settlement on the Northern Prairies, bringing European emigrants to buy the railroad's land and use its rails.

An 1880 Union Pacific advertisement extols the opportunities for new settlers of the railroad's land grants.

Chapter 17

PROSPECTING, SETTLING, AND WONDERMENT

"Prospecting Outfit," photo by C. S. Fly, Tombstone, 1880s.

PROSPECTING

Prospectors scoured the West hoping to find another California gold field. Discoveries from Colorado, Idaho, Montana, Nevada, South Dakota, and, finally, Alaska and the Klondike spurred the settlement of the West as the suppliers to the prospectors moved to the areas of new discoveries, along with merchants, farmers, and all the other people needed to form communities.

C. M. Clark, *A Trip to Pike's Peak and Notes by the Way, with Numerous Illustrations…*, 1861. An account of the Colorado gold rush.

In 1860, Clark became part of the Colorado gold rush, but prospected there without success. He described in detail the frontier towns, which he found distastefully full of gambling, crime, and bad language. His narrative is considered to be an authentic and truthful account of life and travel in Colorado of the day.

The Colorado gold rush began slowly in 1859 with the discovery of gold in what would become Denver. As in California, there was an immediate demand for coinage to eliminate arguments over the fineness and quality of gold; in 1860 Clark, Gruber & Co. minted this $10 coin.

A TRIP

TO

PIKE'S PEAK

AND

NOTES BY THE WAY,

WITH

NUMEROUS ILLUSTRATIONS:

BEING DESCRIPTIVE OF INCIDENTS AND ACCIDENTS THAT ATTENDED THE PIL-
GRIMAGE; OF THE COUNTRY THROUGH KANSAS AND NEBRASKA;
ROCKY MOUNTAINS; MINING REGIONS; MINING
OPERATIONS, ETC., ETC.

By C. M. CLARK, M. D.

"There is a tide in the affairs of men,
That, taken at the flood, leads on
To———."—*Shakspeare.*

Give me facts, for I am no visionary."

CHICAGO:
S. P. ROUNDS' STEAM BOOK AND JOB PRINTING HOUSE, 46 STATE STREET.
1861.

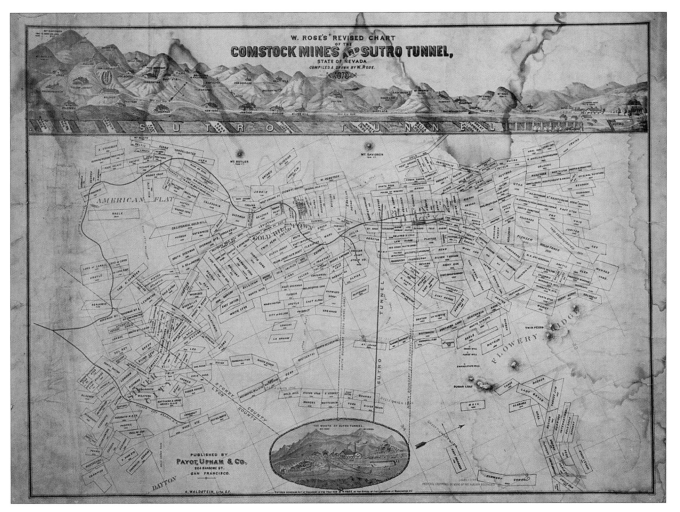

A large map of the Comstock Lode and Sutro Tunnel, illustrating the complex Nevada silver mine, October 1878. The map shows more than 50 mining properties generally running from north to south over a span of about eight miles. At the top is a cross-section of the Sutro Tunnel, which was built to drain water from the mines. Virginia City stood on the mine sites concentrated at center of the right side of the chart; Ophir, the original bonanza mine, was sunk in the very middle of the town. The Comstock Lode was the single greatest find in the country.

Poster advertising the Idaho Steam Packet Company's service to Fort Benton on the Missouri, *ca.* 1865.

The discovery of gold in Montana and Idaho in the mid-1860s greatly stimulated steamboating on the Missouri River. Steamboats were able to proceed as far up the river as Fort Benton, Montana, some 2,300 miles from St. Louis. 22 by 10½ inches.

By 1862, Denver had witnessed the mass migration to Colorado of some 100,000 people between 1858 and 1860 that was triggered by the discovery of gold at the confluence of Cherry Creek and the South Platte River, followed by a dramatic exodus. Only one out of three stayed, as reflected in the census of 1860, which recorded 34,277 residents. Although the population had dropped precipitously, it was by no means snuffed out. Denver in 1862, as described by "Harry" in his letters, was a lively city at its incipience, bubbling with political, judicial, and social intrigue, coping with law and order, and dealing with dispossessed Arapaho and Cheyenne.

"Harry" was a young lawyer, who had come to Denver with his father, a judge traveling the circuit, holding court in Boulder and Colorado City. He wrote about many aspects of life in Colorado:

"Ladies, in such a country as this, unless they keep house, have very little to do, unless it is to gossip. They say Denver is famous for that. Ladies at the hotel seem to be pretty well ennui-ed. There is one beautiful virgin, i.e. mantrap, — of forty summers, who sits at dinner at the next table to us, who is perfectly and bewitchingly excruciating…. I might have fallen in love by this time, but unfortunately I sit with my back to her…. A great many trains are arriving from the States, and they have curious mottoes on their wagon covers. Sometimes they write on it 'Pikes Peak or bust' and if they fail when they go back they put the 'ed' on and make it 'busted'…. Times are brightening, emigration is coming in, families are moving here to remain, business is increasing. I have commenced to earn something, and everybody seems to be in good spirits generally…. A party of Arapahoes came in and encamped

on the Platte. I walked down there in the afternoon and examined their lodges, which are of skins. I did not enter them, although they would have considered it an honor, for very good reasons. The little youngsters are generally in a state of nudity. One of them who could just toddle had an old piece of calico, which he used to wrap around him Indian style. He had not quite learnt the knack, but he managed to get it around him with all the grace…of a big Injun…. Mr Colly, the Indian agent has returned from the Reservation of the Arapahoes and Cheyennes. This war party that is here, he says are Blackfeet, and not Arapahoes. The people begin to fear trouble from the Utes, for these war parties of Arapahoes, every time they have a fight with the Utes, whether they are victorious or not, make straight for some village or city of the whites, and virtually place themselves under our protection. As we have nothing to do with their wars, this running back to us, makes the Utes think us as enemies, and as a consequence trouble is expected…. The citizens are complaining of the city tax now, which is double that of the county. But we need as many improvements that it is necessary. A bridge over the Platte that was swept away last spring, is to be rebuilt, a fire engine is to be bought."

Adolph Sutro proposed to solve the problem of flooding in the Comstock Mines by digging a tunnel four miles from the Carson River to the Comstock Mines, 1,650 feet below the surface. The tunnel took seven years to complete and by that time, 1878, the Comstock was much deeper than 1,650 feet. Nevertheless, Sutro's project did mean that pumps had to raise water only to its level and it would pour downhill to the river.

SETTLING THE WEST

Settlements followed the westward movement, though not in geographic sequence, as the West Coast had many settlements before the Prairies attracted homesteaders. Communities were important, and as soon as possible, churches and schools were established, as well as business to support local activities. Politicians developed out of the communities to bring order and planning for the future.

The Homestead Act of 1862 allowed any adult citizen to claim 160 acres of public land for $10. At the end of five years, if he had not left it for more than six months, it was his.

In 1889, under tremendous pressure from would-be settlers, the government opened two million acres of what had been Indian Territory in Oklahoma. By 1907, millions more acres had been opened, and settlers then occupied all of the United States.

"The Pioneer's Home on the Western Frontier." Lithograph by Currier & Ives, 1867. 25 by 31 inches.

Thomas Jefferson President of the United States of America,

TO ALL TO WHOM THESE PRESENTS SHALL COME, GREETING:

Know Ye, That *Benjamin Ruffner of Shenandoah County Virginia* having deposited in the Treasury a certificate of the Register of the Land-office at *Chilicothe* whereby it appears that *he has made full payment for the West Half* of *Section number Twelve in Township number Fifteen in Range number Eighteen* of the Lands directed to be sold at *Chilicothe* by the act of Congress, entitled "An act providing for the sale of the Lands of the United States in the Territory north-west of the Ohio, and above the mouth of Kentucky river," and of the acts amendatory of the same, **There is granted,** by the United States, unto the said *Benjamin Ruffner the Half* lot or section of land above described: **To have and to hold** the said *Half* lot or section of land, with the appurtenances, unto the said *Benjamin Ruffner his* heirs and assigns forever.

In testimony whereof, I have caused these Letters to be made **Patent,** and the Seal of the United States to be hereunto affixed.

Given under my Hand at the City of Washington, the *Sixth* day of *March* in the year of our Lord one thousand eight hundred and *Six* and of the Independence of the United States of America, the *Thirtieth*

BY THE PRESIDENT,

Thomas Jefferson

James Madison Secretary of State.

As commissioner of the General Land Office, Thomas A. Hendricks in 1856 wrote, *"All the public lands which may be in market and subject to private entry at $1.25 on which there may be no settlement, may be located by any party with military bounty warrants. Second — Ample notice through the public prints will be given when the United States reserved sections, or railroad lands, will be offered at public sale. Third — No lands in the Territory of Nebraska have as yet been offered at public sale."*

Grant of land in "Lands of the United States" in the territory northwest of the Ohio, and above the mouth of the Kentucky River, 1806, signed by Jefferson as President and James Madison as secretary of state.

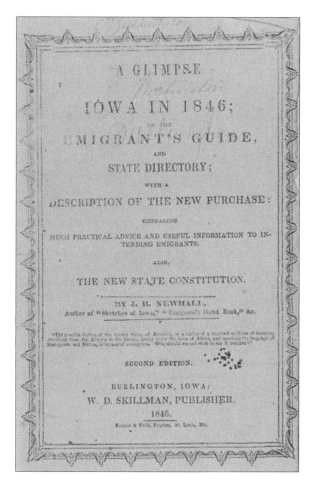

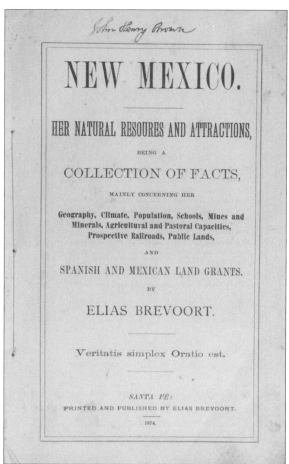

William Marin, an Irish immigrant, wrote from Washington County, Iowa, July 19, 1849, to a friend back home, *"I…am well pleased with the country and think that it is the [best] place for a free man that I have seen…. [Y]ou can suit yourselves in land of any kind either with improvements or no improvements can be for six dollars an acre and there is any quantity of unimproved land which can be had for one dollar and 25 cents per acre. There is thousands of acres of this last sort here covered with the best pasture from 8 to 36 inches long. It can soon make good hay and stock gets fat in summer. If a man in not able to buy this land he can go and improve on it till he is able to pay for it without any rent or tax and a man can get three bushels of corn for a day's work or one bushel and one half of wheat.*

"The State of Society here is good and a man of almost any profession can be suited."

Fort Dodge, Iowa, is described in a letter, 1864:

"Ten years ago there were no buildings in Fort Dodge except the Barracks that were occupied by soldiers, who held a garrison to defend the frontier against the Indians. Civilization has swept the frontier one or two hundred miles further west, & there is no garrison here now:… There are about 800 inhabitants in the village now & 1500 in the town…. Fort Dodge is destined, however, to be one of the largest places in N Western Iowa."

John B. Newhall, *A Glimpse of Iowa in 1846; or, the Emigrants Guide, and State Directory; with a Description of the New Purchase: Embracing Much Practical Advice and Useful Information to Intending Emigrants,* 1846.

New Mexico. *Her Natural Resoures [sic] and Attractions, Being a Collection of Facts, Mainly Concerning Her Geography, Climate, Population, Schools, Mines and Minerals, Agricultural and Pastoral Capacities, Prospective Railroads, Public Lands, and Spanish and Mexican Land Grants,* by Elias Brevoort, Santa Fe, 1874.

The Plan of Operations of the Immigrant Aid Company, 1854, encouraged immigrants to the Kansas Territory, declaring in its preface that "[i]ts duty is to organize immigration to the west and bring it into a system…. The immigrant suffers whenever he goes along into his new home…. All accounts agree that the region of Kansas is the most desirable part of America now open to the immigrant. It is accessible in seven days continuous travel from Boston. Its crops are very bountiful — its soil being well-adapted to the staples of Virginia and Kentucky and especially to the growth of hemp. In its eastern section the woodland and prairie land intermix in proportions very well adapted for the purposes of the settler. Its mineral resources, especially its coal in central and western parts are inexhaustible. A steamboat is already plying on the Kansas River and the territory has uninterrupted steamboat communication with New Orleans…. All the overland immigration in California and Oregon by any of the easier routes passes of necessity through its limits. Whatever roads are built westward must begin in this territory for it is here that the immigrant leaves the Missouri River. The demands for provisions and breadstuff made by immigrants proceeding to California as given to the inhabitants of the neighboring parts of Missouri a market at as good rates as they could have found in the Union. It is impossible that such a region should not fill up rapidly. The immigrant aid company proposes to give confidence to settlers by giving system to immigration."

THE

KANZAS REGION:

Forest, Prairie, Desert, Mountain, Vale, and River.

DESCRIPTIONS OF

SCENERY, CLIMATE, WILD PRODUCTIONS, CAPABILITIES OF
SOIL, AND COMMERCIAL RESOURCES;

INTERSPERSED WITH

INCIDENTS OF TRAVEL,

AND ANECDOTES ILLUSTRATIVE OF THE CHARACTER OF THE TRADERS AND
RED MEN; TO WHICH ARE ADDED

DIRECTIONS AS TO ROUTES, OUTFIT FOR THE PIONEER, AND
SKETCHES OF DESIRABLE LOCALITIES FOR
PRESENT SETTLEMENT.

BY MAX. GREENE.

"FOLLOW LOVE'S FOLDING STAR TO THE EVENING LAND."

NEW YORK:

FOWLER AND WELLS, PUBLISHERS,

308 BROADWAY.

BOSTON: } 142 Washington Street. } 1856. { PHILADELPHIA: { No. 231 Arch Street.

William Tecumseh Sherman, the Union general in the Civil War, had a practical military attitude towards those heading west. In January 1866, he responded to Colonel Bowen in Washington:

"I am…in receipt of the letter…endorsed by you…by the State of Minnesota for the establishment of a Line of Military Posts to Walla Walla Oregon…. [It] is judged both impracticable and unnecessary to guard the Whole Road by costly military posts, but rather to confine travel to one Road, and require emigrants to go in bodies sufficient for self protection. There will be no real danger in travelling from Minnesota to Fort Pierce but there to Virginia City some protection will be necessary. Were we to grant one half the regiments of the Territories, the National Congress would have to increase the Army far beyond any present estimate, and the cost would be beyond all estimates. The People on our Frontiers must conform to the national interests, instead of forcing us to cover them in their wandering propensities."

In a postscript, Sherman wrote, *"Petition re-enclosed."*

Max Greene, *The Kanzas Region: Forest, Prairie, Desert, Mountain, Vale, and River…,* 1856. An extensive work written at the beginning of the settlement of Kansas.

John Haddock set out with a few friends in September 1870 and spent several years traveling on the frontier. His *Journal of Life on the Frontier* contains hundreds of full-page pencil sketches recording his observations and experiences roaming the plains, ranging from a sketch of the town of Golden, Colorado, to scenes of buffalo hunting, roping and branding cattle, and fighting Indians. Many sketches of the interiors of frontier cabins as well as drawings of saloons and seemingly every other aspect of life on the frontier are also included.

"Home Sweet Home."

"The Hunters Camp."

Alfred E. Mathews, *Pencil Sketches of Colorado, Its Cities, Principal Towns and Mountain Scenery...,* 1866.

Mathews' spectacular lithographs of Colorado are among the most lavish of Western views; they depict mining towns and scenes. The artist came to Colorado in 1865. His goal was *"to represent that portion of the country to which interest is attached on account of the rich gold and silver mines; and, if possible, to give non-residents an idea of the beauty and grandeur of the natural scenery in the mountains."*

"Blake Street, Denver, Colorado."

"Denver, City of the Plains."

A Kansas Stock Sale in 1888, *"Terms — Seven Months Credit."*

"Bolles & Bradshaw Horseshoers — And General Blacksmiths."

Buffalo hide coat, *ca.* 1875–1880. After 1880, these coats became prohibitively expensive due to the dwindling buffalo herds. They were replaced by canvas coats with blanket liners.

Colt's first double action revolver, the Model 1877, .38 caliber Lightning.

280

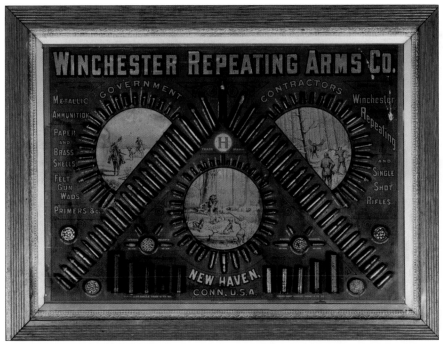

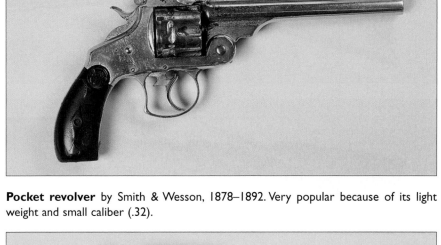

Pocket revolver by Smith & Wesson, 1878–1892. Very popular because of its light weight and small caliber (.32).

Large advertising board containing, under glass, original cartridges made by Winchester. 46½ by 35 inches.

Colt Double Action Model 1878 frontier revolver, .45 caliber.

Colt 1873 Frontier Six Shooter, single action, Winchester 44-40 center fire. The classic Western pistol.

The Winchester Henry Rifle was revolutionary with its 15-round magazine, lever action, and reliability. The .44 caliber Henry competed with the much larger caliber Spencer rifle.

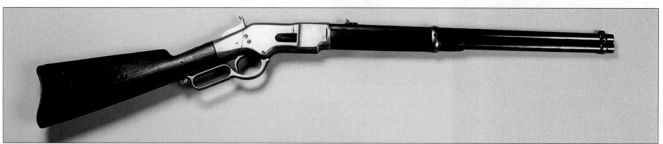

The Winchester Model 1866 Saddle Ring Carbine solved the problem of the Henry Rifle's fragile magazine tube and allowed easy loading through the side of the receiver.

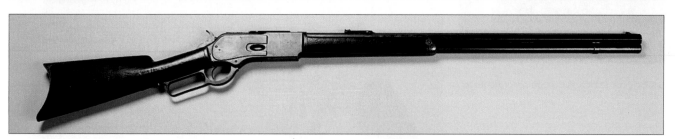

Winchester 1873 Rifle, .38 caliber.

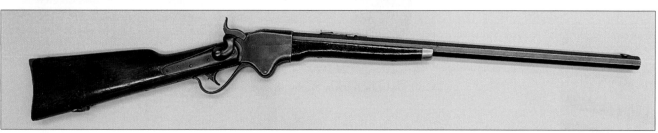

The Spencer Buffalo Rifle, created by many frontier gunsmiths from surplus Civil War Spencer rifles. They installed longer and heavier octagon barrels and other improvements for hunting on the plains. 1870s.

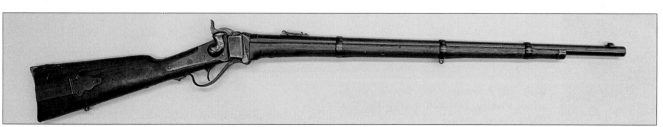

Sharps Model 1874 Military Rifle, reworked by Freund. 45/70 smooth bore or forager. Front sight made from an old coin.

NATURAL WONDERS: YELLOWSTONE

In June of 1871, Frederick Hayden set out to see the Yellowstone country for himself. During the two previous years expeditions had reported on the extraordinary natural wonders, and Hayden, who had established himself with his exhaustive report on his 1870 survey and was a great booster of the future of the West, received a $40,000 grant from Congress for the first official government explorations of Yellowstone.

Thomas Moran, a landscape painter, convinced Hayden to take him on the expedition, which also included the photographer W. H. Jackson. Moran helped the photographer with composition, and Jackson taught Moran how to use a camera. Together, they provided the images that helped an already active campaign to preserve Yellowstone as the first national park. On March 1, 1872, President Grant signed legislation making this area the first national park.

"Yellowstone National Park," a 1904 chromolithograph bird's-eye view of the park. 26 by 12 inches.

The Yellowstone National Park...
by F. V. Hayden. *Illustrated by Chromolithographic Reproductions of Watercolor Sketches,* by Thomas Moran..., Boston, L. Prang & Co., 1876. 15 chromolithographic reproductions of watercolor sketches, 14½ by 10 inches.

One of the great illustrated rarities of Western Americana, with Louis Prang's superb chromolithographic renderings of Thomas Moran's original watercolors of Yellowstone National Park. The illustrations were the first to adequately depict to the world the extraordinary scenes of the Yellowstone, and Moran's rendering of those natural wonders have long been acknowledged as the most skillful depiction of the park's glories. The book's chromolithographer, Louis Prang, was the greatest color printer of his day, and he declared this work to be his masterpiece. Certainly at the time of its production, in 1876, it was the most elaborate and successful work of mechanical color printing ever undertaken. The text was supplied by F. V. Hayden, who directed the geological survey of the park, and was head of U.S. Geological and Geographical survey of the territories.

"Tower Falls & Sulpher Mountain, Yellowstone."

"Great Fall of the Snake River."

THE CASTLE GEYSER, UPPER GEYSER BASIN, YELLOWSTONE NATIONAL PARK.

PRANG'S AMERICAN CHROMO BOSTON.

COPYRIGHT 1874 BY L.PRANG & C.

"Upper Geyser Basin, Yellowstone."

"**Valley of Babbling Waters, Southern Utah.**"

"Falls of the Yellowstone," photograph by W. H. Jackson, 1870s. 9½ by 7 inches. Jackson's photograph brought a sense of reality to western scenery; people were used to romantic paintings until his photographs, which also gave a sense of scale to landscape of unheard of proportions.

Abbot & Downing Nine-Passenger Open Coach, originally operating in Yellowstone National Park. This wagon was used in many major motion pictures including *Paint Your Wagon,* filmed in 1968.

Painting of the classic *Yosemite Valley Scene,* *ca.* 1880, unsigned. 26 by 15 inches.

Josiah Whitney's *The Yosemite Book; A Description of the Yosemite Valley and the Adjacent Region of the Sierra Nevada, and of the Big Trees of California…*, 1868.

An important photographically illustrated work, containing twenty-eight original albumen photographs, originally produced by Carleton T. Watkins in 1866.

"El Capitan and Cathedral Rock."

"The Vernal Falls."

John Muir, *The Mountains of California,* 1894. A vital figure in the growth of environmental consciousness, Muir's writings about the mountains of California and other wild parts of the West were instrumental in the movement for national parks and an appreciation of the value of preserving wilderness.

The pioneer environmentalist John Muir wrote in 1903 in *Our National Parks:*

"The tendency nowadays to wander in wildernesses is delightful to see. Thousands of tired, nerve-shaken, over-civilized people are beginning to find out that going to the mountains is going home, that wildness is a necessity and that mountain parks and reservations are useful not only as fountains of timber and irrigating rivers but as fountains of life. Awakening from the stupefying effects of the vice of over-industry and the deadly apathy of luxury they are trying as best they can to mix and enrich their own little ongoings with those of Nature and to get rid of rust and disease....*

"All the western mountains are still rich in wildness and by means of good roads are being brought nearer to civilization every year. To the sane and free it will hardly seem necessary to cross the continent in search of wild beauty, however easy the way, for they find it in abundance wherever they chance to be. Like Thoreau they see forests and orchards in patches of huckleberry brush and oceans in ponds and drops of dew. Few in these hot, dim, strenuous times are quite sane or free; choked with care like clocks full of dust, laboriously doing so much good and making so much money, — or so little, they are no longer good for themselves."

John Muir, *"Going to the Mountains is going home."*

Colored engraving by J. Smillie of Albert
Bierstadt's painting *The Rocky Mountains,*
1866. 29 by 18¾ inches.

Chapter 18

OUTLAWS AND LAWMEN

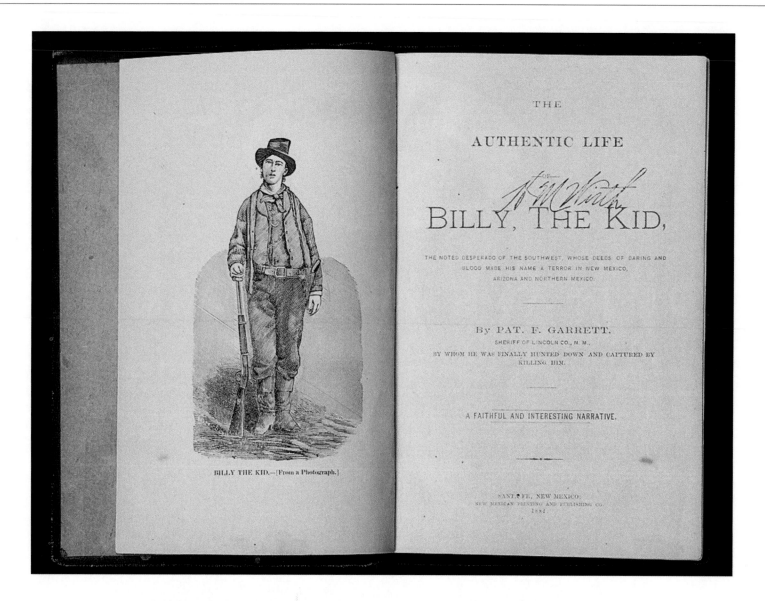

BILLY THE KID.—[From a Photograph.]

THE

AUTHENTIC LIFE

BILLY, THE KID,

THE NOTED DESPERADO OF THE SOUTHWEST, WHOSE DEEDS OF DARING AND
BLOOD MADE HIS NAME A TERROR IN NEW MEXICO,
ARIZONA AND NORTHERN MEXICO.

By PAT. F. GARRETT.

SHERIFF OF LINCOLN CO., N. M.,

BY WHOM HE WAS FINALLY HUNTED DOWN AND CAPTURED BY
KILLING HIM.

A FAITHFUL AND INTERESTING NARRATIVE.

SANTA FE, NEW MEXICO:
NEW MEXICAN PRINTING AND PUBLISHING CO.
1882

Pat Garrett, *The Authentic Life of Billy the Kid, the Noted Desperado of the Southwest, Whose Deeds of Daring and Blood Made His Name a Terror in New Mexico, Arizona, and Northern Mexico…,* Santa Fe, 1882. The most famous outlaw book, written by the man who killed Billy the Kid, was the beginning of a vast outpouring of literature on the outlaw.

The stories of the outlaws and gunfighters created by the media of the time and continuing into our present-day movies and books can make it difficult to distinguish historical facts from popular entertainment. The reality was certainly very violent, and human life was cheap to those who sought out gunfights and robberies.

Many of the outlaws and gunfighters began their careers during the Civil War, often as part of the Confederate guerrilla forces. As outlaws, the James brothers, as well as Cole Younger, employed tactics similar to those they'd used as guerilla fighters with Quantrell's Raiders: intelligence missions scouting robberies, establishing hideouts in advance, and maintaining the support of farmers. To many they represented the lost Confederate cause.

While cattle towns in Kansas attracted many gunfighters, and local businessmen hired other gunfighters as sheriffs and marshals, the mining camps and districts attracted those seeking to get rich quick with their guns rather than with picks and shovels.

Collecting in this area is fairly difficult. Letters by the famous gunfighters and outlaws are with few exceptions very rare as are the reward posters for the major figures. The pistols of this period can be obtained fairly quickly and at relatively reasonable costs. Although difficult to find, the newspapers of this time are the most reasonably priced artifacts of all.

Gunfighter's Fast Draw Bridgeport Rig with a Colt Single Action Army Revolver. .45 caliber. The hammer screw has been replaced with a large screw for a fast draw rig. This consists of a slotted spring steel clasp riveted to a large rectangular steel plate riveted to a brown leather belt. In addition to the manufacturer's name, PAT'D JAN 17 1882 is marked on this steel clasp. Manufactured and shipped in 1887.

PROCLAMATION
OF THE
GOVERNOR OF MISSOURI!
REWARDS
FOR THE ARREST OF
Express and Train Robbers.

STATE OF MISSOURI,
EXECUTIVE DEPARTMENT.

WHEREAS, It has been made known to me, as the Governor of the State of Missouri, that certain parties, whose names are to me unknown, have confederated and banded themselves together for the purpose of committing robberies and other depredations within this State; and

WHEREAS, Said parties did, on or about the Eighth day of October, 1879, stop a train near Glendale, in the county of Jackson, in said State, and, with force and violence, take, steal and carry away the money and other express matter being carried thereon; and

WHEREAS, On the fifteenth day of July 1881, said parties and their confederates did stop a train upon the line of the Chicago, Rock Island and Pacific Railroad, near Winston, in the County of Daviess, in said State, and, with force and violence, take, steal, and carry away the money and other express matter being carried thereon; and, in perpetration of the robbery last aforesaid, the parties engaged therein did kill and murder one WILLIAM WESTFALL, the conductor of the train, together with one JOHN McCULLOCH, who was at the time in the employ of said company, then on said train; and

WHEREAS, FRANK JAMES and JESSE W. JAMES stand indicted in the Circuit Court of said Daviess County, for the murder of JOHN W. SHEETS, and the parties engaged in the robberies and murders aforesaid have fled from justice and have absconded and secreted themselves; and

NOW, THEREFORE, in consideration of the premises, and in lieu of all other rewards heretofore offered for the arrest or conviction of the parties aforesaid, or either of them, by any person or corporation, I, THOMAS T. CRITTENDEN, Governor of the State of Missouri, do hereby offer a reward of five thousand dollars ($5,000.00) for the arrest and conviction of each person participating in either of the robberies or murders aforesaid, excepting the said FRANK JAMES and JESSE W. JAMES; and for the arrest and delivery of said

FRANK JAMES and JESSE W. JAMES,

and each or either of them, to the sheriff of said Daviess County, I hereby offer a reward of five thousand dollars, ($5,000.00,) and for the conviction of either of the parties last aforesaid of participation in either of the murders or robberies above mentioned, I hereby offer a further reward of five thousand dollars, ($5,000.00.)

IN TESTIMONY WHEREOF, I have hereunto set my hand and caused to be affixed the Great Seal of the State of Missouri. Done [SEAL.] at the City of Jefferson on this 28th day of July, A. D. 1881.

THOS. T. CRITTENDEN.

By the Governor:
MICH'L K. McGRATH, Sec'y of State.

BURCH & FERGUSON, STATE PRINTERS, JEFFERSON CITY, MO.

Reward poster for Jesse and Frank James, July 28, 1881.

Colt round barrel conversion .38 rim-fire caliber revolver believed to have been used by Jesse James in the historic James Gang holdup of the First National Bank of Northfield, Minnesota. Accompanied by a letter of provenance dated 1929:

"This genuine old Colt revolver was picked up on the floor of the First National Bank of Northfield Minn. when it was robbed in 1875 by the James Gang. Both Cole and Bob Younger identified this revolver as the property of Jessy [sic] James. It has been made into a .38 caliber metallic cartridge arm in later years as it was originally a powder and ball shooter. It is in perfect condition and was made during the Civil War as the engraving on the cylinder shows. This arm was picked up by Gil Whittier who was Deputy Sheriff of Dakota County at the time of the robbery. As to the validity of all this, the heirs of Mr. Whittier who still are in Minneapolis Minn. will be pleased to corroborate. Further, the present owner who was Junior Warden of Minnesota State Penitentiary at Stillwater Minn. from 1875 until 1883 will be glad to verify the above information. John Ryan."

Jesse James. Photograph taken after his assassination by the Ford brothers on April 3, 1882. A label affixed to the lower margin reads *"Jesse James/Born Feb. 1845, and Killed, St. Joseph."* The photograph was taken by local photographer R. G. Smith after James had been killed by members of his own gang for the $20,000 reward offered by the governor of Missouri. 4 by 5½ inches.

Frank James's playing cards.

Frank James spent several years in jail and had two trials, one for murder, the other for robbery, but managed to be acquitted in both cases. While awaiting his first trial he wrote to his wife from Gallaston, Missouri, in 1883, *"I think my Attys are taking things rather easy, perhaps if their precious time were in any danger they would be a little more hasty to act."*

After being acquitted in the murder trial he was transferred to the Huntsville jail in Alabama and in 1884 described to his wife and son his life in jail and his attempts to make bail.

"I eat breakfast at nine sometimes ten. I never get up before ten. I have buiscuits and steak for breakfast, and at two I have dinner, cabage sweet and white potatoes and frequently oyster soupe, at night I have bread and molasses and sometimes tea. I am getting plenty to eat I almost forgot to say I always have eggs at morning. I spend my time reading smoking and take a nap once and awhile, from night until bedtime which is from nine until eleven…. We have been trying to make arrangements to give bond but as yet have not succeeded… The amount fixed $5,000…well it will be better. Say nothing to anyone about this bond business if we fail to make it I do not want any one to know it."

Jesse James: The Life and Daring Adventures of This Bold Highwayman and Bank Robber, and His No Less Celebrated Brother, Frank James. Together with the Thrilling Exploits of the Younger Boys. Written by…(One Who Dare Not Now Disclose His Identity.) The Only Book Containing the Romantic Life of Jesse James and His Pretty Wife, Who Clung to Him to the Last! Philadelphia: Barclay & Co.

The chapters in this 1882 biography of Jesse James include "Life and Startling Adventures," "Jesse in Love — His Marriage," "Frank James Gets Married," A Seventeen Thousand Dollar Haul," "Escape of Frank and Jesse James," "The Class of People Who Befriended the Outlaws," "The Last Great Train Robbery," "The Younger Family," "The Tragic Death of Jesse James," "The Wife of Jesse James Tells Her Own Story," "Relics of Jesse James…," and "A Terror to His Followers as Well as to the Public at Large."

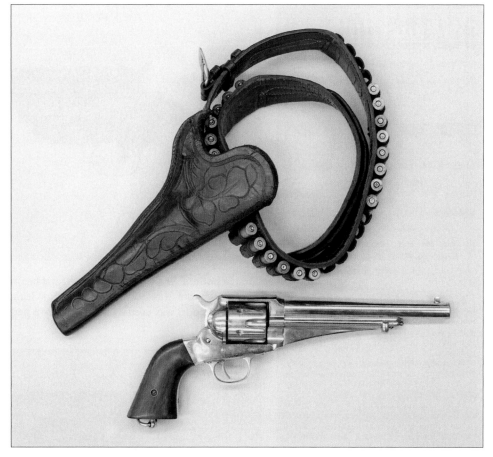

Remington Model 1875 single action Army Frontier Revolver, .44-40 Winchester center fire. Frank James used this model.

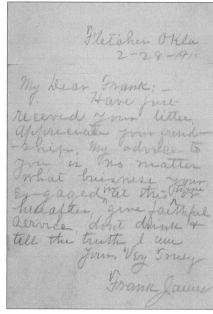

FRANK JAMES. Autograph Letter Signed, Oklahoma, February 28, no year.

"My advice to you is no matter what business you're engaged in at this time or thereafter, give faithful service, don't drink & tell the truth."

299

SAFE IN THE SADDLE.

The Train Robbers Baffle Their Pursuers.

Not the Slightest Trace of the Scoundrels.

The Story Told by One of Their Victims.

An Old Man Beaten and Robbed by Tramps.

New Jersey's Sensation---The Criminal Calendar.

Special Dispatch to the Globe-Democrat.

INDEPENDENCE, Mo., October 10.—There have been no new developments of interest in the Glendale express and train robbery to-day. Officers in large numbers are still scouring the country, and strong hopes of the speedy capture of the thieves are still entertained. The opinion that the gang was under the leadership of the notorious Jesse James is still very strong in this part of the county, as is also the suspicion that the entire gang were former chums of the James and Younger brothers, of this (Clay) and Lafayette Counties. The United States Express Company officials state that they have so far only discovered a loss of about $6,000. The search for the robbers will be diligently kept up, and the officers, as well as the people, are determined that this outrage shall not go unpunished.

DEATH'S HOLD-UP

Dalton Boys Secure in the Embrace of the Grim Highwayman.

CROWDS VIEW THE DEAD BODIES

They Were Emulated by a Desire to Outdo Jesse James.

EMMET DALTON'S STORY

He Says He Is a Cousin of the Younger Brothers, Which Cole Younger Emphatically Denies.

KANSAS CITY, Mo., Oct. 6.—A special to the Star from Coffeyville, Kan., says: The streets are packed today with crowds of excited people from all parts of this section, attracted by the terrible Dalton tragedy of yesterday.

On every street corner, in every alley, stand groups of citizens eagerly discussing the attempted bank robberies of yesterday with its attendant tragical results.

At the city jail an awning has been improvised, under which lie the four dead bandits in the coffins provided by the county, with a guard to see the coffins are not disturbed. Since morning a procession of sightseers have passed in file past the coffins, viewing the bodies. The desperadoes, cold in death, their faces uncovered, seem to possess an attraction for the curious which is almost without parallel.

Among the thousands who have viewed the bodies are many who have known the Daltons for many years, and while their crimes deserve to place them beyond the pale of sympathy, here and there are to be found people who can scarce repress a sigh of regret for the dead men. The stairway leading to the room in which Emmet Dalton lies is at all times surrounded by a dense crowd of men and women, who do their utmost to persuade the guard to let them pass up the stairway to the presence of the wounded man. All sorts of reasons are advanced by these people for their requests, but, with few exceptions, they are not complied with.

The Schofield Smith & Wesson .45 caliber revolver was an improvement on the American model in reliability as well as new features and was adopted by the army in 1875. This model was used by both Virgil Earp and Jesse James.

The Model 1873 Colt single action .45 caliber revolver was very popular with both the military and civilian markets because of its reliability and handling. This model was used by lawmen and outlaws alike, including Wyatt Earp, Jesse James, Bat Masterson, and Billy the Kid as well as by Pat Garrett to shoot Billy the Kid.

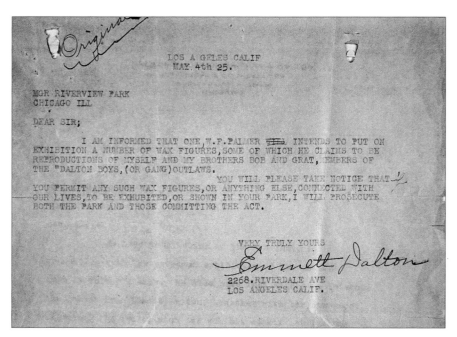

LOS ANGELES CALIF
MAY 4th 25.

MGR RIVERVIEW PARK
CHICAGO ILL

DEAR SIR;

    I AM INFORMED THAT ONE, W.F.PALMER ~~THE~~ INTENDS TO PUT ON
EXHIBITION A NUMBER OF WAX FIGURES,SOME OF WHICH HE CLAIMS TO BE
REPRODUCTIONS OF MYSELF AND MY BROTHERS BOB AND GRAT, EMBERS OF
THE "DALTON BOYS,(OR GANG)OUTLAWS.
                YOU WILL PLEASE TAKE NOTICE THAT
YOU PERMIT ANY SUCH WAX FIGURES,OR ANYTHING ELSE,CONNECTED WITH
OUR LIVES,TO BE EXHUBITED,OR SHOWN IN YOUR PARK,I WILL PROSECUTE
BOTH THE PARK AND THOSE COMMITTING THE ACT.

                VERY TRULY YOURS

                Emmett Dalton

        2268.RIVERDALE AVE
        LOS ANGELES CALIF.

EMMETT DALTON. Typewritten Letter Signed, May 4, 1925. The surviving member of the Dalton Gang acted to block an exhibition of wax figures of the *"Dalton Boys (or Gang) Outlaws."*

TO WHOM IT MAY CONCERN :-

    This is to certify that I have this day appointed
and do hereby commission - *Martin Lohman*
as special deputy sheriff in and for Dona Ana County, New Mexico,
and that the said *Martin Lohman* is duly
qualified to act as such Deputy Sheriff.

    IN WITNESS WHEREOF, I have hereunto set

    my hand and scroll at Las Cruces, New

    Mexico, this the 22nd day of *October*

A.D.1898.

             P.Y. Garrett——(seal)
          Sheriff, Dona Ana County,
          New Mexico.

Territory of New Mexico,)
County of Dona Ana.) ss.

PAT GARRETT. Document Signed, Las Cruces, New Mexico, October 22, 1898. The lawman who killed Billy the Kid appointed Martin Lohman *"as special deputy sheriff in and for Dona Ana County, New Mexico."*

WESTERN DISTRICT OF ARKANSAS,
    April 27 188*7*

    I hereby certify that I have been employed and have acted   *2*   days, as a Guard over
James Shaw
Frank Dalton , a United States prisoner in charge of
             Deputy Marshal, from *Muskogee I.T.*
to *Fort Smith Ark* , being a distance of *80* miles.

                Bob Dalton
        P. O. Address *Fort Smith*
                  Ark

Witness

P. O. Address

BOB DALTON and his brothers, cousins of the Youngers, after a number of unspectacular train robberies, tried to rob two banks in Coffeyville, Kansas, simultaneously. Only Emmett, though badly wounded, survived.

Three Cow-Boys Bite the Dust.

SAN FRANCISCO, October 27.—A Tombstone dispatch says four cow-boys—Ike and Billy Clanton and Frank and Tom McLowery—have been parading the town for several days, drinking heavily and making themselves generally obnoxious. The city marshal arrested Ike Clanton. Soon after his release the four met the marshal and his brothers. The marshal ordered them to give up their weapons, when a fight commenced. About thirty shots were fired rapidly. Both the McLowery boys were killed. Billy Clanton was mortally wounded, dying soon after. Ike was slightly wounded in the shoulder. The officers were, with one slight exception, unhurt.

"Three Cow-Boys Bite the Dust." San Francisco, October 27, 1881. An account of the gunfight at the OK Corral.

Colt Model 1851 Navy .36 caliber. Both Wild Bill Hickok and Cole Younger used this model.

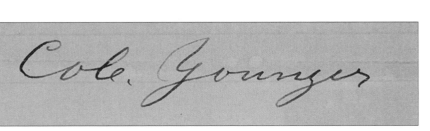

Cole Younger and his brother Bob, as well as Jesse and Frank James, were Confederate guerrillas who became outlaws after the Civil War.

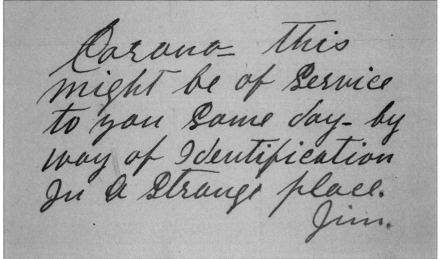

Jim Younger, with his three brothers joined forces with Jesse and Frank James and met his downfall with his brothers in the raid on the banks in Northfield, Minnesota.

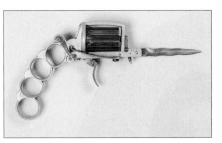

"Apache Knuckleduster" made in France, *ca.* 1880. The blade and brass knuckles fold in.

The Chicago pistol, a gambler's favorite.

The Merwin & Hulbert double action .44 caliber revolver. Pat Garrett and John Wesley Hardin favored this model.

"Wild Bill" Hickok led a colorful life as a gunfighter and was a favorite of the newspapers. He was a sheriff of Ablilene, where he was usually found at his poker table in the town's wildest saloon, the Alamo. In 1876, he was shot in the back while playing poker in a saloon in Deadwood, Dakota. In this handwritten letter, signed "James Butler Hickok," he writes to his sister on April 22, 1858, from Monticello, Kansas, the day after being elected a town constable:

"[I]f I yoused you bad some times when I was angry you must forget it…you did not think that I was in earnest when I spoak of marrying did you[?]…I was only Joking[.] I could not get a wife if was to try[.]…I am homelyer than ever now days and you no that the wiman don't Love homly men…. Waner was here the other day and I sent a letter home by him[.] [H]im and myself drank some Lager together…. [Y]ou ought to see me fishing on my Clame[.] I Can ketch any kind of fish that I was to[.]

"I have fed my fish till they are all tame[.] [T]he girls Comes to my Clame a fishing some times and that I don't like[.] [B]ut I Cant help my self[.] [T]his is a free country[.] [E]vry one dze as he pleases."

and he can keep his thanks
for them that needs them you did
not think that I was in earnest when
I spoke of marrying did you say I
was only Joking I could not get a wife if
was to try for I am homelyer than ever
now days and you no that the women
dont love homly men you to
celurate that oliver never has directed
a letter to me since he left home dont
you think that I would be ungrateful
if I was to feel hard towards him
for it how do you all suppose that
I can wright once a week when you
all cant find time to write
once a month I have answerd every letter
that I have got in a long time
with out much trubble one was
here the other day and I sent
a letter home by him him
and my self drank some
Sugar tho to gether

I hope that you will not have much
trubble with your school this summer if you take
one have you had any high water there
this spring if you haint probibly old
arzy smiths girles has quit going
out to the brige you aught to see
me fishing on my Clame I can
hetch any kind of fish that I
want to I have fed my fish
till they are all tame the girls
comes to my Clame a fishing
some times and that I dont like
but I cant help my self this is
a free country for one acts as
he pleases

from your affectionate
Brother James Butler Wakok

wright to me after
I will answer every one that
is written to me
without fale

$800.00 Reward!
ARREST STAGE ROBBER!

1.

On the 3d of August, 1877, the stage from Fort Ross to Russian River was stopped by one man, who took from the Express box about $300, coin, and a check for $305.52, on Grangers' Bank of San Francisco, in favor of Fisk Bros. The Mail was also robbed. On one of the Way Bills left with the box the Robber wrote as follows:—

"I've labored long and hard for bread—
For honor and for riches—
But on my corns too long you've trod,
You fine haired sons of bitches.
BLACK BART, the P o 8.

Driver, give my respects to our friend, the other driver; but I really had a notion to hang my old disguise hat on his weather eye." (*fac simile.*)

Respectfully
B. B.

It is believed that he went to the Town of Guerneville about daylight next morning.

2.

About one year after above robbery, July 25th, 1878, the Stage from Quincy to Oroville was stopped by one man, and W., F. & Co's box robbed of $379, coin, one Diamond Ring, (said to be worth $200) one Silver Watch, valued at $25. The Mail was also robbed. In the box, when found next day, was the following, (*fac simile*):—

here I lay me down to sleep
to wait the coming morrow
perhaps success perhaps defeat
and everlasting sorrow
I've labored long and hard for bread
for honor and for riches
But on my corns too long yove tred
you fine haired sons of Bitches
let come what will I'll try it on
My condition can't be worse
and if there's money in that Box
Tis munny in my purse
Black Bart
the Po 8

Black Bart, the polite stagecoach bandit who left poems signed *"Black Bart,"* was traced through a laundry mark on a dropped handkerchief.

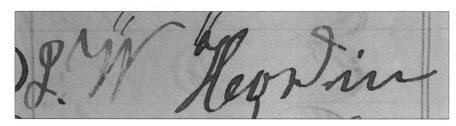

WYATT EARP. A subpoena signed by Earp as constable, June 25, 1870.

JOHN WESLEY HARDIN was an outlaw known to have killed at least 44 men before a sheriff, in 1895, shot him dead.

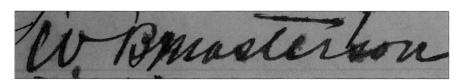

BAT MASTERSON. Legendary gunfighter and sheriff of Dodge City. Signature, "W. B. Masterson" on a document, Dodge City, 1885.

ROY BEAN. The justice of the peace and saloonkeeper who styled himself the *"law west of the Pecos."* Document Signed, Val Verde County, Texas, October 15, 1887. Affidavit for Warrant of Arrest.

Movie poster. 18 by 28¼ inches.

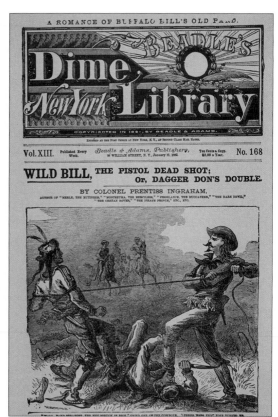

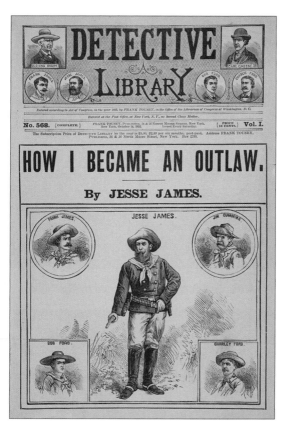

The popularizers of the outlaws and gunfighters, the Dime Novels, published stories that bore no relationship to reality.

Chapter 19

COWBOYS

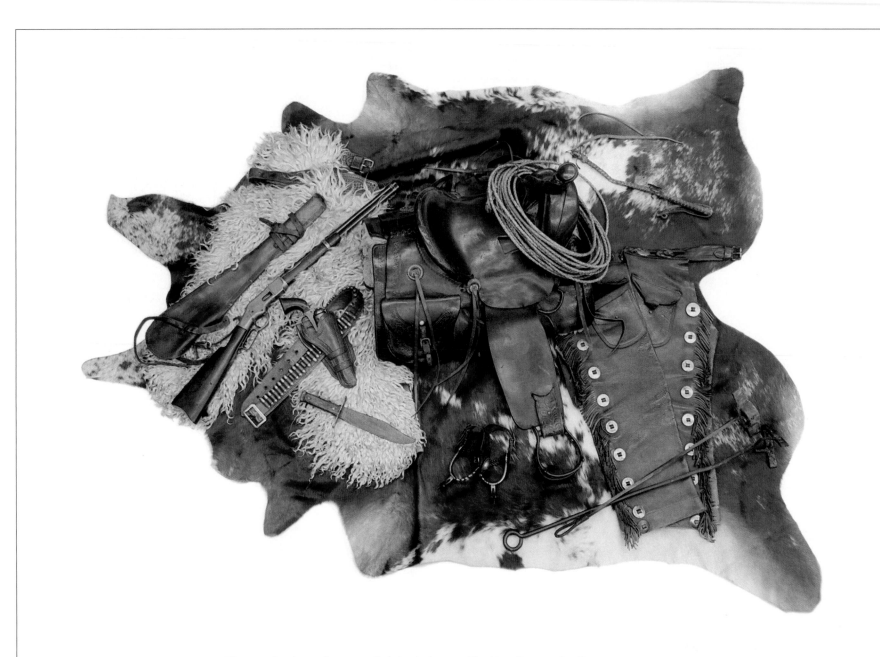

The cowboy's equipment: Colt Single Action .45 caliber Frontier Six Shooter, woolly chaps, bullwhip, lariat, saddle, knives, branding irons, and Winchester rifles.

No area of Western history has been as romanticized as the cowboy. Owen Wister's *The Virginian*, 1902, had a major effect in creating this image as did Dime Novels, Wild West Shows, and, of course, cowboy movies and television shows. The sense of freedom and excitement was undoubtedly as real among cowboys of the 19th century as it is for the cowboys of today. For many, however, the romantic version is the preferred reality.

The cattle business began in Texas in the 1860s. After the Civil War, demand for beef by the Northeastern states increased dramatically, and the advance of the railroads to trail heads like Kansas City, Abilene, and Dodge City made the transport of cattle to the East possible. The great era of the cowboys began to decline by the mid-1880s. The invention of barbed wire in 1874 meant the beginning of the end of the open range, the extension of the railroads ended the long cattle drives, and finally a devastating winter in 1886–1887 killed vast numbers of cattle, as well as ranchers and cowboys. It had become inefficient to have large herds, and ranches did not rebuild after the blizzards. The 25-year heyday of the cowboys still lives on 115 years later in popular entertainment and people's minds.

Cowboy memorabilia is very popular with collectors; early artifacts are rare, but early 20th-century material can be collected from dealers specializing in this area.

The Broncho Buster by Frederic Remington. The artist's first bronze and his most popular. This example was cast during his lifetime [1861–1909], and is number 78. Michael Greenbaum in *Icons of the West, Frederic Remington's Sculpture*, notes, *"It was the rugged frontier character who possessed an 'unearthly wildness,' yet a 'distinct moral fiber,' that Remington depicted in his first bronze subject,* The Broncho Buster. *Copyrighted October 1, 1895, the twenty-four-inch statuette of a cowboy 'breaking in a wild horse' was the first western action bronze of its kind, a frozen moment of nineteenth-century peril and drama. Remington supplied his poignant 'wild rider' with a whip, sharp spurs and an air of confidence.*

"When completed The Broncho Buster *was a technical triumph. The Henry-Bonnard Bronze Co. of New York produced the fine, smooth castings and the work was an immediate success with the public — a quintessential western image.* Harper's Weekly, *the magazine that regularly published Remington's illustrations and stories, ran a photograph and a favorable review on October 19, 1895. 'Remington has stampeded, as it were, to…greater possibilities,' wrote Arthur Hoeber. 'He has struck his gait.'* The Broncho Buster *quickly propelled the artist toward fame and the cowboy to the status of folk hero.* The New York Times *printed the following: 'In point of fact, however, it is an initial effort, and certainly shows genuine taste and talent in that direction. Mr. Remington has long been known as a popular illustrator, whose work in the publications of the day has put him well in the front rank of the men who draw in pen and ink, and in this peculiar field he has been almost without a rival. Now that he has started in another direction, and begun so promisingly, his career will be remarked with still greater interest and subsequent work of this kind will be watched eagerly.'"*

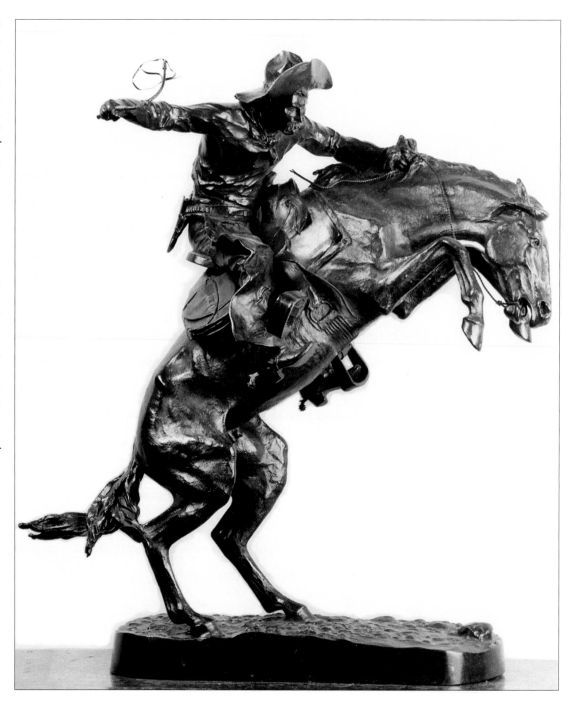

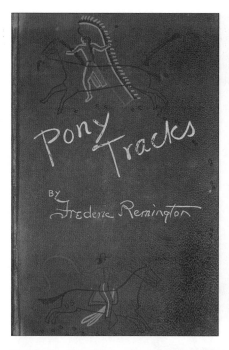

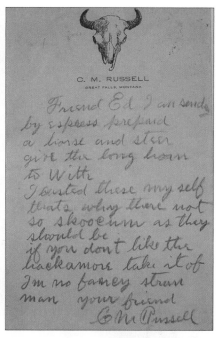

Frederic Remington's *Pony Tracks,* 1895, was his first book with a substantial text; it recounts his adventures in the West, often with the United States Cavalry.

CHARLES M. RUSSELL. Autograph Letter Signed, sending a horse, steer, and longhorn. *"If you don't like the hackamore take it of[f]. Im no fancy straw man."*

FREDERIC REMINGTON. Autograph Letter Signed, 1892, to his publisher.

"I sent some little sketches for the 'Model' article and today ship another — on 'Camping Out' with some sketches.

"I will do you one more article before I go...."

An exceptionally fine pair of spurs.

Personal travel case of Nellie, apparently a saloon entertainer, including her crucifix and small pistol.

Angora woolly chaps by Miles City Saddlery Co, Montana.

"Hands Up!" from Charles M. Russell's *Studies of Western Life,* 1890.

Winchester Model 94 caliber 30/30 saddle ring carbine.

315

"Cowboy Sport. (Roping a Wolf.)"
from Charles M. Russell's *Studies of Western Life*, 1890. This was the first of Russell's
many books on the West.

Chapter 20

INDIAN WARS

"Custer's Last Fight," a lithograph after a painting commissioned by the Anheuser Busch Brewing Association, 1890. Widely distributed by the beer company, this became the most widespread image of Custer's Last Stand. 24 by 38 inches.

The Indian Wars is a period of time that is difficult to define because the European settlers were at war with the Indians, in one way or another, virtually since they arrived on the Atlantic shores. If the Indians didn't cooperate, in the settlers' eyes it was the Indians who were always at fault — the tensions caused by two hundred years of the Indians' being seen as savages who needed to be "saved" by Christian missionaries finally came to a head where there was no place left to drive the Indians, and warfare began in the West.

This was in 1854 in Wyoming, and it became known as the Grattan Massacre. In 1862, the Homestead Act fueled settlement and more Indian problems. The Fetterman Massacre in 1866 was perhaps more a result of the arrogance of army officers than Indian planning. Civil War veterans like Fetterman were looking for something to use their military talents on, and the Indians in the West were the most convenient target.

The following year the Federal Peace Commission found that most violence was caused by whites, not Indians, but despite the implementation of the commission's recommendations (closing various forts, and closing the Bozeman Trail) before long the tide of settlement, or in the case of the Black Hills in South Dakota, 1875–1876, the discovery of gold, pushed the Indians off lands just "given" them by the government. In South Dakota this resulted in the Sioux War and the Custer Massacre.

There is nothing good to be said about this chapter of American history. It is a chapter that interests collectors, reflecting in part the general interest in the plight of the Indians in recent decades. Signatures of Geronimo and Sitting Bull occasionally come on the market at significant prices; forgeries are a serious worry. Letters of army officers, except Custer, are not very expensive. Custer seems to be almost a cult figure and has been for some time. Although theoretically plentiful because he signed many documents and letters in his army positions, Custer material, because of many decades of collector's interest, is not at all common and ranks just below or on a par with Sitting Bull. The guns and other artifacts, unless associated with a major figure, are not expensive.

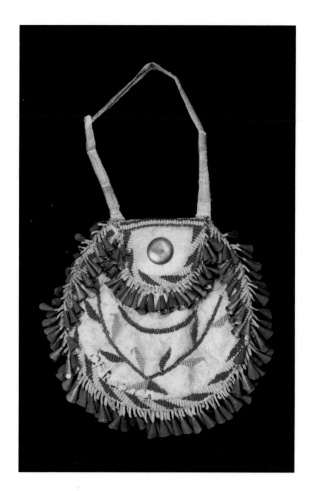

Beaded pouch autographed by Geronimo.

"The Captive White Boy Santiago McKinn." Identified as taken in Geronimo's camp. C. S. Fly, Tombstone, Arizona Territory, *ca.* 1886. 5 by 8 inches.

"Geronimo and Natches mounted, Natches with his hat on; son of Geronimo standing by his side." C. S. Fly, Tombstone, Arizona Territory, *ca.* 1886. 5 by 8 inches.

"Scene in Geronimo's camp, the Apache outlaw and murderer." C. S. Fly,
Tombstone, Arizona Territory, *ca.* 1886. 5 by 8 inches.

"The Council Between General Crook & Geronimo." At the council, Geronimo agreed to surrender but fled that same night; as a result Crook was replaced by Nelson Miles. C. S. Fly, Tombstone, Arizona Territory, *ca.* 1886. 5 by 8 inches.

"Cochise Stronghold, Dragoon, Mt's, Ariz." C. S. Fly, Tombstone, Arizona Territory,
ca. 1886. 5 by 8 inches.

In 1877, at the age of 25, John Clum captured Geronimo; the Apache chief escaped and the Indian problems continued.

In 1929 Clum wrote: *"My story is friendly to the Apaches. My contention is that these Indians, as far back as 1871, displayed qualities which gave assurance of persistent orderly development and material progress under fair and sympathetic direction, and that in spite of the misdirection of their affairs, the great mass of friendly Apaches finally succeeded in subduing and eliminating the renegades of their own race. The subject of the Indians is now prominent because of the rehabilitation of the Indian Bureau, and the Apaches have a new and serious problem in the matter of the substitution of new farming areas in lieu of the many old farms with their irrigation canals which are even now being submerged by the waters gathering behind the new Cooledge Dam. The Apaches always have been, and are now, in sore need of good friends."*

Chum was later Mayor of Tombstone.

Important If True.

SAN FRANCISCO, Sept. 4.—A Nogales, A. T., special says: Information has reached here that Lieut. Clark arrived at Calabasas last night with the intelligence from General Miles that while the latter was marching side by side with Captain Lawton, Geronimo came up saying the Indians were out of provisions and ammunition, they were faint and hungry and would give up their arms and surrender unconditionally.

Hope It's So.

SAN FRANCISCO, Sept. 4.—A Tombstone, Arizona, special says: John Slaughter, owner of San Bernardino ranch, came here to-day and states that Geronimo and his band of forty bucks, squaws and pappooses were captive to Captain Lawton, and were on their way to Fort Bowie.

Account of Geronimo's surrender that appeared in the *El Paso Times,* Sunday Morning, September 5, 1886.

Photograph of Geronimo, signed by him in pencil below the portrait.

326

In 1887, General Bernard J. D. Irwin, a Medal of Honor recipient, wrote a lengthy memoir entitled, *The Chiricahua Apache Indians/A Thrilling Incident in the Early History of Arizona Territory:*

"The usual home...of the Chiricahuas...was in the mountain range situated in the southern part of Arizona.... [T]hey laid in wait ready to pounce upon small parties of incautious travelers en route to Mexico or California. Such parties were usually ambushed; the men slaughtered, and the women and children subjected to bondage and ill-treatment much worse than the most cruel death.

"The chief of the Chiricahuas...was Cachise.... The highway leading to and from Apache Pass was dotted with the graves or...that covered the remains of the victims of this treachery; slaughtered by his bloodthirsty followers....

"Only a few weeks prior to...February, 1861, while Captain Ewell was encamped at the pass, endeavoring to conciliate the Chiricahuas with presents, two young Mexican girls...were rescued by purchase from their cruel fate and restored to their parents.... Two of the men...were killed while defending their wives and children...by... savages who had joined and camped with them during the night, partaken of breakfast, after which...they attempted the destruction of the party whose hospitality they had received only a few moments before! Such was the character of the Apache Indians of Arizona in 1861. One and all were then alike; treacherous, bloodthirsty, and cowardly, and ever on the alert to ambush small parties or incautious travelers when, without risk to themselves, the chances were in favor of their success....

"Lieutenant Bascom having followed the trail of the stolen cattle to the stronghold of the Chiricahuas, marched his command to the mail-station situated within the pass and...Cachise...accompanied by several of his people visited Lieutenant Bascom's camp, but when demand was made upon him for the restoration of the stolen property he scoffed.... Bascom...determined to detain him and...others...as hostages until the tribe should deliver up a captive boy carried off with the herd and surrender the stolen animals.... The Overland mail-coach from California was attacked...that night, but... miraculously, escaped; the driver, with a shattered leg and with one of his passingers shot through the chest....

"There being several wounded men at the station, one of the soldiers volunteered to attempt to lead a mule over the steep and untraveled hill-side...to escape during the night towards Fort Buchanan in quest of aid.... Cachise approached the mail-station with a white flag and called for a talk with the soldiers.... The parley had hardly commenced when a sentinel posted on the roof of the station-house discovered a large number of Indian warriors crouching from view in the ravine close to and behind Cachise. The soldier called out and had scarcely concluded his warning when a dash to surround Bascom's party and to cut off his retreat was made....

"[The men were] captured by the Indians then surrounding and watching the movements of the beleaguered party.... The success of the daring soldier who during the darkness of night stealthily scaled the steep and pathless mountain side and groped his way out to the plain and rode thence to the post was indeed marvelous; surrounded as was the command by several hundred sav-

ages thirsting for the lives of the whole party. Soon after the arrival of the messenger at the post the writer volunteered to take a small but picked number of men and endeavor to reach the pass direct....

"On arriving at the entrance to the canyon a train of five wagons was found in the wash, plundered and burned. To the partially consumed wagon-wheels the naked remains of the eight human bodies were lashed — the unfortunate and unsuspecting victims having been captured were stripped and tied to the vehicles and then slowly tortured to death by the burning of their outfit!

"In reaching the mail-station, where our arrival was hailed with shouts of joy...the wounded were attended, and next morning, after the arrival of the two troops of cavalry [we moved on]....Two more days were spent in seeking the camp or village of Cachise which was found and destroyed... the ghastly remains of six human bodies, upon which the vultures had been banquetting, were discovered.... [T]he skelletons were those of the unfortunate Wallace and his companions and three other prisoners who had fallen into the power of the savages. It was then and there that it was determined to execute an equal number of the Indian warriors confined at the mail-station. The silly fabrication that a game of chance decided their fate is as absurd and groundless....

"From the time our troops first entered Arizona in 1857, until the Chiricahua Apaches were removed in 1886, those indians were open or covert enemies of the white races and during that period the lives of hundreds of our people were sacrificed to the insatiable thirst of the Apache for curious and cowardly assassination. Assuming a state

of quasi friendlin[e]ss when it suited their schemes to do so, the Chiricahua Apaches alternated their marauding raids from one side of the international boundary when playing at peace on the other side. While all other indian tribes in the territory entered into treaties of amity and took to the cultivation of their reservations, those dastardly freebooters rejected every effort made to bring them under treaty obligations; the utmost they would concede to the exercise of authority over them consisted in their willingness to be fed and pampered at government expense while resting upon their anus."

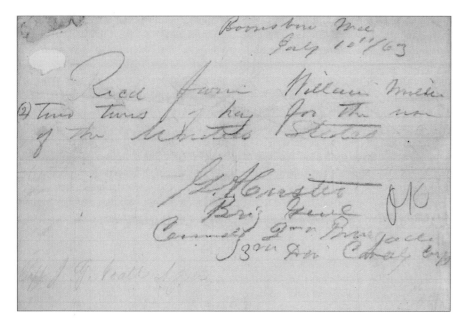

GEORGE A. CUSTER. Autograph Document Signed while serving in the Civil War, July 10, 1863.

TATON KAIYOTONKA, *Sitting Bull*

The above is a true Photo and Autograph of "Sitting Bull," the Sioux Chief at the Custer Massacre.

Copyrighted, 1882, by Bailey, Dix & Mead.

Sitting Bull photograph. *"The above is a true Photo and Autograph of 'Sitting Bull,' the Sioux Chief at the Custer Massacre,"* 1882.

We climbed to the crest of the hill and the Genl. talked with the Crows thro Boyer. The Genl. finally said "I have got mighty good eyes and I can see no Indians" & Boyer replied "If you don't find more Indians in that valley than you ever saw together, before, you may hang me" The Genl. replied, "It would do a dam. sight of good to hang you wouldn't it" This was the second time I ever heard Custer use such an expression the other being in an Indian fight in 1873. We rode back to the command and I hunted for food & drink The officers were called together and the situation discussed, but I was not present. The command then resumed the march I went ahead to the left front, Lieut Harr covering the right front. I got into the hills & a long way from the command. & when at last I rejoined Major Reno with three Troops of

An incredible eyewitness account of the battle of the Little Big Horn by Custer's commander of the Indian scouts, Charles Varnum.

Lieutenant Varnum described his last conversation with Custer ("*the whole valley in front is full of Indians*") while leading his Indian scouts toward Reno's position, his own desperate "final stand," with waves upon waves of mounted Indians attacking and his first sight of Custer's Last Stand.

Varnum began his account, "*[I]n April 1876…I was detailed to organize, enlist and command a detachment of Indian scouts for the Expedition of Genl. A. H. Terry against hostile Sioux Indians. I enlisted about sixty five…. The command left Fort A. Lincoln about the middle of May…. On the 22nd of June Genl. Custer…started up the Rosebud…. [A]fter we camped…the Crow Indians came in and had a long talk with the General…that Crows had reported to him* that there was a high hill in the divide between the Rosebud & Little Big Horn and that there was a 'Crow Nest' near the top, and that when the Sioux were in this country, the Crows used this to watch…on pony stealing expeditions against the Sioux…from the top…when daylight broke…the air was still and clear and they could tell whether the Indians were in camp on the Little Big Horn…. [H]e…wanted an intelligent white man to go with them…. [H]e said he would like to go…. [C]limbed to the crest of the hill where I found the Crows…[who]…said there was a big village in the valley of the Little Big Horn behind a line of bluffs and pointed to a large pony herd. I could not see it. The Indians called my attention to the smoke rising from where Custer had bivouac[k]ed, and did not like it…. I rode out to meet General Custer…. The Genl…said 'I have got mighty good eyes and I can see no Indians' & Boyer replied 'If you don't find more Indians in that valley than you ever saw…you may hang me.'…*

"*The command then resumed the march. I went ahead to the left front…. I got into the hills and a long way from the command, & when at last I rejoined, Major Reno…. I reported to the General, saying I guess he could see about all I could of the situation. 'I don't know, what can you see?' said the General. 'The whole valley in front is full of Indians and you can see them when you take that rise' (pointing to the right front). I asked where Reno was going and he told me he was to attack. I asked if I was to go with him. He said I might…Lt. Wallace was riding with the General as topographical officer. I turned back and shouted… 'Come on Nick, don't stay back with the coffee coolers.' Custer laughed and made no sign to Wallace who joined me…. We rode to overtake Reno…. The Indians were spread across the valley, riding madly in every direction, some times apparently about to charge and then turning and running away only to return again…. I looked back and saw the command dismounting to fight on foot…. [There was] heavy firing…. [M]en were going back to the horses for more ammunition…. [M]en were falling back into the timber & calling out 'they are going to charge.'… The command was on the run…. Indians rode along the column with their Winchester rifles across the pommel of their saddles, pumping them as fast as possible…. [I]t reached the stream. There was no ford but we jumped in and climbed out the best we could….*

"*The Indians had left us for the time being…. We moved to a point that overlooked where Custer's fight took place, but it was covered with Indians riding in every direction. A considerable firing was heard but there was no body of troops in sight. I saw some white objects that I thought were rocks but found afterwards they were naked bodies of men. We fell back along the bluff and the Indians swarmed back on us…. [A] place was selected for the final stand and everything brought inside the lines…. Here we fought it out…. I got busy with my gun on the firing line…. [T]he Indians behind ridges at from about two to five or six hundred yards poured lead into us for twenty or thirty minutes, and then charged us…. [T]he men were ready however with their sights set…. [Ou]r reply…was so effective that it stopped the charge. This was repeated again and again…. [A] few Indians got cover, near the bluff, about two hundred yards down stream, and their fire was very effective. Benteen…suggested we charge them. With a yell we went to it, & that ended all fire from that point. I caught a bullet through the flesh of my leg and another struck my ankle bone on the other foot….*

"*I…with other officers talked over our situation. I suggested that I would try and get away during the night if I could get a good man to go with me & try to get relief…. Late in the afternoon…we noticed groups of Indians assembled on…hills down the river. Their attacks grew less frequent and about sunset almost discontinued…. [T]rumpets were sounded at intervals to attract the attention of any nearby troops. That Custer had been driven off and joined Terry & was approaching was also thought of & discussed…. [W]e learned that Genl. Custer with five troops of the Regiment had all been killed…. It was all sad news to us.*"

Winchester Model 1876 used by Indians, who wrapped the barrel with rawhide to keep the gun from losing parts, which were very difficult to obtain.

Winchester 1873 carbine with Indian tacks and decoration.

A Plains rifle by Joseph Golcher that belonged to Sitting Bull, .42 caliber, 36-inch octagonal barrel, sold to the U.S. Cartridge Company Collection. The catalog entry states, *"This rifle was purchased of a trader, who traded a breechloading rifle for it with Sitting Bull."* It was loaned to the Smithsonian in 1906 and returned to the company in 1931. It was sold at auction in 1942.

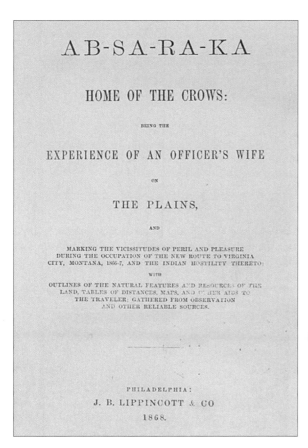

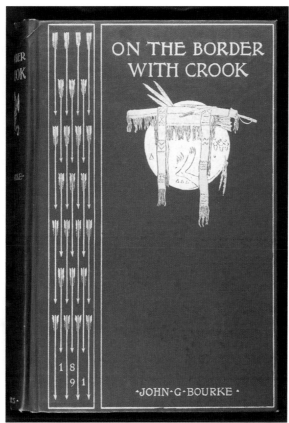

Margaret and Colonel Henry B. Carrington, *Ab-sa-ra-ka Home of the Crows: Being the Experience of an Officer's Wife on the Plains, and Marking the Vicissitudes of Peril and Pleasure During the Occupation of the New Route to Virginia City, Montana, 1866–7, and the Indian Hostility Thereto…,* 1878.

This is the much expanded version of Margaret Carrington's work, first published in 1868 and here almost doubled in size by her husband, Colonel Henry B. Carrington, who added "Indian Affairs on the Plains," covering the period through the Nez Perce War of 1877. An important work by two keen observers of, and participants in, the last days of Indian warfare. Mrs. Carrington accompanied her soldier husband to Wyoming in 1866, where he commanded Fort Phil Kearny at the time of the Fetterman Massacre.

John G. Bourke, *On the Border with Crook,* 1891. Bourke was an aide to General George Crook. By the 1880s, the last Indian wars were coming to a close with the pursuit of the Apache leader Geronimo. Bourke wrote the best book relating to these campaigns, a widely acclaimed account by a soldier who was also an ethnologist.

"A truly great book, on both the Apaches and the Arizona frontier" — Frank Dobie.

A settler in Fort Stanton, New Mexico, C. L. Spring, writing to his sister in 1867 expressed the views of most, if not virtually all, settlers:

"Indians are very quiet…. [N]ot but I expect they will start out on their stealing expeditions this fall and winter. They are the greatest set of thieves you ever saw. These are the Apachae Indians. At fort Summer there is 7000 Navayoe Indians which the Government are a trying to civilize. You would like to see some of the articles that the Squaw make such as dresses Blankets Wollen. They sell Blankets for 100 dollars. I intend to get some of the their things if I can. One captured, a wild squaw and her Pappaws this summer in the Mountains, Killed her Husband. Well this is all about Indians."

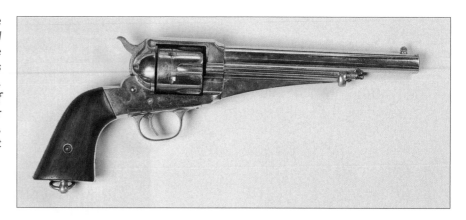

The Colt 1860 Army revolver with the First Model Richards Conversion. In 1870 this invention simplified converting the percussion revolver to the new .44 cartridges. In late 1871 1,200 were issued to cavalry units.

The Remington New Model Army revolver .44 caliber saw extensive use in the Civil War and as a percussion revolver until 1872.

Smith & Wesson No. 3 "American" revolver incorporated several innovations but army field tests in 1871 found it too complex for army use.

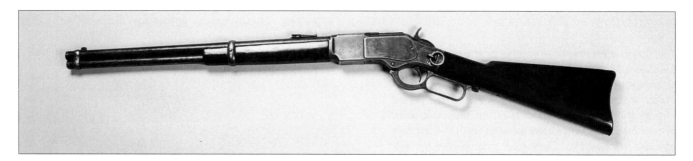

Winchester 1873 Saddle Ring Carbine, .44 caliber.

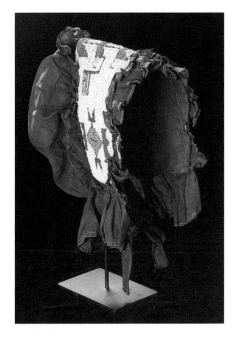

Sioux woman's bonnet with beadwork incorporating an American flag. Late 19th century.

Saddle bags, *ca.* 1904, with Indian beadwork of two U.S. flags on each. The American flag was a frequent theme of beadwork done on reservations.

Five years later, in 1872, the U.S. Army, Department of Arizona issued General Orders No. 9:

"[N]o Apache Indian, who…is absent from his proper reservation or station without written permission from the agent…shall be received back upon, or receive rations at, such post or reservation, except as a prisoner of War…. All Indians, who may become prisoners of War, either by capture or voluntary surrender, shall be turned over at the nearest Military post."

William Tecumseh Sherman, the Union general in the Civil War, went west after the war to eliminate the Indian problem and facilitate Western settlement. In 1874, he wrote, *"[T]he Enemies of the Army were clamoring to our prejudice that we were trying to get up an Indian War…. I don't think you will have much of a war at this time, but it is sure to come sooner or later."*

Medal awarded by the U.S. Army for service in the Indian wars.

Chief Joseph — Nez Perce, by Edward Curtis, 1908. Photogravure printed in sepia tone. Published in Curtis's monumental work *The North American Indian Portfolio,* New York, 1907–1930. 15½ by 10½ inches.

In 1877, Chief Joseph led a long and dramatic struggle after the Nez Perce were driven from their homeland. Chief Joseph almost made it to Canada but was forced into surrender by United States troops. His surrender statement was as eloquent as his situation tragic and the federal government's policy disgraceful:

"Our chiefs are killed....The old men are all dead.... It is cold and we have no blankets, no food.... Hear me, my chiefs. I am tired; my heart is sick and sad. From where the sun now stands, I will fight no more forever."

Chapter 21

KLONDIKE AND ALASKA:
LAST FRONTIERS

A typical cabin.

The Last Frontier — Alaska's self-description — is most appropriate. Up until a few decades ago, Alaska still had homesteading — 160 acres free to anyone who made the improvements. In 1967, I drove to Alaska from Boston — through the Yukon — and there could not have been a better time capsule into the American West. It was all there — people everywhere (excluding Fairbanks and Anchorage) were homesteaders and lived off the land — hunting, fishing, farming, trapping, and even sluicing for gold.

The Yukon gold rush started when gold was discovered outside of Dawson City on the Yukon River in 1896. It was a second chance to strike it rich for everybody who had missed the California gold rush — only getting there was far more difficult than people realized, and the winters were unimaginable.

The pictures of gold seekers carrying their loads up Chilkoot Pass in the Yukon cannot convey the difficulty of the route from the seaport of Skagway, Alaska, to Lake Bennett, where boats were built from available materials to head down the Yukon River to the Klondike. Even in 1967, when I hiked this route, equipment discarded by these dreamers was everywhere. The Oregon Trail was like this in the 1860s. I'm glad I had the chance to experience the Chilkoot Trail before the artifacts and the trail were absorbed by nature.

John Heid was an early miner and attorney. He wrote his sister from Juneau in 1887: "[T]he ships were loaded with excursionists & emigrants to Alaska. There must be at least 50 white women now in Juneau. The town is growing very rapidly and many are making money."

A KLONDIKE PROSPECTOR.

The first issue of the Dawson City, Yukon, newspaper, April 2, 1897.

Archie Hoover left his home in Payola, Kansas, in the spring of 1898 to head for the Klondike gold fields. His diaries are very detailed and give a good sense of how the people supplying those pursuing the dream of gold were very successful. His initial description of Skagway suggests he was somewhat overwhelmed by the number of restaurants, saloons, and bakeries. There was no shortage of businesses to supply those headed to the Klondike. He has an early indication that by the spring of 1898, as the hordes from the south began to arrive in the Yukon, that it was already late in the game.

"Skagway is very quiet now, the rush seems to be about over. It will start up again though as soon as the ice gets off the harbor."

They camped just outside the town and then began to explore the road to White Pass. The original trail had deteriorated to the point where it was unusable but there was an alternative.

"This road is a new wagon road built by Brackett. The old trail is impassable now and Brackett Road is the only practical one from Skagway so he has a monopoly and charges cent and a half per pound toll accordingly…. We are dickering with a man named McConnell to haul our outfit to the snowline, from there we will sled it to Lake Bennet, if possible, if not we will pack it over."

On May 2, McConnell carted 900 pounds up the pass while Hoover and his partner carried packs of 60 to 75 pounds each. Along the trail they *"noticed a bright rosy-cheeked boy…."* Hoover continues, *"In coming closer I was surprised to find the boy was a girl. This was the first specimen of the emancipated Klondike Miss that I had seen."* Despite hiring a cart to move the bulk of their supplies, they had a very difficult time getting over the pass.

"I was awfully tired and thought I had never passed a worse day but it was until the next one. We were about ten hours in making eleven miles" — and this was before they hit the snowline.

The melting snow caused them to sink into the thawing ground. Hoover described a scene of chaos as new shiploads of gold seekers continued to start on the trail to go over White Pass. But Hoover and the other gold seekers had to go on.

Colt 1878 Double Action Frontier .45, Alaska Model with a bigger trigger guard enabling it to be used with gloves.

Robert Service, the most famous author of the Klondike, writes about the origin of one of his most famous poems, "The Cremation of Sam McGee," and reminisces about the Klondike: *"I was always a lone wolf in the Yukon and made few friends…. I still think of these great guys who made the Yukon what it was, even if it was tough."*

MONTE-CARLO, Monaco

28th Octr. 1938

Dear Mr. Griffith:

Many thanks for your long and interesting letter. After a stretch of nearly half a century I find it hard to remember names. I remember a Griffith who was Manager for Pat Burns, but I suppose it was not you.

I do not belong to a Press Cutting Agency, as I hate to see my name in print. Nevertheless I thank you for the cuttings you send, also for your nice little verse. The Sourdoughs in the picture look so profoundly respectable they give me an inferiority complex. I only hope they are not disgracing the Fraternity by drinking <u>soft</u> drinks.

As regards the McGrew and Mc'Gee items, they need be identified with noone living or dead. Both were written as recitations for Smoking Concerts. The first id a stock melodramatic story I gave a Yukon setting; the second, an after dinner story I heard someone tell. I have long since grown out of them.

I was always a lone wolf in the Yukon and made few friends. Some of those I remember best are: Congdon, the M.P., Clem Burns, Billy MacGinnis, Sheriff Eilbeek, Judge MacCauley, Vic Grant, Doc Gillis, and greatest Yukoner of them all, Colonel Joe Boyle. Good sports, every one. One does not meet many of the real Sourdough brand, these days. I am sixty five and can't go the pace any more, but I still think of these great guys, who made the Youkon what it was, even if it was tough.

Many men, including Stanley Scearce have written books on the early days, but few have found publishers. I had one sent to me recently written by an Englishman called ANSELL which seems authentic, and by his account he must have been a tough nut.

I knew many of the old-timers, Bob Henderson, Skookum Jim and Dawson Charlie, Chief Isaac, Joe Clark, Pinkert and Curley Munro, Geo Black Frank Lowe, Tredgold, the Administration crowd, the tenderloin crowd, Diamond tooth Gertie and the Oregon Mare, the saloon stiff crowd, Murry Eads and Tom O'Brian Doig of the Bank, Big Alec Macdonald, and Big Jock Mac D. the men from the creeks, ever so many I cannot remember for the moment but must now be dead.

Well, thanking you again for your letter. Much that I seen since has somewhat eclipsed my Yukon experience but I still think if it with fond remembrance.

Sincerely

Robert. W. Service

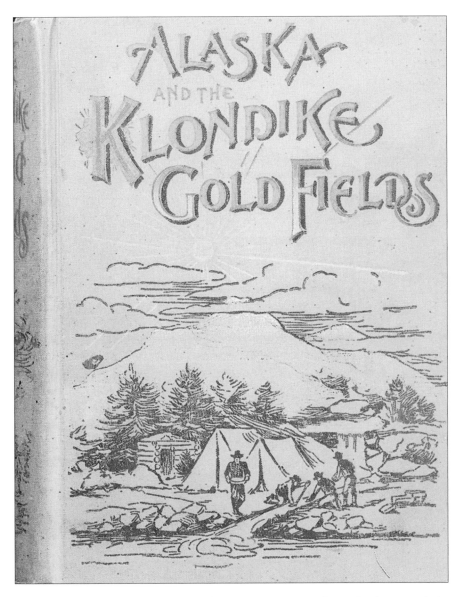

A standard guide, published in 1897, containing material on the history of the Klondike gold fields, routes, and modes of transportation used to reach them, life in Dawson City, resources of Alaska, and how to find gold.

The Official Guide to Klondike Country and Gold Fields of Alaska, 1897.

"'Klondike or bust!' This country has been seized with the gold fever.... Men and even women talk of little else. In nearly every city parties are being organized to invade the Klondike district. Experienced miners who have spent years in Alaska advised them that the road would be set with hardships...but this friendly counsel has no effect stemming the rush.... Corroborative evidence of the richness of the new fields was received in Seattle in the shape of two million dollars with of gold dust and now the cry...is raised in all parts of the land. There is nothing like the site of gold to insight a desire for possession of it."

A paragraph entitled *"Richest the World Has Known"* states, "Today the eyes of the world have turned toward our frozen acquisition in the north for within its borders has been discovered an El Dorado.... A gold bearing district...richer...than any the world has know with the possible exception of California."

Subsequent sections include *"Poor Man's Mines"* and *"Tender Feet Are Winners."* The latter notes that *"the big strikes were made by tender feet.... [F]ortune seemed to smile on the inexperienced men who went into the mining districts late last year as nearly all of them were the most fortunate.... Single individuals have taken out in two and a half months gold to the value of over $150,000."*

The next section, entitled *"Made a Thousand Dollars a Day,"* is followed by *"Big Wages for Laborers,"* which declares, *"If a man is strong healthy and wants to work he can find employment at good wages. Several men worked on an interest...and during the winter realized from $5,000–$10,000 each."* The guide continues with additional sections, including *"Has All the Gold He Wants."*

"Welcome to Camp Montauran."

Chapter 22

The West of the 20th Century

"Canon de Chelley," by Edward Curtis, in the original frame.

The turn of the 20th century saw the West being romanticized in magazines, in books, and particularly in Buffalo Bill's Wild West Show and Congress of Rough Riders. The art of Charles M. Russell and Frederick Remington did much to preserve the image of the cowboy in the popular imagination, while Edward Curtis spent most of his life preserving the images of the Indians and their way of life in photographs. Ansel Adams in *Taos Pueblo* established the style that he would use for decades in portraying the West.

Popular entertainment, including movies and television, created a very unrealistic view of the West until recently, when films such as *Unforgiven* and, earlier, *McCabe and Mrs. Miller*, attempted to show what life there was really like.

Edward Curtis. *The North American Indian Portfolio.* Photogravures printed in sepia tone, New York, 1907–1930. 15½ by 10½ inches.

Edward Curtis began his monumental survey of Native American life in 1907. It was funded by the financier J. Pierpont Morgan and enthusiastically supported by President Theodore Roosevelt. Today, Curtis is widely recognized and admired for these striking early photographic images. The *North American Indian Portfolio* is remarkable for its melding of aesthetic considerations and ethnographic information.

"A Zuni Governor," 1908.

"Medicine Crow — Apsaroke."

"Wolf — Apsaroke."

"Horse Capture — Atsina."

"White Shield — Arikara."

Photograph inscribed by Edward Curtis for his father in the original frame.

Buffalo Bill (William F. Cody) was the greatest showman to bring the highly romanticized West to the rest of the world.

WILLIAM F. CODY — BUFFALO BILL. Autograph Letter Signed, Woonsocket [Rhode Island], July 3, 1907.

"I am really in a desperate position. I have been telegraphing the parties who I owe for time, but they say that they must have part of it at once or for[e]close, and that might cause others to do the same, and if so, it means ruin to me in every way. My credit reputation and my valuable property sold at a sacrifice, and every newspaper in the country saying laws broke; whether I could stand up under such a blow is more than I can say."

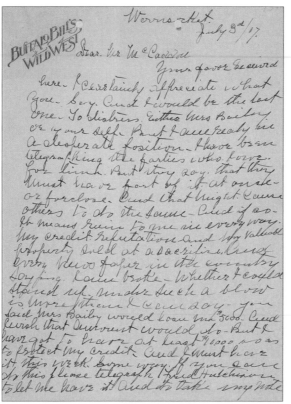

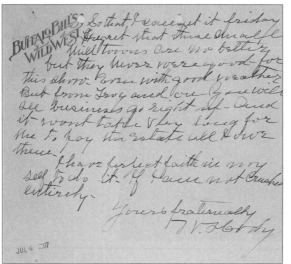

The sharpshooter Annie Oakley was the most popular member of Buffalo Bill's Wild West Show.

Late in his life, the American photographer William Henry Jackson voiced his disapproval of Cody, who had died fifteen years before in 1917: *"As you know I have no great admiration for Buffalo Bill himself and hardly think he merits this nation-wide recognition — I do wish, however, their efforts might be turned into some such testimonial to the Buffalo of the Plains."*

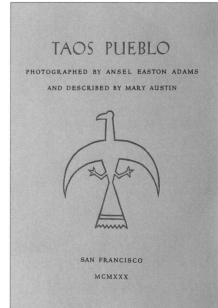

Ansel Adams and Mary Austin, *Taos Pueblo,* 1930. Probably the most famous of modern photographic works on the West, their collected photographs distilled the romance and naturalism that many Americans found in the Indian pueblos of New Mexico, and defined the style that was to make Adams the most popular of photographers of the American West.

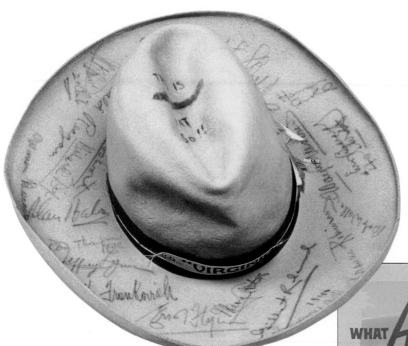

A cowboy hat from the Hollywood film premiere of the Civil War Western *Virginia City,* signed by many members of the cast and attendees of the premiere, including Errol Flynn, Alan Hale, Ronald Reagan, Fred Astaire, and Mary Astor.

Index

A

Abbot & Downing, 288
Abrahams, M. A., 187
Adams, Ansel, 345, 351
Adirondack Mountains, depiction of, 39
Alamo, Battle of, 150, 155
Alaska, 335–342
Allen, Samuel, 221
Allyn, Edward, 224
Ambrose, Stephen E., 64
American Express Company, 248
American Fur Company, 69, 78–81, 90,
    156–157
American Indians. *See* Indians
American Revolution, 23
Andros, Sir Edmund, 16
Anheuser Busch Brewing Association, 318
annuities. *See* Indians, treaties and
    negotiations
Allen and Thurber revolver, 236
Apache tribe, 100, 110, 327.
    See also Geronimo
Appalachian Mountains, 21–42
Arikara tribe, 66
Ashley, William Henry, 69, 80
Astor, John Jacob, 69, 80–82, 90
Atherton, Robert, 202
Audubon, John James, 41–42
Austin, Mary, 351
Austin, Moses, 149
Austin, Stephen A., 149–151

B

Babington, Anthony, 12
Baldwin & Co., 230

Barnett muskets, 75
Bass, Sam, 160
Bean, Roy, 307
Bean, Walter, 167
Bear Flag Revolt, 165
Beard, James H., 192
beaver tall hat, 74
Bellingham, Richard, 16
Bierstadt, Albert, 292
Billy the Kid, 294
Bingham, G. C., 58
Birds of America (by John James Audubon),
    41–42
Black Bart, 306
Blackfoot tribe, 98, 106, 109, 113, 116
boats. *See* clipper ships; steamboats
Bodmer, Karl, 116–117, 244
Bonneville, Benjamin, 131
Boone, Daniel, 23, 35
Booth, T. D., 192
Bourke, John G., 331
bowie knives (*ca.* 1850s), 82–83
Breck, James Lloyd, 88
Brewerton, George, 180–181
Bridger, Jim, 82, 212
Bringhurst, Newell, 260
Broadhead, Daniel, 29
Bronck, Jonas, 17
Bronco Buster, The, 312
Buffalo Bill, 350
Buffalo Bill's Wild West Show, 345, 350
buffalo hunters, 262
Bullock, William, 17
Butterfield, Henry, 247

C

California, 163–170, 291
    map of (1690), 170
    map of (1846), 175
    purchase of, 161
    route to. *See* Overland Trail
California gold rush, 217–240
    Chinese immigrants, 233, 255
    crime, and, 236–238
    pictorial letters, 228–229
Californios, 165–166
Canadian fur trade, 69–70, 76–77, 138
Canyon de Chelley, 344
Carrington, Margaret and Colonel
    Henry B., 331
Carson, Kit, 129–130, 165, 180
cartography. *See* maps
Casement, Jack, 259
Catlin, George, 118–119, 122
cattle business, 311
Central Pacific Railroad, 219, 255, 257–258
Charles I, King (Spain), 4–5
Cheyenne tribe, 96, 103, 107, 112, 113
Chilkoot Pass, 337
Chinese immigrants to California, 233, 255
Chiricahua Apache Indians, 327
Choris, Louis, 144
Chouteau, Pierre, Jr., 81
Chouteau, Rene Auguste, 80
Christ, D. B., 182–183
Christian missionaries. *See* missionaries
chromolithography, 284
Cimmaron revolver, 160
Clark, C. M., 270
Clark, George Rogers, 23, 35–36

Clark, William. *See* Lewis and Clark
expedition
Clinton, Dewitt, 40
clipper ships, 244
clothing
beaver tall hat, 74
cowboy hat, 352
cowboys, 314
Indian, 98–101
pioneers, 19th century, 34
Sioux bonnet (late 19th century), 334
western settlers, 280
Clum, John, 326
coal mining, 169
Cochise, 325, 327
Cody, William F. ("Buffalo Bill"), 350
coins and currency. *See also* tokens
California gold rush, 230–232
colonial, 15, 18
Colorado gold rush, 270
French colonies (1721), 48
Mormon, 210–211
North West Company's 1820 Beaver
Token, 76
Oregon Exchange Company, 203
Russian-American Company, 169
Colden, Cadwallader, 26
Collot's map of America (1804), 50
Colorado, depictions of, 278–279
Colorado gold rush, 270
Colorado River, map of (1745), 127
Colt guns, 236, 248, 280–281, 296–297,
300, 302, 310, 330, 340
Columbus, Christopher, 2–3, 8–9
Columbus, Luis, 8
Committee of Vigilance of San Francisco,
237–238
communications
Overland Mail, 246–250
Pony Express, 250–252, 254
telegraph, 253–254
Wells Fargo & Co., 242, 245, 248–249

Comstock Lode, 271–272
Concord Western stagecoaches, 242–243
Cook, Captain James, 134, 139
copper, discovery of, 18
Cornell, Ezra, 254
Cortéz, Hernando, 4–5
cowboys, 309–316
crime and outlaws, 293–308
California gold rush, 238
guns, 296–300, 302
Crocker, Charles, 219
Crockett, Davy, 37
Crooks, Ramsey, 79
Crow tribe, 95, 96, 100
Cumberland Gap, 23, 35
Cuming, Fortescue, 38
currency. *See* coins and currency;
tokens
Currier & Ives, 172, 186, 216, 264, 273
Curtis, Edward, 334, 344–349
Custer, General George A., 318–320,
328–329

D
Dalton Gang, 300–301
Dana, Richard Henry, 169
Danckerts, Justus, 170
Davion, Albert, 9
Dawson City, Yukon, 335–342
De Bry, Theodor, 6
De Smet, Pierre, 98
De Tonty, Henry, 72
Delaware River, settlement of, 19
Denver, Colorado, 272, 278–279
Deringer, Henry, 55
desert, Southwest as, 135
Dime Novels, 308, 311
Dimick, D. E., 68
Disturnell, John, 222
dolls, Indian, 112
Donner Party, 178–179
Dubuque, Julien, 52

Dunbar, Edward E., 220
Dunmyer, Jonathan, 33

E
Earp, Wyatt, 307
eastern settlements, 1–10
Edward, David B., 154
Eldredge, Horace, 215
Elizabeth, Queen, 12
Emory, William H., 136, 143
Endicott, John, 16
environmentalism. *See* Muir, John
Erie Canal, 40
expeditions
Appalachian region, 21–42
early, 1–10
Northwest Passage, 135, 138
Northwest settlement, 193–204
Rocky Mountains, 143, 172–173, 292
scientific, 133–146
Southwest, 135

F
Fargo, William. *See* Wells Fargo & Co.
Ferdinand, King (Spain), 2
Fetterman Massacre, 319
Filson, John, 35, 38
Flathead Nation, 93
Flintlock Springfield carbine, 106
Florida peninsula, map of (16th century),
7
Fly, C. S., 322–325
Fort Christina, Delaware, 19
forty-niners. *See* California gold rush
Francks, H., 204
Franklin, Benjamin, 23, 25
Fremont, John C., 135, 165–166
French and Indian War (1755–1763), 45
fur trade, 45, 67–84
location of in America, 71
medals for. *See* medals, Indian trade
regulation of sale of furs, 74

fur trade companies
American Fur Company, 69, 78–81,
90, 156–157
Hudson's Bay Company, 69–70, 72–73,
75–76, 81
North West Trading Company, 69–70,
76–77, 138
Rocky Mountain Fur Company, 70, 82

G
Gage, Thomas, 27
Gambrel, William (and brothers),
174, 189, 234–236
Garrett, Pat, 294, 301
Geronimo, 319, 321–326
Giguiere, Robert, 71
Golcher, Joseph, 330
gold
coins, 203, 210–211, 230–232, 270
and early exploration period, 5
Northern California, 169
panning for. *See* California gold rush
prospecting for, 268–272
recovered from SS *Central America*,
226–227
gold rushes
Alaska gold rush, 335–342
California gold rush, 217–240
Colorado gold rush, 270
Gookin, M. S., 225
Grand Canyon, 132, 136
grants of land
on Long Island, 61
Louisiana, 47
New Mexico, 275
in Northwest, 274
Oregon and California, 178
for railroads, 266
Texas, 149, 152, 155, 157, 159
Yellowstone National Park, 283
Grattan Massacre, 319
Gravier, Jacques, 10

Great Salt Lake Valley, Utah, 146, 206, 213, 216
Greenbaum, Michael, 312
Greene, Max, 276
Gregg, Josiah, 124
Grenville, Lord, 49
Grozelier, Leopold, 185
gunfighters, 293–308
guns, 106. *See also specific manufacturer name*
  Alaska, 340
  Appalachian region, 33–34
  buffalo hunters (railroads), 262
  California gold rush, 235–236
  cowboys, 310, 314–315
  fur trade, 68, 75, 82–83
  gunfighters, 296–300, 302–303
  Indian Wars, 330, 332
  Lewis and Clark expedition (1805), 65
  Mississippi River Valley (1759–1784), 55
  Texas, 160
  Wells Fargo & Co., issued to, 248–249
  western settlers and miners, 280–282

H
Haddock, John, 277
Hall, James, 120
Hamilton, James, 159
Hardin, John Wesley, 307
Harpers Ferry, 65
Hastings, Lansford W., 178
Hawaiian Islands, Captain James Cook in, 134, 139
Hawken, Jacob and Samuel, 83
Hawken guns, 70, 83
Hayden, Ferdinand, 136, 260
Hayden, Frederick V., 283–287
Heid, John, 338
Henderson, M. P., 245
Hendricks, Thomas A., 274
Hennepin, Louis, 4

Henry, Alexander, 77
Hernisz, Stanislas, 233
Herrera, Antonio de, 9
Hickok, "Wild Bill," 302, 304–305
Higley, Dr. Samuel, 18
Holladay, Ben, 248
Holley, Mary Austin, 152–153
Holm, Campanius, 19
Homestead Act of 1862, 273, 319
Hoover, Archie, 339
Hopkins, Mark, 219
Houston, Sam, 149–150, 156–157
Hudson's Bay Company, 69–70, 72–73, 75–76, 81
Humphrys, Henry, 194
Huntington, Collis, 219

I
Imlay, Gilbert, 25
Independence, Missouri, 173–174
Indian artifacts
  ceremonial objects, 102, 106–111
  clothing, 98–101
  currency, 15
  musical instruments, 110–111
  tomahawks, 75, 93. *See also* guns
  trade jewelry, 88–92
Indian Peace Medals
  English Indian Peace Medal, 114
  George II Indian Peace Medal, 18
  George III Indian Peace Medal, 115
  George Washington Indian Peace Medals, 30
  Grant Peace Medal, 115
  Jefferson Indian Peace Medal, 66
  Lincoln Peace Medal, 115
  Louis XVI Indian Peace Medal, 114
  Monroe Peace Medal, 115
  Pierce Indian Peace Medal, 115
  Season Medal (*ca.* 1796), 62
  Treaty of Grenville Medal, 31
Indian Removal Act (1830), 47

Indian tribes. *See specific tribes by name*
Indian warfare, intertribal, 87
Indian warfare against settlers, 317–334
  Appalachian Mountains, 23, 28
  Louisiana, 52–53
  in Northwest, 194, 202
  Oregon Trail, 183
  Santa Fe, 130–131
Indians, in general, 85–122
  depictions of, 6, 84, 86, 96, 116–122
  Lewis and Clark expedition, 62–63, 66
  Quakers and, 18
  religious conversion of, 88, 98
  Six Nations, 26, 28
  treaties and negotiations, 23, 29–31, 45–46, 93–95
Iowa, 275
Iroquois tribe, 100
Irving, Washington, ii
Irwin, General Bernard J. D., 327
Isabella, Queen (Spain), 2

J
Jackson, Andrew, 40, 47
Jackson, William Henry, 136, 283, 288, 350
Jamaica, 8
James brothers (Jesse and Frank), 295–300, 302, 308
James, Edwin, 143
Jay, John, 49–51
Jay's Treaty, 46, 49
Jefferson Indian Peace Medal, 65
Jefferson, Thomas, 18, 29, 52–53
  Louisiana Purchase, 61
  Notes on the State of Virginia, 18
jewelry, Indian, 88–92
Johnson, Overton, 177
Johnson, Theodore T., 223
Johnson, William, 26
Jones, Dr. James L., 83
Jones, Mayor John B., 160

Joseph, Chief, 334
Joutel, Henri, 48

K
Kansas, 276
Kearny, General Stephen Watts, 126, 165–166
Kelley, Hall J., 194, 198
Kendall, George W., 158, 161–162
Kenton, Simon, 35
Kentucky, 35–36
  map (1793), 38
Kern, Edward, 168
Kills-Eagle, 96
King, Clarence, 136
King, S. D., 190
Klondike, 335–342
knives. *See also* guns; tomahawks
  California gold rush, 221
  Indian, 113

L
La Perouse, Jean-Francois, 140–141
La Salle (La Sieur Robert Cavalier), 48
land grants
  on Long Island, 61
  Louisiana, 47
  New Mexico, 275
  in Northwest, 274
  Oregon and California, 178
  for railroads, 266
  Texas, 149, 152, 155, 157, 159
  Yellowstone National Park, 283
Last Frontier, Alaska as, 335–342
Latter Day Saints. *See* Mormons
Laudonniere, Rene de, 6
lawmen and outlaws, 294–308
Le Count, Cookes, 232
Le Moyne, Jacques, 6
Leigh Manor, 12
Leonard, Zenas, 176
Lewis and Clark expedition, 59–66, 135

Lewis, Henry, 57
Lewis, Meriwether. *See* Lewis and Clark expedition
Linforth, James, 213
Lisa, Manuel, 69, 80
lithography, as method of book illustration, 144
Little Big Horn, battle of, 329
Livingston, Robert R., 63
Long, Stephen H., 135
Los Angeles, 180–181
Louis XIV, King (France), 48
Louisiana
    land grants, 47
    Louisiana Purchase, 61
    New Orleans, map of (1770), 48
Louisiana and Mississippi River Valley, 43–58
Louisiana Purchase, 63
Lucero, Pablo, 128
Lum, James, 238

M
MacKenzie, Alexander, 135, 137–138
Mackinac (originally Michilimackinac), 71
mail and communications
    Overland Mail, 246–250
    Pony Express, 250–252, 254
    Wells Fargo & Co., 242, 245, 248–249
Mallory, Henry H., 234
Mandan tribe, 66, 119
Manifest Destiny and the Mexican War, 161
maps
    California, as island (1690), 170
    Comstock Lode and Sutro Tunnel (1878), 271
    Delaware River, Swedish settlement of (1702), 19
    Florida peninsula (16th century), 7
    Kentucky (1793), 38
    Lewis and Clark expedition, 60

maps *(continued)*
    Mississippi River Valley (1759–1784), 44
    New England, 14
    New Mexico (1745), 127
    New Orleans (1770), 48
    North America (1732), 22
    North America (1755), 32
    North America (1804), 50
    Oregon (1830), 198
    San Francisco Bay (1846), 168
    Texas (1833), 152
    Texas (1836), 154
    Texas, Oregon, California (1846), 175
    Union Pacific route (1867), 265
Marin, William, 275
Marshall, James W., 210, 218–220
Massachusetts and New England, 12–16
Masterson, Bat, 307
Mathews, Alfred E., 278–279
Maurer, Evan M., 96
Maximilian, Prince Alexander, 116–117
McKinn, Santiago, 321
McLeod, Archibald, 76
medals, Indian fur trade
    American Fur Company, 81
    Hudson's Bay Company, 73
    Pierre Chouteau, Jr., & Company, 81
Medals, Indian Peace
    English Indian Peace Medal, 114
    George II Indian Peace Medal, 18
    George III Indian Peace Medal, 115
    George Washington Indian Peace Medals, 30
    Grant Peace Medal, 115
    Jefferson Indian Peace Medal, 66
    Lincoln Peace Medal, 115
    Louis XVI Indian Peace Medal, 114
    Monroe Peace Medal, 115
    Pierce Indian Peace Medal, 115
    Season Medal (*ca.* 1796), 62
    Treaty of Grenville Medal, 31

medals, Indian Wars service, 333
Merwin & Hulbert revolver, 303
Metis tribe, 104
Mexican War, 161–162
Michaux, F. A., 36
Michilimackinac (Mackinac), 71
Miles, Nelson, 324
Miller, Alfred Jacob, 84
mining and prospecting
    Alaska gold rush, 335–342
    California gold rush, 217–240
    coal mining, 169
    Colorado gold rush, 270
    depictions of mining towns, 278–279
    gold and silver mines, 239, 271
    guns, 280–282
    miners' courts, 238
    Northern California, 169
missionaries, 9
    California, 164–168
    religious conversion of Indians, 88, 98
    Santa Fe, 125
Mississippi River Valley (1759–1784), 43–58
    depictions of, 57–58
    map (1759–1784), 44
    navigation rights, 46, 49, 51, 61
Missouri, 173–174
Mitchell, S. Augustus, 175
M'Kenney, Thomas L., 120
moccasins, Indian, 101
modern (20th-century) West, 343–352
Moffat & Co., 231
Moll, Peter and Daniel, 33
Mollhausen, H. B., 128
Monroe, James, 63
Moran, Thomas, 132, 283–287
Mormons, 205–216. *See also* Young, Brigham
    coins and currency, 210–211
Morse, Samuel, 253
Mousley, Washington, 215

movies and the romanticized West, viii, 345, 352
mud wagon coaches, 245
Muir, John, 245, 291
muskets, 75. *See also* guns; *gun manufacturers by name*

N
Napoleon, offer to sell Louisiana, 61
Natches, 322
national parks, 283, 299
natives. *See* entries at Indian
natural wonders of West, 283–292
Nebel, Carl, 161–162
New England, 12–16
    early exploration of New World, 1–10
New Mexico, 275, 351. *See also* Santa Fe
    annexation of, 161
    map of (1745), 127
New Orleans. *See* Louisiana
New York, 17
    Erie Canal, 40
Newhall, John B., 275
Nez Perce, 334
Nicholson, J. A., 202
Nicolls, Richard, 17
Norris, Gregg & Norris, 230
North West Trading Company, 69–70, 76–77, 138
Northern Pacific Railroad, 266
Northwest Coast, exploration of. *See* Vancouver, George
Northwest Passage, 135, 138
Northwestern settlement, 193–204. *See also* Oregon and Northwestern settlement
Notes on the State of Virginia, 18

O
Oakley, Annie, 350
Ohio, 36
OK Corral, gunfight at, 302

Oliphant, Laurence, 56
Omaha tribe, 66
Oneida tribe, 26
Onondaga tribe, 26
Ordinances of 1785 and 1787, 24, 45
Oregon and Northwestern settlement,
        193–204
    map of (1830), 198
    map of (1846), 175
Osages tribe, 63
Osborne, R. M., 63
Overland Mail, 246–250
Overland Trail (Oregon Trail), 171–192
depictions of, 184–188, 192

p

Pacific Coast, first expedition to.
        See Lewis and Clark
Pacific Company, the, 230
Pacific explorations, 134, 135, 139–141,
        144, 145
Pacific Fur Company. See Astor,
        John Jacob
Pacific Rail Road, 159
Palóu, Francisco, 164, 167
Panama, as route to California, 174, 190
panning for gold. See gold rushes
Parkman, Francis, 179
Pattie, James O., 175
Payne, George, 224
Penn, William, 13, 20
Pennsylvania, 20
Pennsylvania Quakers. See Quakers
Philadelphia Mint, 230
Pickford, Nicholas, 155
pictographs of Indians, 96
pictorial letter sheets, 228–229
Pike, Zebulon, 135, 142
Pinckney Treaty, 46
Pioneer Stage Line, 242
pipe tomahawks, 75, 93. See also guns
pipes, Indian, 102

pistols. See guns; also pistol manufacturers
        by name
Pittman, Philip, 48
Plate, A. J., 235
Plymouth, Massachusetts, 13
Pony Express, 250–252
Popple, Henry, 22
powder horns, 33–34, 73, 104.
        See also guns
Powell, John Wesley, 136
Prang, Louis, 284
Prescott, William, 5
Proclamation of 1763, 23
Promontory, Utah, 255, 263
prospecting. See mining and prospecting
Putnam, Rufus, 39

Q

Quakers, 18. See also Penn, William

R

railroads, ix, 255–266
        Central Pacific Railroad, 219, 255,
            257–258
        Northern Pacific Railroad, 266
        Union Pacific Railroad, 255, 259,
            261, 265–266
Raleigh, Sir Walter, 12–13
rattles, Indian, 110–111
Red Jacket, Chief, 94
Reed, James F., 179
Regan, John, 56
religious conversion of Indians, 88, 98
religious settlements. See Mormons;
        Quakers
Remington, Frederic, 312–313, 345
Remington guns, 55, 299, 330
rendezvous (fur trade), 70, 82
revolvers. See guns; also revolver
        manufacturers by name
rifles. See guns; also rifle manufacturers
        by name

Rocky Mountain Fur Company, 70, 82
Rocky Mountains, 143, 172–173, 292
    route across. See Overland Trail
romanticized vision of the West, viii,
        345, 352
Russell, Andrew J., 260–261, 263
Russell, Charles M., 313, 315–316, 345

S

Salem, Massachusetts, 16
Salt Lake, Utah, 146
Salt Lake Valley, Utah, 146, 206, 213,
        216
San Francisco, 167–168, 224.
        See also Mormons
    Committee of Vigilance, 237–238
    depictions of, 140–141, 144–145, 232
    map of (1846), 168
Sandwich Islands, Captain James Cook
        in, 134, 139
Santa Anna, 149–150, 155
Santa Fe, 123–132, 191
Santa Fe Trail, 174–175
Schindler, Zeno, 188
Schoolcraft, Henry R., 54
Schultz & Co, 232
scientific exploration, 133–146
Seneca Indians, 94
Serra, Father Junipero, 164
Service, Robert, 340
settlements. See also missionaries
        eastern, 11–20
        prohibitions on (1763), 23, 29
        western, 273–282
Seymour, Samuel, 143
Sharps rifles, 262, 282
Sherman, William Tecumseh, 276, 333
Sibley, Hiram, 253–254
silver
        artifacts from early exploration, 5
        gold and silver mines, 239, 271
        Indian trade jewelry, 88–92

silver (continued)
        Northern California, 169
Sioux tribe, 96, 113, 183
Sioux War, 319
Sitting Bull, 319–320, 328
Six Nations, Indian, 26, 28.
        See also Indians
Sloat, Commodore John Drake, 165
Slocum, John, 158
Smith, Captain John, 13–14
Smith, Joseph, 173, 207–208
Smith & Wesson revolvers, 281, 300,
        332
South Pass, Wyoming, 173
Southwest, as "Great Desert," 135
Spanish colonization of California,
        164–165
Spaulding, Eliza, 173
Spencer rifles, 262, 282
SS Central America, 226–227
St. Clair, General Arthur, 46, 53
stagecoach travel, 242–250, 288
        Black Bart, 306
stamps, 250–251
Stanford, Leland, 219, 258
Stansbury, Howard, 146
steamboats, 169, 244
Stockton, Robert F., 165–166
Stuart, J. E. B., 131
Stuart, Robert, 78–80, 82, 173
Stuyvesant, Peter, 17
Suhtai tribe, 107
surveys. See maps
Sutro, Adolph, 272
Sutro Tunnel, 271–272
Sutter, John, 219–220
Sutter's Mill. See California gold rush

T

Tapis, Estevan, 168
Taylor, Bayard, 238
telegraph, 253–254

Texas, 147–162
    maps of, 152, 154, 175
    Mexican War, 161–162
    war for independence, 149–150, 155
Texas Rangers, 160–161
Thayer, A. P., 202
The Bronco Buster, 312
tokens. *See also* coins
    Overland Trail, 185, 187
    San Francisco, 232
tomahawks, 75, 93
trade jewelry, Indian, 88–92
transcontinental railroad, 255–266
transcontinental transportation, 241–266
travel. *See* railroads; stagecoach travel
Travis, William Barret, 155
treaties with Indians, 23, 29–31, 45–46,
    93–95. *See also entries at* Indian
Treaty of Grenville, 31, 46
Treaty of Hell Gate, 93
Trumbull, John, 62
twentieth-century West, 343–352

U
Union Pacific Railroad, 255, 259, 261,
    265–266
Utah, depictions of, 146. *See also*
    Great Salt Lake Valley

V
Vail, Alfred, 253
Vancouver, George, 194, 196–197
Varnum, Charles, 329
Veragua, Duke of, 8
Virginia, 12–13, 17–18
Visscher, Claes, 170
voyageurs. *See* fur trade

W
Wade, Jeptha H., 253
wagons. *See* stagecoach travel
wampum, 15
warfare, Indian, 87, 317–334
    Appalachian Mountains, 23, 28
    Louisiana, 52–53

warfare, Indian (*continued*)
    in Northwest, 194, 202
    Oregon Trail, 183
    Santa Fe, 130–131
Warre, Captain Henry, 200–201
warrior-artists, 96
Washington, George, 23, 30, 51
Wass, Molitor & Co., 231
water route across America (Northwest
    Passage), 135, 138
Watkins, Carleton T., 290
weapons. *See* guns; *also gun manufacturers
    by name*; knives; tomahawks
Wells Fargo & Co., 242, 245, 248–249
Western Concord stagecoach, 242–243
Western Union Telegraph Company, 254
Whitman, Marcus, 195
Whitman, Narcissa, 173
Whitney, Asa, 257
Whitney, Josiah, 290
Wi-Jun-Jon, 119
Wild West Show, 345, 350

Williams, Roger, 13
Winchester rifles, 262, 282, 310, 315,
    330, 332
Winter, William, 177
Winthrop, John, 16
Wister, Owen, 311
Worsley, Benjamin, 19
Wyoming, 173

Y
Yeates, Jasper, 27
Yellowstone National Park, 283–288
Yosemite Valley, depiction of, 289–290
Young, Brigham, 207, 209, 214–215,
    259–260
Younger brothers (Cole and Jim), 295,
    302
Yukon (Alaska) gold rush, 335–342